Forschung & Studium Anglistik 3

Herausgegeben von
Wolf-Dietrich Bald, Rudolf Emons und Leonhard Lipka

Leonhard Lipka

An Outline of English Lexicology

Lexical Structure, Word Semantics, and Word-Formation

L.L.: English Lexicology. Lexical structure, word semantics and word formation. Narr Studienbücher, Tüb. 2002. XXIV + 243 S, div. Abb. u. Tab.

Max Niemeyer Verlag Tübingen 1990

R: Catherine J. Caws, Word 43, 1992, 491-5 (gut)

CIP-Titelaufnahme der Deutschen Bibliothek

Lipka, Leonhard :
An outline of English lexicology : lexical structure, word semantics, and word-formation / Leonhard Lipka. – Tübingen : Niemeyer, 1990
(Forschung & [und] Studium Anglistik ; 3)
NE: GT

ISBN 3-484-41003-5 ISSN 0178-7861

Printed in Germany.
Satz: Johanna Boy, Regensburg
Druck: Weihert-Druck GmbH, Darmstadt

Contents

Preface

The reader of this book may perhaps not be a word-lover, lexicomaniac, or "into" lexicophilia – a characteristic propensity of some language users, recently discussed in the quarterly *English Today* (*ET* 10, 1987:2). However, even if he is not afflicted with this "disease", he will not be able to escape the fundamental insight that the 'lexicon', lexis, or vocabulary of a language is its most basic level and its most important instrument of communication. It is obvious that we communicate with texts – but these may be simple words like *Fire*! or *Stop*! We categorize extralinguistic reality by means of the concept-forming power of the word, and such categorization is always culture-dependent, since different cultures and languages have different needs and values which are reflected in the words they coin, as frozen pieces of reality. The word as a coin is a frequently used metaphor in many languages. However, the 'lexicon' does not consist of a closed set of items; it contains various productive processes (like word-formation, metaphor, and metonymy), which are tendencies rather than hard-and-fast rules. This creative aspect of the 'lexicon' will not be neglected here. I will regard the treasure of the English vocabulary mainly from a synchronic point of view, and wherever appropriate, material from other languages will be drawn upon, in particular from German, but also from Romance and occasionally from less familiar non-European languages.

There are some basic issues in the discussion of the human word-store and its use by various speech communities which play an important role in research and in this *Outline of English Lexicology*. The most important of these issues are: the distinction between linguistic and extralinguistic (or encyclopedic) knowledge; the assumption of components of meaning, or semantic features; the holistic view of word meaning as gestalt or prototypes; the question of the language-immanent vs. referential or pragmatic approaches to semantics; and the role of interdisciplinary influences and connections between linguistics and sociology, psychology, artificial intelligence, and semiotics. Many of these controversial points are still hotly debated (cf. Hüllen/Schulze 1988) and they will all be addressed in this book. Although the focus here is on structural phenomena and relations, the conception underlying this book is basically pragmatic, sociolinguistic, cognitive, textual, and procedural. Formalization is regarded as a means, not as an end in itself and is restricted to a necessary minimum. I hope any apparent contradictions arising from this perspective will be resolved by reference to these larger issues.

This book is intended as a comprehensive and up-to-date survey of the "state of the art" in English and general lexicology and lexicography (cf. Lipka 1989b).

Chapter I discusses general problems of the vocabulary and dictionaries of English, while chapter II introduces basic notions about words: models of the linguistic sign, kinds of meaning, and the concepts *morpheme, word*, and *lexeme*. Chapters III and IV treat the internal structure of words (word-formation, semantic features, componential analysis) and the structure of the lexicon (paradigmatic and syntagmatic relations between words). The critical evaluation of research on morphological and semantic structure, the question of polysemy vs. homonymy, lexical rules, and sense-relations is combined with new suggestions on a typology of semantic features, the advantages of Prototype Semantics, the notion of semantic processes, and the distinction between *lexemes* and *lexical units*. The concepts *collocation, lexical sets*, and *lexical fields* are stressed and words are considered both in context and in the mind. The consequences of lexical research for lexicography, language learning, and language teaching are considered in chapter VI. The book aims to strike a balance between applied and theoretical approaches to lexis, word meaning and the vocabulary of English.

After a period of long neclect, the field of lexicology has recently been rediscovered (cf. Lipka 1975a) and attracted the attention of a large numer of scholars (cf. Hüllen/Schulze 1988). Conferences and workshops have been organized, e.g. at Essen, Groningen, Tucson, and Hamburg and books have appeared on topics such as (in chronological order): word-formation and semantics (Kastovsky 1982a), contemporary English lexicology (Hansen et al. ^{2}1985, Tournier 1985, 1988), lexical semantics (Cruse 1986), vocabulary (Carter 1987), words in the mind (Aitchison 1987), and words and their meaning (Jackson 1988). A series of monographs is about to be published under the title of *Oxford Studies in Lexicography and Lexicology*. So why another book on the subject?

Let me try to justify my own attempt by referring to the above mentioned monographs. The first two, which originally appeared the same year (1982), are almost exclusively language-immanent approaches (which also holds for Cruse's book), although they are excellent treatments of the wide ground they cover. They are furthermore limited by the language they are written in, as are Tournier (1985) and (1988) by his use of French (in spite of his amazing comprehensiveness in the earlier book). Cruse (1986) is restricted to lexical semantics (in the tradition of Lyons (1968) and (1977)), while Carter's book gives "applied perspectives" as part of a series with "a practical point of view" (in the words of its editor). Aitchison (1987: vii) focuses on psycholinguistic aspects, and gives a highly competent, convincing, comprehensive, and readable survey of "recent findings on the mental lexicon", defined as "the human word-store". Finally, Jackson (1988: vii) concentrates on English dictionaries and is conceived "as a workbook and as a textbook", which results in a most reliable but also rather elementary treatment of the subject.

Acknowledgements

This book developed out of lectures I gave in 1976, 1981, 1985, and 1987. An earlier manuscript is referred to in Kastovsky (1982a: 308) as Lipka (1977c). Some parts have appeared elsewhere in previous versions (see the bibliography). Many people have contributed to the book in one way or another, and I would like to thank all of them, friends, colleagues, and students sincerely. My linguistic roots go back to American and European structuralism, to which I was introduced in the early sixties at Tübingen University by Hans Marchand and Eugenio Coseriu. I am grateful for discussions and comments to Helmut Gneuss, Jürgen Esser, Andrea Brosch-Heiler, Eva Leitzke, Hans-Jörg Schmid, and Arthur Mettinger, who read large parts of the manuscript at various stages. Special thanks are due to Wolf-Dietrich Bald and Dieter Kastovsky for their detailed criticism and constructive suggestions for the improvement of the whole book. These often resulted in footnotes and additional examples, which is also the case for many of the most helpful comments provided by Graham Pascoe. I am particularly indebted to him, furthermore, for additional illustrative material, meticulous corrections, and numerous suggestions for improvement, also with regard to style and the readability of the text. He read through the whole typescript very carefully and thoroughly. Helga Kerlikowsky, who patiently and competently typed draft after draft, and Birgitta Zeller, who provided support, help, and advice for publication, also deserve my sincere thanks and gratitude. Finally, I would like to thank my wife for her patience, interest, and constant encouragement. Without her support this book would not have been written.

October 1989

Leonhard Lipka
University of Munich

Chapter I

General Problems. Words, Words, Words

1.1. Introduction

Surprisingly enough, the term *lexicology* is not to be found in most medium-sized dictionaries and in various handbooks (e.g. Lyons 1977) and English grammars (with the exception of the *Longman Dictionary of Contemporary English* (LDCE) ²1987 and Quirk et al. 1985). Only *lexicography*, explained as 'dictionary-making' or 'the writing and making of dictionaries', is usually mentioned. Apparently this situation is now changing.[1] *Lexicology* might be defined as the study of the *lexicon* or *lexis* (specified as the vocabulary or total stock of words of a language). LDCE ²1987 has the following entry:

> **lexicology** ... *n* [U] *tech* the study of the meaning and uses of words.

What is most important, however, is that in lexicology the stock of words or lexical items is not simply regarded as a list of isolated elements. Lexicologists try to find out generalizations and regularities and especially consider relations between elements (see chapters II and IV). Lexicology is therefore concerned with structures, not with a mere agglomeration of words (cf. Jackson 1988: 222).

In order to illustrate this approach I will draw on some entries from dictionaries and use as a starting point a remark made by Fillmore (1978:167f.) in his article "On the Organization of Semantic Information in the Lexicon". Discussing the characteristics of the language of law, he points out:

> The difference between *jail* and *prison* in many states is determined by the duration of the incarceration ... less than one year, it's a jail; a year or more, it's a prison.

So in the legal language of some parts of the United States the two lexical items *jail* and *prison* could be said to be differentiated by a distinctive feature [over/under one year]. In other areas and in ordinary language, the two words seem to be largely synonymous.

A relation of synonymy also seems to hold in the following quotations from two dictionaries, where one item (namely *jail*) is defined in terms of the other

---

[1] Cf. the title of the new *Oxford Studies in Lexicography and Lexicology*, and Jackson (1988:239ff.) with the chapter 16 "Lexicology, Lexicography and Semantics" containing an extensive discussion of Ullmann's view of lexicology as a branch or "basic division of linguistic science". See also diagram (1) p. 6. It is perhaps significant that *lexicology* is not contained in the Lancaster-Oslo-Bergen (LOB) Corpus of contemporary British English.

(namely *prison*). Let us first look at a partial quotation (slightly modified) from the revised LDCE ²1987:

> **Jail**[1] || also **Gaol** *BrE* ... *n* ... a place where criminals are kept as part of their punishment; prison
> **Jail**[2] || also **Gaol** *BrE* – *v* [T] to put in jail ...
> **Jailbird** ... *n infml* a person who has spent a lot of time in prison
> **Jailbreak** ... *n* an escape from prison ...
> **Jailer** ... *n esp. old use* a person who is in charge of a prison or prisoners

A number of interesting relations can be found in these entries between lexical items and also some of their constituents. Obviously, there are variants of items, too, and it is interesting to see, how these are treated in another dictionary. I will only give a short excerpt from the *Concise Oxford Dictionary of Current English* (COD 1982):

> **Gaol** ... **Jail**, *n.*, & *v. t.* (**G-** in official use, **G-** and **J-** in literary use, **J-** in U.S.). **1.** *n.* public prison for detention of persons committed by process of law; confinement in this, ... **2.** *v. t.* put in gaol ...

For the LDCE *jail* is the normal variant, and the British English (*BrE*) *gaol* is the marked option. For the COD the American variant is the marked one, and further distinctions are drawn concerning official and literary use.

Another interesting difference is the treatment of the distinction between the noun and the formally identical verb in the two dictionaries. In the LDCE *jail*, noun, and *jail*, verb, are considered as homonyms and distinguished by raised numbers.[2] In the COD, however, *gaol* is treated as one lexical entry with two meanings, and we therefore have a relationship of polysemy.

Synonymy and homonymy are counted among paradigmatic lexical relations (see 4.2.), since the lexical items so related stand in a relationship of opposition or contrast to each other. Polysemy is a relationship internal to a lexical entry or word (see 3.1., 4.2.1.). But we may also say that $jail_1$ and $jail_2$ are derivationally connected and that $jail_2$ is a denominal verb derived from the noun $jail_1$. We are then concerned with word-formation processes (see 3.2.). This could be justified by pointing out that the meaning of the verb necessarily contains the meaning of the noun, and that the latter is included in the paraphrase 'to put in jail'. Since the derivation is not formally expressed by a suffix, it is customary to speak in such cases of zero-derivation (see 3.2.2.). That this specific pattern is a productive word-formative process can be seen from examples such as *to bag, to bottle, to box, to dock,* and *to kennel.*

There are also the synonymous verbs *to imprison* and *to incarcerate* 'to imprison' (LDCE). The latter is marked as "formal" (*fml*) in the LDCE and "literal or figurative" in the COD. Only the COD gives a further zero-derived verb *to prison* 'imprison', labelled "poetical or dialect". Here, a so-called 'zero-

---

[2] In the following replaced by subscripts, in order to avoid confusion with the raised numbers for footnotes.

morpheme'[3] (usually symbolized as ø) may be postulated (see 3.2.2.), since an overt derivational suffix (parallel to *–ate*) is missing which expresses the meaning elements 'put into'. *To imprison* may be analysed as a prefixal derivative, a zero-derivative with a prefix, or a zero-derivative with a discontinuous morpheme representable as: *im/prison/ø* 'to put (= ø) into (= im) prison'.

It should be obvious from these examples that the use of such 'labels' (e.g. *fml*), for indicating limitations of usage, is far from identical in the two dictionaries (see 2.2.5.). For example the LDCE makes many more and finer distinctions with regard to regional varieties of English. It is also clear that the use of an item in legal language may be very different from the use of the same item when labelled *infml*. We will have a closer look at the varieties of English later (see 1.3.). However, it should be stressed here that lexical variation and the restriction of items to specific varieties must not be neglected in lexicology, as has so often been the case in the past.

The relevance of syntagmatic lexical relations can also be seen from the above examples (see 4.3.). Here elements are not contrasted or substituted for each other, but combined. This is the case with *jail* and *bird* which yield the so-called compound *jailbird*. The second constituent has to be understood metaphorically (see 3.4.2.). This is not at all unusual, since animal names are often transferred to human beings (cf. *ass, goose, fox, rat*). Furthermore, *bird* in slang can denote a girl or woman, and in informal language also a male person (e.g. *He's a dear old bird*). Only the COD also gives the synonymous *prisonbird* (cf. Ger *Galgenvogel*).

The next syntagma *jailbreak* can either be interpreted as a regular compound, since the second constituent may stand for the whole combination in the sense 'escape from prison'. It could also be regarded as a so-called pseudo-compound, with a 'zero-morpheme', analysable as *jail/break/ø* – parallel to the overt derivation *prison/break/ing* which also means 'escape from prison'.

There is also a syntagmatic relationship between *jail* and the suffix *-er* in *jailer*. The same systematic relationship is to be found in the combination of the synonym *prison* and the identical suffix *-er*, resulting in *prisoner*. However, *prisoner* is 'a person kept in a prison' (LDCE), not one 'in charge of a prison'. From the point of view of the system of the language, it could equally well be the other way round, namely that the *jailer* was inside and the *prisoner* outside the prison. Basically, the suffix only denotes someone who has something to do with what is denoted by the derivative base. In my opinion, the fact that specific irregular meanings have become customary in a language can best be captured with the concept of 'norm' in the sense of Coseriu (see 3.2.5.). With regard to the results of word-formation processes the concept of 'lexicalization' can also be profitably used in this respect (see 3.2.5.).

---

[3] This is a lexicalized technical term which should actually be replaced by *zero-allomorph* (cf. Bußmann [2]1990).

Before starting a thorough discussion of paradigmatic and syntagmatic lexical relations[4] – which presupposes a detailed investigation of the nature of the linguistic sign and of the internal structure of words – we must have a look at some general problems. These concern the general notion of the structure of the English 'lexicon', the problem of varieties of English, and a survey of the most important dictionaries of English.

1.2. The Structure of the English Lexicon

In what sense can we say that the 'lexicon' of English is structured, or has *structure*? What does *lexicon* mean in the technical sense in which it is used here? Why do we not simply speak of the *vocabulary* of English? What does one understand by *lexical structure*?

In her book *Modern English Structure* Barbara Strang (²1968:215) makes the following remark:

> While grammar is the domain of systems, lexis is the domain of vast lists of formal items about which rather little generalization can be made.

Although it is true that, historically speaking, the vocabulary of a language is an accumulation of words, I would claim – against Strang – that it is not merely a list of items. It is certainly possible to make a number of important generalizations. The 'lexicon' is not simply an inventory of unconnected, isolated elements, but it definitely has a structure. There are various types of relations and connections between the elements (see 4.2. and 4.3.) and we may establish (at least partial) regularities and recognize clear, if partly incomplete, patterns (cf. Jackson 1988:243f.).

If we consider language as a system of signs, or, following Saussure, as a structure of interdependent elements, then we may distinguish at least two types of structure in the 'lexicon': external (to the word) and internal structure. Full words may substitute for each other, i.e. be in opposition, or they may combine with each other. Such paradigmatic and syntagmatic relations constitute external structure (see ch. 4). We may also look at the internal structure of lexical items, which are either morphologically complex (such as compounds, or prefixal and suffixal derivatives) or simple (see ch. III). In the last case, although there is no superficial, morphological regularity visible, we may nevertheless find and postulate underlying semantic structure.

Such a structuralist approach, in the sense of Saussure, however, has serious limitations. It is restricted to purely language-immanent relationships. Thus, it

---

[4] Loosely defined here as the substitution or association and the combination of words; see 4.2. and 4.3. and cf. Jackson (1988:96, 244), Carter (1987:158). In Lyons (1981:91) the terms *substitutional* and *combinatorial* (relations) are introduced as equivalents for the Saussurean *paradigmatic* and *syntagmatic*.

abstracts from and cannot capture certain so-called pragmatic factors, which have been rediscovered in recent linguistics (cf. Lipka 1975a). For example a language-immanent approach cannot account for certain metaphorical and metonymic relationships in the lexicon (see 3.4.2.). We will return to these aspects in connection with the various models of the linguistic sign and also elsewhere.

Lexicon is defined in the LDCE ([1]1978) as

> a dictionary, esp. of an ancient language

and in the COD ([6]1976) as

> dictionary, esp. of Greek, Hebrew, Syriac, or Arabic; (fig.) vocabulary of a person, of a language, of a branch of knowledge, etc.

Obviously, the first definition is rather narrow and does not cover the way I have used *lexicon* so far. The second part of the definition in the COD comes close to it (but cf. LDCE [2]1987); the first part, containing the synonym *dictionary*, is not of much use.

Two things should be pointed out here: both terms, *lexicon* and *dictionary*, have been used as technical terms in the literature, and there is no single "correct" use of *lexicon* or *dictionary*. To take up the last point first, I claim that such words are "notational terms". I here follow Enkvist (1973:17), who points out that *style* "is a notational term rather than a linguistic prime" and can be defined differently in different frameworks. Within the theory of transformational-generative grammar (or TG), Chomsky, Katz, and Weinreich have used *dictionary* in different ways (cf. Lipka 1972:37, 84f.). Weinreich even postulates a distinction between a "simplex dictionary" and a "complex dictionary".

In the following, I will use *lexicon* in two senses that are not always sharply distinguished: a) for a metalinguistic level, or a subcomponent in a linguistic model (basically compatible with a variety of theories of language); and b) in the sense of vocabulary as seen from a systematic, synchronic point of view. I will deal with the two aspects in turn. Let me first illustrate sense a) with the analogy of the following position of *lexicology* in the classical structuralist model in Ullmann's *Principles of Semantics* ([2]1957:39) here reproduced as diagram (1). The justified criticism of the model voiced in Jackson (1988: 241ff.) may be disregarded for our purposes. It is certainly true that lexicology must include both the study of individual words and their structure (see ch. III) and of the overall structure of the vocabulary as a whole (see ch. IV), and that it cannot describe either from a purely formal point of view, without considering semantic aspects and relations.

(1)

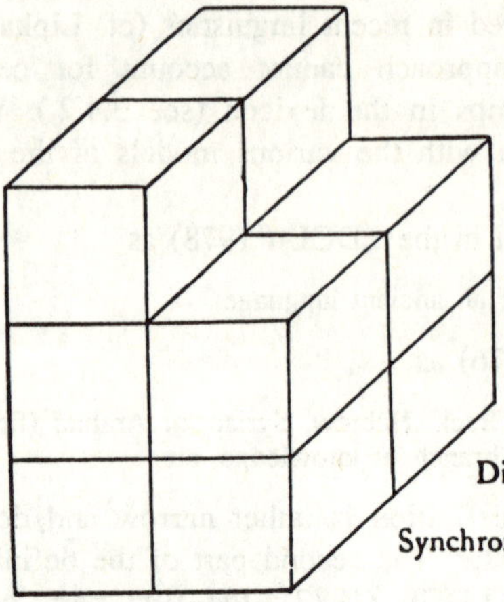

In this three-dimensional linguistic model,[5] *lexicology*, as the discipline concerned with lexis or the lexicon, is represented as a level in between phonology and syntax. All three levels, phonology, lexicology, and syntax are subsystems of the entire language system. They may be described at a particular point in time, i.e. synchronically, or in their historical evolution, i.e. diachronically. Phonology, which is concerned with the sound system of the language, has a formal, but no semantic aspect.[6] Lexicology has both a morphological and a semantic dimension, and both may be regarded from a diachronic or a synchronic point of view. The same holds for syntax, which is concerned with larger linguistic units. Ullmann (²1957 : 31) explicitly relates the distinction between "morphology" and "semantics" to the duality of form and meaning and to Saussure's "signifiant" and "signifié" (see 2.1.1.).

He clearly states that his diagram is only a possible representation of the various disciplines of linguistics and their interrelation. Here the lexicon is an organic and essential part of a structuralist model. In generative grammar both the status of the lexicon as a component as well as its scope are rather controversial. In particular, there is a controversy between the so-called "lexicalists" and the "transformationalists" (cf. Lipka 1975 : 207–209, Kastovsky 1982a : 220 ff.). The former argue for a very comprehensive lexicon that contains as a list not only simple words and idiomatic expressions but also compounds and derivatives. According to the transformationalists (whose position Chomsky

[5] Cf. also the three-dimensional "language block" (*Sprachklotz*) for the representation of the levels, historical stages, and varieties of the English language used in Bald (1988 : 129).

[6] This view obviously disregards onomatopoeia and attitudinal meaning related to prosody.

himself had shared in early TG), complex words are derived by a productive mechanism of so-called "transformations". Such complex lexical items therefore need not be separately listed in the lexicon.

The second sense b) of *lexicon*, with stress on the systematic and synchronic point of view, distinguishes my approach from other descriptions of the vocabulary of English. Naturally, to adopt such different perspectives is perfectly legitimate. As an example of such a different view of the English word-stock I will briefly mention Manfred Scheler's (1977) *Der Englische Wortschatz*. The author is mainly concerned with the following points: the etymological heterogeneity of the English vocabulary (as his most important focus), the problem of the mixing of languages with its causes and consequences, and finally specific forms of the English vocabulary and its stratification. His approach is therefore primarily historical, and it is partly based on the results of the *Chronological English Dictionary* (CED) by Finkenstaedt, Leisi and Wolff (1970).[7] There is no comparable full-scale treatment of the word-stock of English by a British or American author (but cf. Baugh/Cable 1978, esp. ch. 4.7.8. and 10).

I will draw in the following on the approach to the vocabulary of English in Ernst Leisi's (^{7}1985) book *Das heutige Englisch*. There are two relevant chapters namely II, "Der gemischte Wortschatz", on the mixed vocabulary, and V, "Die Schichtung des Englischen", on the stratification of English. Leisi's treatment can be characterized as a synchronic description on a historical basis. He distinguishes various historical strata and deals with the consequences of language-contact. In chapter V he discusses a purely synchronic star-shaped model of the stratification of the English vocabulary (see diagram (2) p. 10), based on a diagram in the *Shorter Oxford English Dictionary* (SOED). Common etymological origin and period of adopting loanwords, as well as stylistic stratification (in a wide sense of *style*) result in groups or categories of words and thus permit generalizations and impose a sort of structure on the vocabulary.

According to Leisi, contemporary English is a unique mixture of Germanic and Romance elements and this mixing has resulted in the international character of the vocabulary. Its great richness allows far finer differentiation in comparison with other languages. For example German *Tier* corresponds to either *animal* or *beast* in English. *Wagen* can be rendered by a series of English translations, such as *car, cart, carriage,* and *chariot*. As equivalents of *nachdenken* or *überlegen*, English has *think, reflect, meditate, ponder,* and *cogitate*. Clearly, the structure of the vocabulary is different in both languages.[8]

---

7 Cf. Jackson (1988 : 242 f.) where this dictionary is mentioned as an example of a practical answer to lexicology's legitimate question about the overall structure of the vocabulary. Its early use of computational methods is also stressed.

8 But cf. Farrell (^{3}1977 : vii): "The fact that German lacks terms of such wide application as 'take', 'way', 'leave', 'keep', 'power' (to mention only a few of the more notorious), and must therefore use specific terms, perhaps to a greater extent than even French ...". G. Pascoe is of the opinion that German

This is also true for the negative consequences of the mixing of languages. Leisi treats these under the headings "Dissoziation" and "hard words". "Dissoziation" (dissociation) describes the phenomenon that words are unrelated or not associated with each other, which is typical of English as opposed to German. Thus for example in German *mündlich* and *Dreifuß* are related ("vergesellschaftet" or "konsoziiert") to *Mund, drei,* and *Fuß.* The English equivalents *oral* and *tripod,* however, are completely unrelated to *mouth, three,* and *foot.* Other examples of the dissociation of the English vocabulary are *appendix,* as opposed to *Blinddarm, hippopotamus* as opposed to *Nilpferd* or *Flußpferd,* and *syringe* as opposed to *Spritze.*

Leisi (⁷1985 : 68 f.) uses the term *hard words* (following a tradition in English lexicography) for words of Latin or Greek origin that pose problems for those ignorant of classical languages. This may lead to more or less funny mistakes and erroneous use, so-called malapropisms. Thus, for example *epitaph* and *epithet* may be easily confused as well as *illiterate* and *illegitimate. Allegory, alligator,* and *atheist* are further examples. Besides social consequences of such difficulties Leisi also sees change of meaning as a result of the problem of hard words.[9]

It is certainly true that all languages are mixtures to a greater or lesser extent. Comparing English to German and French, however, Leisi (⁷1985 : 58) comes to the conclusion that the present-day English vocabulary is unique in this respect.[10]

A brief look at the various historical strata may perhaps not be out of place. Through cultural contact with the Romans, partly already on the Continent, and also through the influence of Christianity, a very early stratum of Latin-Greek words entered the language. This origin is no longer felt by the normal speaker today in words such as *dish, cheese, mint, pound, devil.* The same holds for some Scandinavian words from about the 10th century that today belong to the central core of the vocabulary. This means that their frequency is very high. The stratum contains: *they, them, their, sky, skin, skill, ill, die, cast,* and *take.* They partly supersede a number of Old English words such as *heofon* 'sky, heaven', *steorfan* 'die', and *niman* 'take'.

A more radical change and profound influence on the English vocabulary occurred in the wake of the Norman conquest of 1066. Until the 15th century a great number of French words were adopted that belonged especially to the areas of court, state, law, and church (another possible generalization) such as: *sovereign, country, minister, parliament, noble, honour, justice, religion, service,*

---

has more "generalisation gaps" than English, which cause German learners usage-problems, since they lack what he calls "the small wide words of English", e.g. *box, pull, move, get, stop.*

[9] Some of the examples he gives are: *sensible, pathetic, emergency, premises, realize,* and for recent shifts of meaning: *alibi, allergic, facility.*

[10] G. Pascoe justly points out that Persian and Japanese are certainly similar, with a native "base" plus a huge admixture of words from another source even less closely related than in English.

virtue, vice, pity, beauty and also *preach, arch,* and *chaste*. The influx was strongest before 1400 but continued up to the 17th century.

These early words are distinguished from later French loans, such as *champagne* and *machine*, by phonological peculiarities of the latter, namely the pronunciation [ ] instead of [t]. In Leisi's ([7]1985:60) opinion the adoption of French words at various times prepared the ground for the invasion of learned words of Latin and Greek origin during the humanistic period.

We mentioned before that as a positive result of the mixing of languages, the possibility of distinguishing fine nuances of meaning arises. Leisi ([7]1985: 68) points out that the distinction between *manly, masculine, male, virile* is not parallel to that between *womanly, womanish, female, feminine*. It must be added that it is impossible to capture the exact differences of meaning, unless we consider the combining potential of these words, the so-called collocations (see 4.3.5.). Thus, for example, *masculine* can be combined with *style, woman*, and *pronoun*, but *male* cannot.

We have so far considered various historical strata in the English vocabulary. In contrast to this analysis on the basis of etymological criteria, we will now look at the synchronic stratification of English. Although Leisi speaks of 'stratum' ("Schichtung") in this context, this is perhaps not a very fortunate term. It would be better to speak of areas or zones, since *stratum* implies the existence of various horizontal levels on top of each other. For the structure of the vocabulary discussed in the following, the metaphors of circles or zones, however, seem more appropriate. We can establish a relatively clear-cut centre or core. The peripheries, however, are rather vague and fuzzy. The zones also overlap and penetrate mutually in various ways. This is related to the problem of varieties of English, which we will discuss in greater detail later.

The simple image of stratum may have some justification in the explanation of sociolectal differences in the vocabulary. Sociologists often do not only speak of classes, but also of strata and social stratification. How difficult it is to reach general and permanent agreement in this field can be seen from a concrete example mentioned in Leisi's book ([7]1985:182). In 1954, Alan S.C. Ross introduced a distinction between two kinds of words in British English: *U* (for upper class) vs. *non-U* (for non-upper class), which were said to be linguistic "class-indicators". For example he labelled *ill, cycle, mirror, dentures* as "non-U", while *sick, bike, looking-glass, false teeth* were claimed to be "U". The distinction between *U* and *non-U* soon became part of the public consciousness in Britain and the whole business quickly developed into a sort of party game. The linguistic situation was already changed by the heated discussion itself and by the eagerness of many people to be considered as *U*-speakers. There was a revival of the *U* vs. *non-U* debate around 1979. What is more important, however, than discussing further individual examples, is to realize that the simple image of two distinct layers or strata in society and language is far too simplistic. Reality is far more complex, as we will see when discussing varieties of English in 1.3. Furthermore, there is often an interrelationship between various regional, social, and situational parameters which results in the choice of a specific lexical item (cf. Lipka 1988a). A glance at the pair *ill/sick* alone will show that there are crucial differences between British and American English, but also within each geographical variety, depending on specific collocations – cf. *illness, sickness, be sick* (on the boat), *sick leave, sick parade* = AmE *sick call* (see 4.3.5).

In the following I would like to give a traditional, synchronic survey of the structure of the English vocabulary based on a diagram given in the introduction to the *Shorter Oxford English Dictionary* (SOED [3]1973 : x). This is also discussed in Leisi's book ([7]1985 : 187 f.) and should be related to the treatment of varieties of English in 1.3. Here is a slightly modified version of the original diagram:

(2)

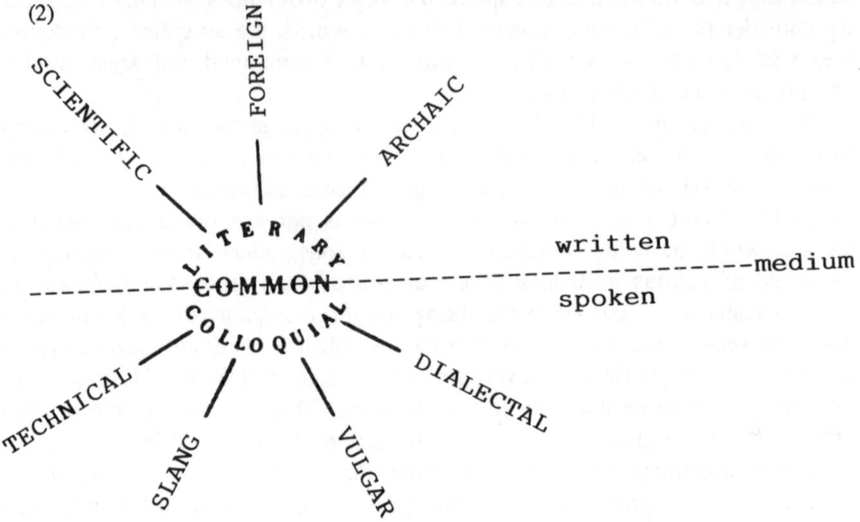

The representation starts out from the assumption that the vocabulary of English contains a large central area, which is common to all media, styles, and social classes. This concept of common English, symbolized by COMMON, is equivalent, with respect to the lexicon, to the "common core" treated in the *University Grammar of English* (Quirk/Greenbaum 1973 : 1 ff.; cf. Quirk et al. 1985 : 16 ff.), which is present in all varieties of English. This central area, which contains words like e.g. *come, father, chair, good, bad, very*, is labelled "Common English" by the editors of the SOED.

Above and below we have the neighbouring areas of "Literary" and "Colloquial". Connected with these in a radial manner are further areas of the vocabulary, which are also related to each other in content, according to the opinion of the editors of the Oxford Dictionary.

The literary vocabulary contains scientific, foreign and archaic words such as *Weltanschauung* or *blasé*. The transition from other "literary" words such as *firmament, similitude, whence, whither* to the outer areas is gradual and fluid. On the other side "Colloquial" English contains dialectal and vulgar elements, as well as words from slang and technical language. We should add that the term *slang* is often used for special languages of specific groups, e.g. in *army slang, public school slang, navy slang, RAF slang*. There are thus no clear boundaries between *slang* in this sense and *technical language*.

It is true, in general, that all categories used in this diagram have no sharp boundaries. Thus "Colloquial", "Slang", and "Vulgar" cannot be precisely and unambiguously defined. In the diagram they are consequently close neighbours. The areas of vocabulary denoted by them merge and interpenetrate. The radial lines connect the peripheral and the central areas of the vocabulary. The further we get to the periphery, the more we are removed from the common vocabulary of "Common English".

Leisi ([7]1985:187f.) draws attention to the fact that if we start out with Archaic and turn right in a circle, until we get to Foreign, we always find an inherent connection between the labels. Archaic words are often alive in dialects, dialectal and vulgar expressions both belong to popular language, etc. He further points out that if we draw a line through COMMON, this would divide written English above from spoken English below. Vocabulary is thus assigned in equal parts to the two media.

In the following I would like to give an example of the general treatment of lexical structure, not restricted to the vocabulary of English. As a model approach, I will discuss the following schema (3), adapted from Coseriu (1970: 166) (cf. also Coseriu/Geckeler 1981:56). He basically proposes the following model for describing and analysing lexical structure (with my modifications):

(3)

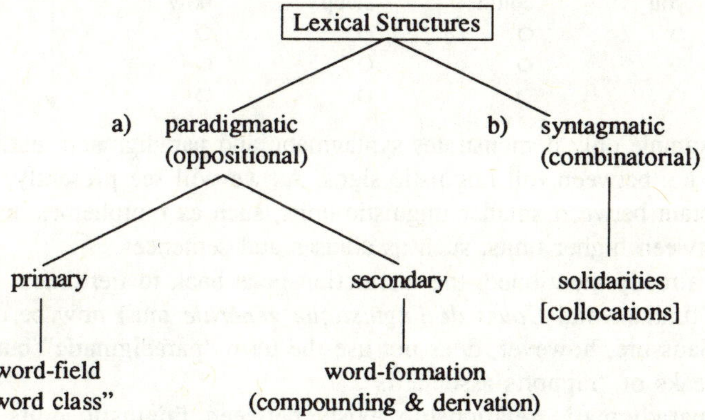

For the moment, the following explanation of diagram (3) should suffice. Paradigmatic structures comprise words which can be substituted for each other in a specific slot in a sentence. They necessarily belong to the same syntactic class (see 4.2.). Syntagmatic structures, which Coseriu labels 'solidarities' ("Solidaritäten"), comprise the relationships between words which are systematically and conventionally combined in a sentence (see 4.3.). Examples for the latter are *blond* and *hair* or *bark* and *dog*. Coseriu distinguishes three types of solidarities but does not mention collocations. Word-fields (his "Wortfeld") are primary paradigmatic structures consisting of lexical items that share a common zone of meaning and are in direct opposition to each other (see 4.2.4.). "Word class" in Coseriu's sense (marked by inverted commas, here and in the English version of 1981 labelled 'lexical class') are classes of lexical items that contain the same very general semantic feature, called a 'classeme' ("Klassem") by Coseriu (see 4.3.). Examples of such classes are animate beings, objects, humans, and animals. Secondary paradigmatic structures comprise the traditional field of word-formation (see 3.2.).

Let us now have a closer look at the fundamental distinction between paradigmatic and syntagmatic relationships in the lexicon (cf. Lipka 1972:32 f.). This distinction basically derives from the linear nature of linguistic substance, what Saussure (1916:103) called the "caractère linéaire du signifiant". This linearity goes back to the fact that speech sounds follow each other in time. Successive linguistic elements that are combined were called "syntagme" by Saussure. In English, both *syntagma* and sometimes *syntagm* are used as equivalent terms. Elements that are in opposition or contrast in the same position in a syntagma are said to be in a paradigmatic relationship. One can also say that they can be substituted for each other and form a paradigm. The different relationships and the resulting two dimensions may be illustrated with the following simple example adopted from Crystal ([2]1985 : 163):

(4)	He ———	can ———	go ———	tomorrow	←→ syntagmatic relationships
	she	may	come	soon	↕ paradigmatic relationships
	I	will	ask	next	
	you	could	sleep	now	
	o	o	o	o	
	o	o	o	o	
	o	o	o	o	

This example only demonstrates syntagmatic and paradigmatic relations between words, i.e. between full linguistic signs. As we will see presently, the relations also obtain between smaller linguistic units, such as morphemes and phonemes, and between higher units, such as clauses and sentences.

As already mentioned, the distinction goes back to Ferdinand de Saussure, whose fundamental *Cours de linguistique générale* must now be quoted explicitly. Saussure, however, does not use the term "paradigmatic" but "associatif" and speaks of "rapports associatifs".

A paradigmatic relationship exists between linguistic units that can be substituted for each other in the same syntagma. These units are often said to be in *opposition*. Sometimes a finer terminological *distinction* is made between *opposition* and *contrast*. In this case *opposition* is reserved for paradigmatic relationships, while *contrast* is only used for preceding and following elements in syntagmatic relation (cf. Kastovsky 1982a:22). It will be immediately obvious that again these are notational terms, if we consider that Lyons (1977:279) uses both for paradigmatic meaning relations, with *contrast* being "the most general term" and *opposition* denoting "dichotomous, or binary contrasts" (see 4.2.3.). Syntagmatic relations exist between elements of the language system that are combined, i.e. that co-occur. On the lexical and syntactic level the result of such a combination is therefore often called *syntagma*, which is equivalent to *construction* used in American structuralism.

Some further illustration may perhaps be useful. On the phonological level, the English phonemes /i/, /e/, and /æ/ in the words *pit, pet*, and *pat* stand in paradigmatic relation, since they may be substituted for each other as in (5a). Each of these phonemes, however, is in syntagmatic relation with the English phonemes /p/ and /t/ in all three words. On the lexical level the distinction can be illustrated as in (5b):

(5a) pit /i/	(5b) the *old* man
pet /e/	the *tall* m a n
pat /æ/	the old w o m a n .

The adjectives *old* and *tall* as well as the nouns *man* and *woman* are in paradigmatic relationship. The article, the adjective, and the noun, however, are syntagmatically related in all three cases. The following example has been taken over in modified form from Leech (^{2}1981:15), who uses it for a different purpose:[11]

(6a) They *cast* stones at the *police*

↕ ↕

(6b) They *chucked* stones at the *cops*

The relation between the italicized verbs and nouns marked by vertical arrows is paradigmatic; the relation between the verbs and the nouns in both sentences (6a) and (6b), however, is a syntagmatic one.

As a sort of summary of my general remarks on the structure of the lexicon let me give the following diagram representing lexical structure and relations:

[11] G. Pascoe rightly argues that Leech's example has certain drawbacks and instead proposes: (a) *The comestibles were unsatisfactory* (over-formal or mock-formal), (b) *The food was poor* (neutral), (c) *The grub was chronic* (schoolchildren's slang).

(7)

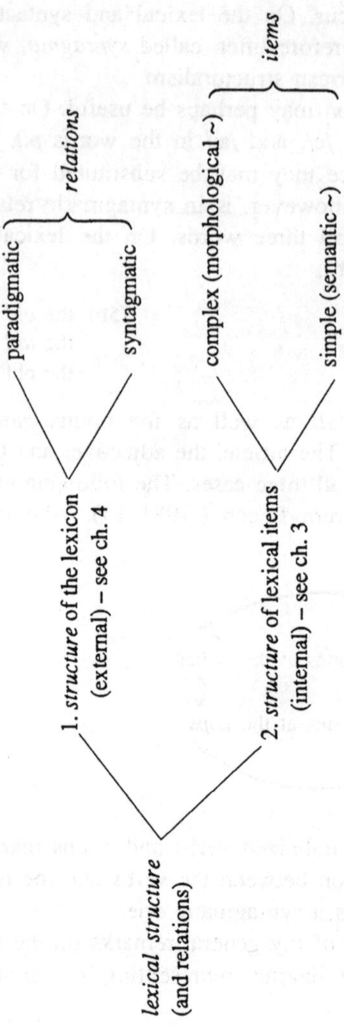

1.3. Varieties of English

We now come to varieties of English and their relevance for the lexicon (cf. Quirk et al. 1985 : 15 ff.). We have already seen in diagram (2) that the vocabulary of English is far from being homogeneous. This also holds for other linguistic levels. It will immediately become clear that no language approaches the completely homogeneous system postulated by many linguistic theories and models.

We have noted that the vocabulary of English has a temporal dimension visible in its stratification through various influences at different times. English has changed so much that it is even relevant to ask whether English before the Norman Conquest in 1066 can be said to be the same language as modern English. Obviously the language of Shakespeare compared to present-day English shows many more correspondences and equivalents than Old English. Nevertheless, there are very important differences that are often overlooked, due to the frequent formal similarity of words. A precise analysis in many cases shows considerable discrepancy of meaning between words used by Shakespeare and formally identical contemporary words. As part of our literary heritage, such words and their use in famous quotations simultaneously belong to Early Modern English and the contemporary language.

Besides the temporal dimension, the geographic dimension of a language naturally also plays a very important role. The differences between British English and American English immediately come to mind. I will restrict myself to the level of the lexicon. In many descriptions of the English language and in some school grammars we find pairs of lists such as the following (cf. Leisi [7]1985:226, but also the illustrations in LDCE 2 s.v. *house, kitchen*).

> AmE: *railroad, conductor, baggage, package, gas(oline), truck, sidewalk*, as opposed to BrE: *railway, guard, luggage, parcel, petrol, lorry, pavement.*

It is rarely mentioned that a number of British words are perfectly acceptable in many areas in America. On the other hand numerous Americanisms have become quite familiar in Britain, due to an increase in transatlantic travel and the influence of broadcast media. At Heathrow Airport, for example, the signs read *baggage* not *luggage*. In many cases the original American flavour has been lost completely, especially for younger British speakers.

Before the Second World War some Americans insisted on referring to "the American language" instead of "the English language in America". Today, nobody seriously claims that these are two different languages. Nevertheless, there is a grain of salt in the well-known saying by George Bernard Shaw that Britain and America are two nations divided by a common language. We can conclude that the differences between British and American English are on the same level as those between other varieties of English, although the two might be regarded as the most important "national standards".

Basically, the assumption that language is a homogeneous system, which goes back to Saussure's *langue*, echoed in Chomsky's *competence*, is always an abstraction. The idealization is particularly evident in Chomsky's (1965:3) claim that linguistic theory is concerned

> with an ideal speaker-listener, in a completely homogeneous speech-community, who knows its language perfectly.

As a rule, every speaker has at his or her disposal several variants of a language, which becomes particularly apparent in phonology and the choice of words. Especially in times of great mobility many members of a speech community are subject to varying linguistic influences, which are most clearly noticeable in the vocabulary.

Consequently, as a rule, every single speaker has his or her very personal language. This language form of the single speaker is nowadays generally called *idiolect.* As opposed to this, *dialect* is the language form of a particular group of speakers. The term *dialect* is currently often used in a broad sense, i.e. both for a regional, geographical variety, as well as for a social subclass of a speech community (cf. Wächtler 1977:37–45). The neutral term *variety* is frequently preferred today since it lacks the negative connotations, or shades of meaning, of *dialect.* Sometimes a terminological distinction is made between *dialect,* used for the regional varieties (cf. Quirk et al. 1985:16), and *social dialect,* or *social-class dialect,* for the language of a socially determined group of speakers.

In Strang (^{2}1968:19) *dialect* is used for both a geographical and social subsection of speakers of a language, and a scale of *idiolect – dialect – language* is set up. This is said to intersect with three other parameters necessary for the description of language variation: 1. *medium*, 2. social role, labelled '*style*' (with inverted commas to mark the technical sense), and 3. *register.* All these are obviously notational terms, and it is not justified to speak of the "correct" definition of *register.* The mistaken belief that such terms only have a single correct definition, in my opinion, is a result of the process of 'hypostatization' (cf. Lipka 1975:200, 212; 1977).[12] By this term I mean, following Leisi, that the existence of a word implies the existence of a single entity denoted by it. For Strang both *medium* (denoting the distinction between writing and speech) and '*style*' depend on the user of the language (cf. ^{2}1968: 21). The third type of variety, *register,* according to Strang, does not depend on the user but on the use of language (cf. Quirk et al. 1985:16). An example of this would be the lexical item *drop goal* in talking about rugby. According to Strang, *register* is not merely a matter of lexical forms, but may also be realized by phonological and grammatical features.

The distinction between "user" vs. "use of language" has a long tradition in British linguistics in the analysis of language variation (cf. Wächtler 1977: 27–30). It is sometimes equated with the opposition between "dialectal varieties", which are relatively permanent, and "diatypic varieties", which depend on situations. The former can be further subdivided into diachronic, diatopic and diastratic varieties, according to variation in time, place, and social class. The diatypic varieties are often referred to as *registers.* Halliday (1978: 31, 35, 142f.) and others consider *register* as a complex notion determined by the three variables: 1. *field*, 2. *tenor*, and 3. *mode of discourse.* It is said that the configuration of all three variables taken together determines situation-types and the "context of situation". The three situational features correspond to: 1. subject matter plus type of social action, i.e. what is actually taking place (*field*), 2. role relationships, i.e. who is taking part (*tenor*), and 3. symbolic organi-

[12] Other alternatives for this admittedly clumsy term, such as *hypostasis* or *reification,* do not seem to have caught on. I believe that the reverse of the medal of this phenomenon is the "concept-forming power of the word" mentioned in Leech (^{2}1981:32).

zation, i.e. what part the language is playing (*mode*) (cf. Lipka 1988b). For Halliday (1978:132f., 143f.) subject matter is only one element of *field*. As he points out, while one is engaged in gardening or playing football, one hardly uses words from this area. However, when talking about these subjects, the relevant terminology is very important.

We shall now look at the explicit classification of varieties of English as given by Quirk/Greenbaum (1973:1ff.) in the UGE. The variety classes distinguished there are not restricted to the vocabulary. I will tentatively illustrate the respective limitations of words to certain areas by using the "labels" employed for this purpose in the LDCE. There are evident connections with the distinction between 'denotation' and 'connotation' that will be discussed later (cf. 2.2.).

In the following diagram (8), I have added to the variety classes distinguished by the UGE some more or less equivalent terms from other approaches (cf. Lipka 1988a). Partial equivalences are symbolized by . So-called "labels" used in the two editions of the LDCE have also been included.[13]

(8)	1.	Region (geographical variation)		*AmE, NEngE*
	2.	Education and social standing		*lit, sl*
	3.	Subject matter	register/field	*law, med*
	4.	Medium	mode	*lit, poet*
	5.	Attitude	'style'/tenor	*fml, humour*
	6.	Interference		*Fr, Ger*

Before considering the relevance of this schema for the structure of the lexicon in greater detail, I should like to explain the distinctions as made by the UGE. The grammar points out that there are numerous varieties of the English language and that what is normally meant by *English* is the "common core" realized in the different spoken or written froms of the language.[14] There is, thus, a set of grammatical and other characteristics common to all "variety classes". Within each class, further subdivision is possible and so there are

[13] According to the LDCE 2 (^{2}1987:F45) the purpose of the labels is to indicate that "the use of a word is limited in some way", e.g. to informal situations (*infml*), to technical legal language (*law*), or to specific regions such as the North of England (*NEngE*), etc. (see the list of abbreviations p. 189f.). The LDCE has labels for: region, special fields or subjects, situations, time (*old-fash, old use, rare, becoming rare*), attitude (e.g. *apprec, pomp*), and "other limitations on use" namely *dial* (local speech of a particular area), *nonstandard* ("regarded as incorrect"), *taboo* (very offensive), and *tdmk* (trademark). Two additional devices for helping to choose the right word in the LDCE 2 are the so-called "Usage Notes" and "Language Notes", both containing (besides other things) pragmatic information.

[14] In the LDCE 2, *English*, defined as 'the language of Britain, the US, Australia, etc.' is still marked as an uncountable noun. In recent usage, especially by linguists, the word can be pluralized, and *Englishes* appears in the title of articles and books, a form likewise not yet recorded in Howard (1985).

varieties within varieties. Naturally, these are closely interrelated. Also, each of the six kinds of variety is related to the other variety classes. Clearly, there are many parallels to the distinctions made in the vocabulary by the SOED, as represented in diagram (2). Here is a closer look at the distinction of the six classes.

1. "Region"

For geographical or regional variation the term *dialect* is traditionally used. As we have seen, this is a notational term that is not at all unambiguous. It is often used for socially determined variants of a language (but not in Quirk et al. 1985, for example). Sometimes there is close interdependence between the two variety classes 1 and 2. Thus, Cockney is really the dialect of a particular social class living in a particular part of London. Regional variation in language seems to be predominantly realized on the phonological level. This is often referred to as *accent*, although the term may also refer to variety class 6 "Interference". We may speak of a *Welsh* or *Scottish accent*, but also of a noticeable *German* or *French accent*. A dialect, or rather a regional variety, may also be distinguished by different lexical or grammatical features.

It has to be noted that there is regionally different familiarity with specific variants of English. Thus, an Englishman will hear an American Southener first as an American and may perhaps then classify him as a Southener in addition. On the other hand, he may be able to distinguish within Great Britain between Irish, Scots, Northern, Midland, Welsh, South-Western, and may perhaps recognize several London varieties. In North America, however, many people are able to distinguish between Canadian, New England, Midland and Southern.

With regard to lexical variants, we have already seen a number of examples of differences between British and American English. Another regional variety, namely Scottish English, is perhaps less well known, although words such as *loch, kirk, bonnie, lassie, wee* are certainly not only familiar to British speakers. It may be difficult (cf. Lyons 1977: 619) to decide whether these are purely dialectal variants, or whether they have a more specific descriptive meaning than their corresponding stylistically neutral equivalents (*lake, church* etc.). Less well known is e.g. *outwith* meaning 'outside', which may be found in formal written Scottish texts.

Besides British and American English, the UGE distinguishes several other "national standards of English". Scots, Irish English, and Canadian English are comparable to these two overwhelmingly predominant standards. South African English, New Zealand English and Australian English are in a different position in several respects. Although they are similar in orthography and grammar to British English, there are considerable differences in the lexicon and the phonology.

2. "Education and Social Standing"

Within geographically different forms of English there is considerable variation depending on education and social standing. This is sometimes referred to as *sociolect* or *social dialect*. Although there is some correlation between uneducated speech and regional dialect, the two are certainly not coterminous. As an example of uneducated English the UGE mentions the double negative. Educated English is often referred to as *Standard English* which, however, is clearly a notational term. There is a partial correspondence between educated and literary English as well as between uneducated and so-called substandard and slang (see diagram (2) p. 10).

With regard to the lexicon, the stratum of words of Greek and Latin origin must be mentioned here. "Hard words" are a problem mainly for the uneducated. The distinction betwenn *U*-words (such as *lavatory* and *rich*) and *non-U*-words (such as *toilet* and *wealthy*) is a matter of social standing.[15]

3. "Subject Matter"

The UGE points out that varieties according to subject matter are often referred to as "registers". We have already seen that this is a notational term, and that it may be considered, for example by Halliday, as a complex notion involving further variables. Both Strang and Halliday define *register* as a "variety according to use". More precisely, for Halliday "subject matter" is only one element in the contexual variable *field*. In Quirk et al. (1985:16) class 3 is consistently replaced by "field of discourse" (see diagram (9) p. 23).

The use of particular lexical items is one of the most typical characteristics of language variation according to subject matter or field of discourse. The UGE mentions law, cookery, engineering, and football in this connection. It also points out that there are certain interrelations and dependencies between specific varieties. Thus, for example, a well-formed legal sentence presupposes an educated variety of English. Such connections, however, are not limited to relations between the classes 2 and 3. There are also correlations with other classes, as, for example, the following one.

4. "Medium"

This term is usually employed to distinguish the spoken from the written variety of a language. Further subdivision is possible (cf. Lipka (1988b) for the distinctions made by Crystal and Davy, such as between "simple medium" vs. "complex medium"). Thus, a dictation is "spoken to be written", while a radio news bulletin is "written to be spoken". Many legal expressions and specific

---

[15] See p. 9 for the distinction between *U* and *non-U*. Words of Greek or Latin origin are not necessarily "hard words" (e.g. *angel, church, devil, mint, parson*) and it is sociolinguistically revealing that *U*-words tend to have an Anglo-Saxon etymology (such as *looking-glass, false teeth*).

grammatical peculiarities are only found in written texts, such as documents and contracts.

Obviously, the choice of medium depends on the situation in which language is used. The written medium normally presupposes the physical absence of the addressee. There are also differences in the devices used for the transmission of spoken and written language. In print we have various typographical means, as well as headings and paragraphs, for structuring the message. The spoken language, on the other hand, makes use of devices such as intonation and speech tempo, as well as extralinguistic communication signals, like gestures and eye contact.

In Halliday's theory, *mode* is the equivalent of *medium*, although it comprises further elements of the "symbolic organization". Here, textual functions such as expository, didactic, persuasive are included as well as the concept of "genre" (Halliday 1978:144f.).

With regard to the lexicon, literary and poetical words are relevant here, which occur practically only in the written language. Also, archaic and extinct words are normally only found in writing and hardly in the spoken medium. Clearly there is a close relationship here with variety class 2. In French, the differences between the spoken and the written medium are even more important. Here we have practically two different languages co-existing side by side, the so-called *code parlé* and the *code écrit*.

5. "Attitude"

In this variety class, according to the UGE, linguistic form may be determined by the speaker's or writer's attitude to the hearer or reader (the addressee), to the subject matter, or to the purpose of the message. The UGE points out that this variety is often marked by the ambiguous label *style*. We must add that Halliday's *tenor* is a more precise equivalent, although it does not include attitude to the subject matter. The UGE distinguishes five variants of attitude along the following scale: rigid / FORMAL / neutral / INFORMAL / familiar (of which only the two in capitals are explicitly marked).

With regard to the lexicon, finer distinctions are usually drawn in many dictionaries. There are different kinds and different degrees of formality and informality. From the point of view of etymology it is noteworthy that formal words are normally of classical or Romance origin, while informal words usually derive from Anglo-Saxon (cf. four-letter words).

There is a problem here sometimes, parallel to the one mentioned in connection with variety class 1, namely whether we have to do with two formally distinct variants of the same word, or with two denotationally different lexical items. For example Leech (^{2}1981:14) mentions as "synonyms with ... stylistic overtones": *steed* (poetic), *horse* (general), *nag* (slang). According to this, *horse* would be stylistically neutral or unmarked, while both *steed* and *nag* are stylistic variants of *horse*. However, *nag* is defined in the COD as "small riding-horse or pony; (colloq.) horse". The OALD compresses this twofold definition of *nag* into: "(colloq.) (usu old) horse". The LDCE 1 (1978), gives two distinct definitions: "1 *not fml* a horse that is old or in bad condition 2 *infml, esp. derog* a horse, esp. one which races". If we take the second definition in the LDCE and COD,[16] and the one in the OALD without the qualification "usu old", then *nag* is simply a stylistically marked variant of horse (see 2.2.5.). If, on the other hand, we consider a *nag* to be a horse that is either small, old, in bad condition, or one which races, then *nag* has a meaning or denotation different from *horse*. The example demonstrates the problem of the delimitation of meaning, the so-called "fuzziness" of meaning that will be further discussed in 2.1. and 2.2. The dictionaries try to capture this by using labels such as "usu" or "esp". A label such as *derog* clearly refers to attitude towards the thing talked about (here: dislike), while *humor* denotes attitude more towards the addressee than towards subject matter.

6. "Interference"

This class (set off from the others by a broken line in the UGE) is in fact rather different and, as the authors state, "on a very different basis" (UGE 1973: 7). It refers to contact with a foreign language and includes varieties caused by the traces left by a speaker's native language when speaking English. An example of grammatical interference given by the UGE is the utterance *I am here since Thursday* made by a Frenchman. The grammar points out that certain varieties of English spoken in India, Pakistan, and some African countries, might be considered as almost reaching the status of a national standard. This shows that there is considerable overlap with the other variety classes. Also, pidgins and creoles are relevant here.

On the level of the lexicon, interference is probably more important than on the phonological level. In this connection loan-words and loan-translations must be mentioned as the result of interference. The so-called "false friends" also belong here, for example when Ger *sensibel, brav, pathetisch* are identified with E *sensible, brave*, and *pathetic* (cf. Pascoe and Pascoe 1985). Interference can further cause change of meaning, as for example in Ger *realisieren* and *kontrollieren*, which have acquired the additional meanings 'notice' and 'command, influence' under the influence of E *realize* and *control*.

As already mentioned, there exists a great deal of overlap and interrelation between the variety classes. The UGE points out that certain subjects can hardly be handled in writing, while others (e.g. legal statutes) must be handled in this medium. It is further observed that for certain topics (e.g. funerals) informal language would be inappropriate and distasteful. Nevertheless, attitudinal varieties possess a great deal of independence, compared to other varieties. The parameters used for defining the six variety classes are not absolute either. They are graded and variable and there are varieties within each variety.

---

16 This is missing in the LDCE 2 (1987), where the noun *nag* (denoting a horse) only has the entry: "*infml* a horse, esp. one that is old or in bad condition". See 2.2.5 (p. 64) and the remarks on *foal* and *Fohlen/Füllen* p. 155, 157.

A few further points must be made with regard to the subject of this book. Not all variety classes are equally relevant for the lexicon. Idiolectal variation will be disregarded here, although it is perfectly legitimate to establish concordances of the usage of words by authors such as Chaucer, Shakespeare, or Byron. The choice of specific lexical items by an individual may be crucial in textual studies, for example for establishing authorship. Temporal variation is completely neglected by the classification in the UGE; but cf. LDCE (^{2}1987: F46). However, most speakers of a language are definitely able to distinguish archaic, obsolete, or obsolescent words from recent coinings, new words, and neologisms generally. Lyons (1977: 621) has coined the expression "diachrony-in-synchrony" for this phenomenon. Language change is probably most rapid on the lexical level (cf. Strang ^{2}1968: 227 ff.). This is one of the reasons for the frequent characterization of the lexicon as an open set or list, as opposed to the closed systems of grammar. It also forces lexicographers to revise their dictionaries at certain intervals, and even induces some of them to write dictionaries of "New English" (see 1.4.).

There are also dictionaries of Americanisms and other regional varieties of English. Geographical variation is tied up with another vexing problem: some words are identical in form, but have a different meaning in various parts of the English-speaking world. This is well known in the case of the names of certain bakery products, such as *biscuits, cookies*, and *scones* (cf. Lehrer 1974: 65) which do not mean the same in America, England, and Scotland. In German, equally, e.g. *Wecken* may denote a roll in some parts of the country, while it refers to a loaf of bread in others. A *crumpet*, in the sense of 'cake', is sweet in Scotland (equivalent to an English *pancake*), while it is unsweetened in England. The word has a further meaning, not geographically restricted, denoting 'a (sexually desirable) woman' that must be considered a metaphorical extension of meaning (see 3.4.2.). In this sense it is labelled "*BrE infml & often humor*" in the LDCE (1978), but "sl." in the COD, which shows how variation according to "attitude" may be classified differently. Further examples of regional variation from other semantic fields are: *bucket*, which to some people in Scotland is 'a dustbin', and *chapel*, which denotes a place of worship 'for non-conformists' in England and Wales, and 'for Roman Catholics' in Scotland.

In the second type of varieties (social class or standing), usually two different items are used as a shibboleth (*U* or *non-U*). But within this type, there are also lexical items with identical form and different referent. Thus *dinner* is the chief meal eaten 'at midday' by some people and 'in the evening' in other social classes in Britain.

In Quirk et al. (1985: 15 ff.), the underlying model for the treatment of varieties of English has been considerably simplified, with a noticeable influence of Hallidayan ideas. Thus, there are only five types left and "field of discourse" (defined as "type of activity engaged in through language") replaces "subject matter". If the distinction between "variety according to user" and "variety according to use" (which is stressed throughout the text) is furthermore incorporated into the schema, the following diagram with five parameters results:

(9)	(a)	region	user
	(b)	social group	
	(c)	*field of discourse*	language use
	(d)	medium	
	(e)	attitude	

These distinctions are certainly justified from the point of view of a grammar. However, as already mentioned, the discarded category "Interference" is particularly relevant for the lexicon, especially from a diachronic point of view.

Most entries in any dictionary will be neutral with regard to the six variety classes. In other words, the items can be used anywhere in the world where English is spoken or written. This also holds for the entries in the LDCE. If, however, the usage of a word is limited or restricted to a particular geographical area, subject matter, or type of discourse, this is marked by the label. Sometimes several labels can be combined, which is not surprising if we think of Strang's remarks about the overlap of different scales and the reference to the interdependence of variety classes in the UGE. Here are two examples. *Gramophone* is defined in the LDCE (1978) as 'record player' and marked: *BrE becoming rare* (cf. Strang ^{2}1968:220). In the second edition of the dictionary, the label changes to *old-fash.* The marking of a regional variety is in 1978 combined with one of restricted frequency of use, which refers to diachrony-in-synchrony. *Gran* is explained as 'grandmother' and labelled *BrE infml*, a combined reference to the variety classes 1 and 5.

In the following, some further correlations between the labels of the LDCE (both editions) and the variety classes in the UGE will be mentioned for illustration.

1. *Pommy* is defined as 'an Englishman' (in 1978) and (in non-sexist language in 1987) as 'an English person'. In both editions of the LDCE it is marked (for "region") as Australian and New Zealand English. It furthermore belongs to slang and is therefore assigned to both variety classes 1 and 5. It has the additional label *often derog*, defined as words which show that "the speaker dislikes or disapproves of something". This is clearly a matter of "attitude". *Beck*, meaning 'stream', is characterized as a word used in the North of England (*NEngE*) and is obviously related to Ger *Bach*, although definitely a Scandinavian loanword.
2. It is much more difficult to find examples for illustrating the second variety class ("education and social standing") in the LDCE. *Fag*, defined as 'a young pupil who has to do jobs for an older student' and characterized as "in certain English public schools" by the LDCE, certainly applies to both aspects of the variety class 2. However, there is no specific label to indicate this. There are certain interdependences which allow us, probably, to relate both the labels *lit* (for literary) and *sl* (for slang) to variety class 2. But the association is not a necessary one.

Although it cannot be seen from the label, *wireless*, which belongs to a conservative speech variant, must probably be included in this group. Also, literary *lambent* 'softly shining' is certainly restricted to educated English. On the other hand, the slang noun *fag* 'cigarette'[17] a homonym of the above-mentioned *fag* and the verb *to fag* 'work hard', can probably be associated with the other end of the social class scale, although its use is certainly also situationally conditioned. The verb *to clock* 'to strike', homonymous with the zero-derived denominal verb (in *I clocked him while he ran a mile*) in the expression *I'll clock you one*, will certainly not be considered as belonging to the educated English of the upper classes.

The examples just mentioned clearly reveal the problems of discussing words in isolation, without linguistic or extralinguistic context (see 5.1.). Today, a terminological distinction is often made between *co-text* (linguistic context) and *context* (extralinguistic context, including context of situation). The choice of a lexical item or lexical unit is not only determined by the language user's more or less permanent property of belonging to a specific social group, but also by the situation of language use (see diagram (9), and cf. Lipka 1988a: 320 f.). Not only educated speakers have more than one level or "style" at their disposal, a phenomenon which is well known in sociolinguistics under the term *code-switching* (cf. Halliday 1978:65). According to situation, all speakers may rapidly move from one 'code' to another – here *code* denotes different language varieties or even, in multilingual societies, entirely different languages (e.g. Spanish and Guarani).

3. Decisions on the next class ("subject matter") are easier to make. For this, there is quite a range of labels in any dictionary. Words from legal or medical language are clearly marked. Words used by specialists in various other subjects are labelled *tech*. We are obviously concerned here with 'register' or 'field'. Lexical items used predominantly in the Bible (labelled *bibl*) clearly also belong to variety class 3. Here, temporal variation is involved at the same time.
4. In contrast to the preceding group, assignment to the next class ("medium") is not entirely unproblematic. In my opinion, we can assume that literary and poetical expressions, as well as obsolete words, can

[17] To be precise, according to the LDCE 2 there are four lexical items *fag*, namely three nouns marked as 1. *BrE sl* ('cigarette'), 2. *AmE derog sl* ('homosexual man'), 3. *infml, esp. BrE,* and a verb 4. marked as *infml, esp. BrE.* The dictionary gives two meanings each for noun 3. and the verb 4., so that in my terminology they both consist of two lexical units: 3a) 'chore' (as in *Cleaning the oven is a real fag*), 3b) 'young pupil who has to do jobs for an older pupil'; 4a) 'to do jobs for an older pupil', 4b) 'to work hard'. The verb 4a) can be interpreted as a zero-derivative from the noun 3b) which is equivalent to Ger *Fuchs* (in student fraternities). Transatlantic misunderstandings may arise, e.g. when *Lord Smith was my fag at Eton* is said by a British speaker to an American (cf. Moss 1973).

normally be assigned to the written medium. Again, we can see the overlapping of categories. *Velocipede* in the meaning 'bicycle' has the label *obs*, defined in the LDCE as "often found in old books". It is therefore correlated with the written medium. Incidentally, the COD gives two different meanings of the noun: 1. "(Hist.) Light vehicle propelled by rider, esp. early form of bicycle", and, with a symbol marking it as "Chiefly U.S.", 2. "Child's tricycle". Obsolete words may be used intentionally in spoken language, which results normally in a humorous effect. This is why *velocipede* is labelled "old use or humorous" in LDCE.

5. Lexical items marked by the label *humor* may definitely also be assigned to variety class 5 ("attitude"), since they pertain to 'attitude', 'style', or 'tenor'. As with the group indicating regional variation, the LDCE here has a wide range of finely differentiated labels. This can be seen from the following examples. A negative or positive attitude is characterized by the pair of labels *derog/apprec* (derogatory/appreciative) as implied by words like *brat* 'child', and *cosy*. Polite words for things that for some reason or another are regarded as unpleasant, are marked *euph* (euphemistic). Examples are: *senior citizen* 'old person', *charlady* 'cleaner', and *cloakroom* 'toilet'. Today the expression *industrial action* is often used instead of *strike*. Besides neutral words that are unmarked, the LDCE in 1978 distinguished three degrees of formality: *fml/not fml/infml*, which are replaced in the second edition by *infml/fml/sl. Nag*, when meaning an old or bad horse, is labelled *not fml* in 1978, but is marked *infml* in the second edition of the LDCE. Words that should be avoided in formal society or in conversation with foreigners and children are marked *taboo*. Items that "show a foolishly self-important attitude" are labelled *pomp* (pompous), such as *to pen* 'write with a pen'.

   There are two particular areas, within the variety class 5 of attitude, which are not marked by the system of labels used in the LDCE: racist terms and sexist language. These have become extremely important for good English in the 1980s (cf. Howard 1985 and the differences between the two editions of the LDCE). Certain words are considered offensive by certain groups of people, but this is only pointed out in the "usage notes" of the dictionary. For example, *black* is the word preferred by many black people today, but *coloured*, and especially *negro* are considered to be offensive. Many women resent the words *chairman* and *spokesman*, when used referring to both sexes, and prefer to say *She/he is our new chairperson* or *She/he agreed to act as spokesperson.* These two examples are only given in the latest LDCE (1987) and exemplify clear cases of language change (s.v. *black* and *person*, but cf. also Howard (1985) esp. *sexist language*). The problems of the new, non-discriminatory title *Ms* are discussed in great detail by Howard and mentioned in the LDCE also in the "language notes" on "addressing people".

6. The last group of items, related to variety class 6, "interference", consists of words that have been borrowed from other languages and that are

still felt to be foreign. They are frequently pronounced in an un-English way. Here, we may have labels which refer to the language of origin (*Fr, Ger, It, Sp*), but the origin may also be named in the definition itself. This is illustrated by the treatment of *détente, Zeitgeist, Herr, Sauerkraut*, and *paella* in the two editions of the LDCE.

Obviously, words contained in the class interference frequently also belong to other variety classes. Thus, loans from certain languages often belong to certain topics, i.e. there is a relationship with class 3. For example English, like many other European languages, has borrowed a number of expressions from the register of music from Italian. In this field, terms like *andante, da capo*, and *piano* have become so familiar that they are not marked by the label *It* in the LDCE at all. In general, the dictionary does not contain a specific technical label *music* (but cf. *law, med, naut*), but in a number of cases "in music" is added in brackets.

A mistake due to interference which is unfortunately often made by German linguists is the use of Ger *linguistisch* in the sense of 'sprachlich', due to the convergence of both *linguistisch* and *sprachlich* in the English lexical item *linguistic*. One could even argue that this is an instance of language change (extension of meaning) in the technical register of linguistics.

This brings to a close our discussion of the marking of varieties of English in a modern dictionary. We have seen that all variety classes distinguished in the UGE can be correlated with specific labels in the LDCE. We have noted some quite fine distinctions, particularly in the first and fifth class. It is important, however, to repeat that the majority of entries in dictionaries are neutral with respect to variety classes. Furthermore, even those words that are marked by specific labels often belong to the "common core" of English, at least with regard to the passive vocabulary of many speakers.

1.4. Dictionaries of English

An outline of English lexicology would not be complete without a sketch of the most important and most relevant English dictionaries (cf. Strang [2]1968: 215 ff.; Marchand [2]1969:457f.; Scheler 1977:170; Standop 1985, Höhlein et al. 1987:9ff.). We will have a look at the great tradition in English lexicography, consider some medium or concise dictionaries (beyond the pocket dictionary) in greater detail, and look at various dictionaries for specific purposes.

Completeness is clearly impossible in this field, and there is rapid change and development in the publication of dictionaries, as in the lexicon itself, reflected in the dictionaries. We will only be concerned with unilingual dictionaries.

Leech ([2]1981:204) sees the dictionary as "a store of all the *particular* facts about a language" [his emphasis], stresses its "open-ended" nature, and distinguishes between "practical" and "theoretical" dictionaries. He uses the term *lexicon* in the sense of the "inbuilt dictionary", as part of the competence of the native speaker, and identifies it with the "theoretical dictionary" (^{2}1981: 207). He further raises the question of how much "encyclopedic information about the referents" (^{2}1981: 205 f.) dictionary definitions should contain.

It is an old and knotty problem how to distinguish between linguistic and encyclopedic knowledge (cf. Lipka 1972 : 49, 56; Hüllen/Schulze 1988), to which we will return in connection with the discussion of language, meaning, and reality in 2.1. and 2.2. In principle, knowledge of language and knowledge of the world have to be separated, but it is not always easy to draw a neat line in specific cases. This is tied up with the problem of the "fuzzy" nature of language to which we will return.

In dealing with practical dictionaries, we have to keep in mind that they are not "the true repositories of lexical knowledge" as the man-in-the-street believes, and that a "reverent attitude to dictionary authority is mere superstition" (Strang ^{2}1968 :217). As Strang points out, in the layman's view a dictionary is not a work written by somebody. This false impression is further enhanced by the fact that most titles of dictionaries do not mention an author. The absence of an author definitely contributes to the awe-inspiring authority of the dictionary, especially if the lack of originator is coupled with the illustrious name of Oxford.

It is contained in the title of a series of reference books that derive from the most comprehensive and impressive work of English lexicography, the *Oxford English Dictionary* (OED). It has rightly been referred to as the greatest dictionary ever written for any language. Although it certainly cannot be up-to-date (due to its history and its genesis) it is without any doubt a most astonishing achievement and an inexhaustible storehouse of knowledge about the English language.[18]

A glance at its history will reveal why the OED is unique (cf. McArthur 1986:124ff.). Around the middle of the last century it was felt in England that existing dictionaries of the language werde inadequate. So the Philological Society in London, around 1850, started the project of a new dictionary. For this purpose, in 1879 a contract was signed with the old and famous Oxford University Press for the financing and publication of the dictionary. During the long and eventful years of writing and publishing, several editors were in charge of the process. The most important of these was probably James A. H. Murray.

[18] To be sure, "the OED can only be understood as a product of 19th century philology" and the use of the first edition as "a safe standard of vocabulary in the second half of the twentieth century" is doubtful (Finkenstaedt/Wolff 1973:21, 23). Its editors always tended to be conservative (cf. Marsden 1985:28), which is most obvious from the fact that Americanisms only began to be admitted in the 1933 Supplement, other Englishes were only recognized in the second Supplement (1972ff.), sexual terms ("dirty words") were excluded up to its first volume (1972), and the inclusion of racial terminology made the second volume (1976) notorious. For the reliability of the OED's first citations and voluntary readers cf. Schäfer (1980; esp. 3–5).

But neither a single editor nor the entire Philological Society could have managed to complete this immense project single-handed. The plan (which was in fact carried out) was to give for every word of the English language and for each of its meanings, quotations from actual written texts. To find such examples by the systematic reading of texts could only be done by the help of many volunteer readers, over the course of years and years. The material contributed by hundreds of readers formed the basis of the editing of the dictionary. At one point there were over 800 of them (cf. *The Compact Edition of the OED:* vii) and all in all 2,000 readers sent in 5 million quotations over a period of 70 years (cf. McArthur 1986:131). In 1884 the first instalment of the dictionary, originally entitled *A New English Dictionary on Historical Principles*, was issued.[19] This title is responsible for the abbreviation NED, still occasionally used today. The final part with the letter Z appeared in 1928. Thus the whole project had taken exactly 70 years since the resolution of the Philological Society calling for a new dictionary was passed in 1858. However, the undertaking was not completed with the issuing of the last instalment.[20] In 1933 an important supplement volume appeared containing new and omitted words, as well as corrections necessitated during the long publication process. The completed work treats more than 400,000 words and phrases. Together with the 1933 supplement it is bound in 13 large volumes, occupying 16,570 pages. Since the original format of the huge work takes up an enormous space, a micrographic reproduction in two volumes was produced in 1971. It bears the title *The Compact Edition of the Oxford English Dictionary*. Most of it can only be read with a magnifying glass, but it is sold at a reasonable price which individuals can afford.

But this was by no means the end of what McArthur (1986:124) calls "the unendable dictionary". In 1957 the New Zealand scholar Robert W. Burchfield became editor of the new supplements to the dictionary (OEDS) which led to a shift of viewpoint away from the original "Britocentric" approach (cf. Weiner 1987). In 1984 Edmund Weiner (responsible for the computerization of the OED) was appointed co-editor of the *New Oxford English Dictionary*, which aims at integrating the OED and its supplements into an electronic database, publicly available both online and on compact disc.[21] This new "electronic OED" can

---

[19] A "Historical Thesaurus of English", based on the OED and its supplements, has been in preparation at the university of Glasgow, under the direction of M.L. Samuels, for a number of years. Modern electronic equipment (machine-readable data, a mainframe computer) is being used for storage, processing, and classification and it is hoped that the project will be completed in the early 1990s. Section I, "The External World", including "Land, Water, The Extraterrestrial Universe, Mankind, etc.", is largely completed. Other sections are: II "The Mind" and III "Society".

[20] The original ten-volume work (NED) was later (1933) reprinted and bound in twelve volumes (as the OED) plus Supplement (vol. 13).

[21] This first computerized edition of the OED on CD-ROM (Compact Disc Read Only Memory) has been available since late 1988 and contains the original twelve-volume OED (thus not including the new Supplements) on a single

be revised and up-dated continuously and rapidly. It favours an "inclusive approach" (Weiner 1987) and attempts to become the historical dictionary of every variety of World English.

As we have seen already, the rate of language change is greatest in the area of the lexicon (cf. the example *gramophone* discussed in Strang (^{2}1968: 220)). This development has caused a need for constant revision and publication of further supplementary volumes in the past. Under the title *A Supplement to the Oxford English Dictionary* (OEDS) four volumes were published in 1972, 1976, 1981, and 1986. They incorporate and replace the 1933 Supplement and contain new words adopted into the language since the publication of the OED. They are based on a collection of quotations from literary, scientific, and technical works, as well as from newspapers and magazines.

In 1987, sixteen years after the publication of *The Compact Edition* (vols. I and II), the four new supplement volumes edited by R. W. Burchfield (OEDS) were also published in a reduced compacted version (as vol. III), thus completing the printed output of what an Oxford University Press release praises as "the culmination of about 130 years' work on the complete Dictionary". In 1989, a second edition of the OED was produced in twenty volumes (the OED 2), conflated by computer, integrating the supplements, thus making available all the wealth of material (over half a million words and 2,4 million quotations, including some 5,000 new entries) in a single alphabetical sequence, on 21, 728 pages. The OED 2 has further been improved by many corrections and a modernized, standardized phonetic transcription (IPA).

The OED claims to record every word in the English language and to give quotations for each of its "senses", "about one for each century" in which the word was not extinct. Beginning with its earliest appearance in Old English or at a later period, all recorded spellings, uses, and meanings are registered, in order to account for the history of the word as completely as possible. An attempt is also made to register the latest occurrence of words that have died out. However, words that were already extinct by 1150 are not included.

This short sketch can certainly not do justice to the OED. But it is necessary to draw attention to some further dictionaries derived from the OED. Besides the *Compact Edition* there is a shortened version in two volumes, containing about one sixth of the material of the OED, entitled *The Shorter Oxford English Dictionary on Historical Principles* (SOED). This in turn is the basis for a dictionary published in 1970, which lists the English vocabulary not in alphabetical but in chronological order, and bears the title *A Chronological English Dictionary* (CED). It was prepared by Th. Finkenstaedt, E. Leisi, and D. Wolff and contains the 81,000 main entries of the SOED listed according

---

compact disc. In addition there are indexes for etymology, definition, labels (parts of speech, topics, registers etc.), and quotations (date, author, work) – which may also be combined – for electronic searches. Considerable space is devoted to several aspects of the second edition of the OED (1989) in twenty columes (OED 2) in *ET* 19 and 20 (1989).

to first occurrence and etymological origin. It further includes material from the 1963 edition of *The Advanced Learner's Dictionary of Current English* (ALD) and the *General Service List of English Words* (GSL) (see below).

The smallest and therefore most up-to-date dictionary based on the OED and its Supplements is *The Concise Oxford Dictionary of Current English* (COD). In spite of this origin, the COD used to contain relatively few quotations, illustrative sentences, or collocations, i.e. co-occurrences of lexical items. The latest editions, however, have adapted more to the pressure of competing dictionaries of comparable size and price. Furthermore, the long tradition in which it stands, also is a burden in some respects. Thus, the COD can definitely be characterized as conservative in spite of the inclusion of recent usage. This is particularly evident in the strange, unorthodox scheme for the notation of pronunciation (replaced by IPA in OED 2), for which also the intended non-specialized native speaker readership is responsible. The symbols of the International Phonetic Alphabet (IPA) are not used, but the transcription follows the orthographic conventions of English, which facilitates use by the layman.

But the COD has other, positive aspects. First of all, it explicitly tries to separate linguistic and encyclopedic information. This can be seen from the following quotation from the preface to the first edition, reprinted in later editions (^{7}1982:ix):

> The book is designed as a dictionary, and not as an encyclopaedia [sic!]; that is, the uses of words and phrases as such are its subject-matter, and it is concerned with giving information about the things for which those words and phrases stand only so far as correct use of the words depends upon knowledge of the things.

Another advantage is that, as a rule, we find an etymology for every word. The contents are by no means adapted to the needs of the advanced learners only, as in some other dictionaries, but also include many learned and technical words. It is further remarkable, how far recent usage has been incorporated in the latest edition.

Other medium dictionaries of comparable size will be considered later (cf. Standop 1985, Hartmann 1987, and Summers 1988). Although the *Oxford Advanced Learner's Dictionary of Current English* (OALD), originally compiled in 1942 by A. S. Hornby (with the help of others), is also published by Oxford University Press, it is indirectly related to the preceding work. The characterization "Advanced Learner's" in the title is somewhat misleading (but cf. Cowie 1987). It is definitely profitable for other users as well. In contrast to earlier editions, the fully revised one of 1989 (Cowie 1989) has returned to the transcription system used by Gimson and now conforms to the notation found in the *English Pronouncing Dictionary* (EPD). Compared to the COD, the OALD is rather restricted to more basic vocabulary and contains fewer learned and technical words, and of course no etymology. On the other hand it is modern and up-to-date and is distinguished by its clarity. It further contains many typical examples and collocations and very useful illustrations (cf. Ilson 1987). Another helpful feature found in most modern dictionaries (automatically incorporated in computer programms for word processing today) is the marking of word-divisions at the end of a line. Three advantages of the OALD may be particularly emphasized: 1. It contains simple but nevertheless exact definitions and paraphrases of the concepts, 2. each definition and different use is illustrated with an example, i.e. the word is shown in a typical context, 3. valuable grammatical information is provided. In the latest edition, a new simpler verb classification scheme is introduced. Nouns are marked with special symbols according to whether they are countable or uncountable. As in most recent dictionaries, a number of useful appendices are added at the end.

Another important medium-sized dictionary that is not derived from the OED is the *Longman Dictionary of Contemporary English* (LDCE). It was first published in 1978 as a completely new, original work, which uses the findings of modern linguistics to give a more precise description of language. The editors have frequently had recourse to the material of the Survey of English Usage at University College London. This is a representative corpus set up for the analysis and description of the contemporary language, containing examples of many varieties of English. There are very important and symptomatic changes and improvements in the second edition of 1987.

The LDCE is comparable in scope to the OALD and has many original features. It also contains grammatical information on word classes, countability, and the construction potential of verbs. As in the OALD, illustrations are used, besides definitions, for the explanation of the words treated. Syllable structure is also indicated, which is relevant for end-of-line divisions. The use of words is demonstrated in extensive typical contexts, and collocations are shown in three different ways: in example sentences, by explanation in the so-called Usage Notes, and by typographic emphasis if the collocation is idiomatic or found very often. The revised edition is furthermore improved by additional "Language Notes", i.e. tables which incorporate pragmatic aspects into the dictionary and provide useful information on addressing people, apologies, criticism and praise, invitations and offers, politeness, thanks, the use of articles, collocations, modals, phrasal verbs, prepositions etc. It also consistently attempts to avoid racist and sexist language (see 1.3.). Neologisms and natural and typical usage in the 1980s are captured by constant updating of the Longman Citation Corpus.

There are two features of this dictionary which were unique in 1978. First "Usage Notes" are appended to many entries in both editions. Thus, e.g. under *fastness* we learn that there is no noun formed from *fast* when it means *quick*, and that instead *speed* or *quickness* is used. The note following *hire* not only provides information on the differences between British and American English, but also on the nouns that may be combined with *hire* in contrast to the usual collocations of *rent, lease, charter, appoint, engage,* and *employ.*

The second peculiarity (revolutionary in 1978) is the controlled basic vocabulary used for the definition of the main entries. Every single word in the definitions was checked by computer to ensure that it belongs to the list of approximately 2,000 words selected on the basis of frequency studies (also with reference to the GSL). The list of this defining vocabulary is printed at the end of the book. When a word had to be used that is less common and does not belong to the special list of 2,000 words, it is marked by small capital letters. The careful labelling of different varieties of contemporary English, especially the detailed coverage of different national varieties, have already been discussed.

A third example of medium British dictionaries free from the burden of tradition is the *Collins Dictionary of the English Language* (COLLINS), first published in 1979. A slightly revised edition appeared in 1986. It pays considerable attention to geographical variation and has special consultants for Scottish English, Caribbean English, Australian English etc. The COLLINS is larger than the COD, which is due in part to the fact that it contains a great deal of encyclopedic information. This may be illustrated by the following entries: *Brenner Pass* 'a pass over the E Alps, between Austria and Italy. Highest point: 1,372 m'; *Bretagne* 'the French name for Britanny'; *Bridge ... Frank* '1879–1941, English composer ...'; *Bridge of Sighs* 'a covered 16th-century bridge in Venice ...'.

With its special focus on varieties of English, it is not surprising that the COLLINS (like the LDCE) should have developed a neat system of "restrictive labels", subclassified into "temporal" (*Archaic, Obsolete*), "usage" (*Slang, Informal, Taboo, Facetious, Euphemistic, Not standard*), "connotative" (*Derogatory, Offensive*), "subject-field" (*Astronomy, Banking* etc.), and "national and regional labels" (*Austral., Brit., Canadian, Caribbean, Irish, N.Z., S. African, Scot., U.S.*). In this context it is worth mentioning that a proposal for a consistent abbreviated labelling system for the world's Englishes has been proposed in Görlach (1987).

In the foreword to the COLLINS, the publishers claim in 1979 that:

> For the first time in a major dictionary of this kind, computer technology has been used from the inception of the work.

This feature, they continue:

> made it possible to survey every field of human activity subject by subject, defining technical as well as everyday vocabulary in an exceptionally short time.

Closely related to the new possibilities of the computer age, and particularly interesting in comparison with the quotation from the COD given above, is the following statement in the foreword to the second edition (1986:vii):

> Parallel to this concern with the contemporary language went a comprehensive treatment of modern science and technology, the most thorough and encyclopedic of any general single-volume dictionary to date. This encyclopedic approach was extended by a generous provision of biographical and geographical entries that provided information on people and places of cultural importance on an international scale.

I will return to this conflict between purely linguistic and encyclopedic knowledge, and the possibility of their separation, repeatedly in this book. In the development of linguistics, it is paralleled with a shift of attitude from a strictly structuralist to a more comprehensive cognitive and interdisciplinary point of view.

Let us now turn to a fourth medium-sized dictionary of contemporary English, produced by the same publisher, the *COBUILD English Language Dictionary,* which was unique in many ways when it appeared in 1987 (incidentally, our counting could be renumbered on good grounds, if we considered the second edition of the LDCE as a different, fifth book. It is really a *new* edition, with a woman Della Summers as a new Editorial Director, with a more progressive attitude, where women feature as protagonists in many of the examples given). A number of features of the COBUILD are quite exceptional, which make it a kind of "odd man out".[22]

The COBUILD (an acronym which stands for Collins Birmingham University International Language Database) is derived from computerized evidence from spoken and written actual texts. Both the LDCE and the COBUILD are thus based on citations corpora.[23] Since in the latter, the examples are only slightly adapted, we find a high percentage of proper names (e.g. *12 million pounds spent by Courtauld's in modernizing its old Greenfield factory* under *modernize*), which are often not very helpful for the user's understanding of the definitions. As discussed in the introduction by the Editor-in-Chief, John Sinclair, "The dictionary is designed to read like ordinary English", collocations are stressed (see 4.3.5.), social and geographical variety is considered, and warnings are given to avoid offensive racist and "sexist talk". The first-mentioned characteristic, which results in a sort of "folk definition", is considerably, and perhaps unnecessarily, space-consuming. Finally, a unique positive feature of the dictionary must also be mentioned, which is especially relevant with respect to sense-relations (see 4.2.3.): a system of semantic cross-referencing with the help of special symbols for synonyms (=), antonyms (≠), and superordinate terms (⥣).

The highly competitive market for dictionaries aimed at students of English as a foreign language (cf. Summers 1988) has also produced a number of other

---

[22] Most reviews have been rather critical of the striking departures from lexicographical standards, e.g. the fact that grammatical information is put into a so-called "extra column", to the right of the definitions, while the claimed "user-friendliness" of the definitions has been criticized as a waste of space and a mixture of condescension and chumminess. Thus the entry for *to nudge* reads: "When you nudge someone, you push or poke them, usally with your elbow, in order to draw their attention to something or to make them move". Homographs are not distinguised (s.v. *lead*) and there is also a single lemma only for different word classes (s.v. *open, twist*). The indication of pronunciation, a mixture of broad and narrow transcription, is also problematic. For a comparison of OALD, LDCE, and COBUILD cf. Jackson (1988:181ff.) and Summers (1988).

[23] As appears from the "Corpus Acknowledgements" in the COBUILD (1987:xxii), the bulk of quotations derives from texts produced in the 1970s and 1980s, with a very few earlier sources going back as far as 1945. Cf. Carter (1987:140–142).

books, of which only *The Penguin Wordmaster Dictionary* (1987), compiled by M. H. Manser and N. D. Turton, can be mentioned here in closing. It is described by the publishers as a combination of thesaurus, usage guide, lexicon, and historical survey, with boxed notes about usage and etymology.

Diagram (10) gives a survey of British and American dictionaries (the latter to be discussed on the following pages) most relevant for our purposes.[24] It includes as an example of a particularly useful medium-sized American dictionary the college edition of *Webster's New World Dictionary of the American Language*, with the new editor-in-chief V. E. Neufeldt in charge of the latest edition 1988. This has nothing to do with WEBSTER's THIRD (W 3), since the name Webster is not protected by American law. Originally published in 1953, the college edition was based on an earlier two-volume encyclopedic edition which first appeared in 1951.

The schema does not contain dictionaries of synonyms, or other specialized works of reference. Since, however, synonyms are especially important in our context (see 4.2.3.1.), a few remarks on the topic may not be out of place here. A useful book, which also draws on the favourable connotations of the name Webster, is *Webster's New Dictionary of Synonyms*, latest edition 1973. As the subtitle indicates (see bibliography Gove [4]1973), it further deals with other sense-relations, in particular antonyms. For the German user, the *Englische Synonymik für Studierende und Lehrer* ([3]1968) may be very helpful, originally written in 1951 by H.-W. Klein alone. The newest relevant (British) publication is the *Longman Synonym Dictionary* (1986), with editor-in-chief Laurence Urdang, a renowned lexicographer. An extremely useful contrastive dictionary of synonyms, particularly helpful for the English learner of German, is Farrell ([2]1977).

---

[24] The *Longman Dictionary of the English Language* (= Gay et al. 1984) is not counted among the medium-sized dictionaries here and is also often too technical. E.g. the noun *foal* is defined as two lexical units: 1. "the young of an animal of the horse family; *esp* one under one year", and 2. "a horse up to the first January after its birth". Is this perhaps explainable from the fact that there are even two consultants for the field of horse-riding? It is extremely instructive to compare entries for this item in various dictionaries.

(10)

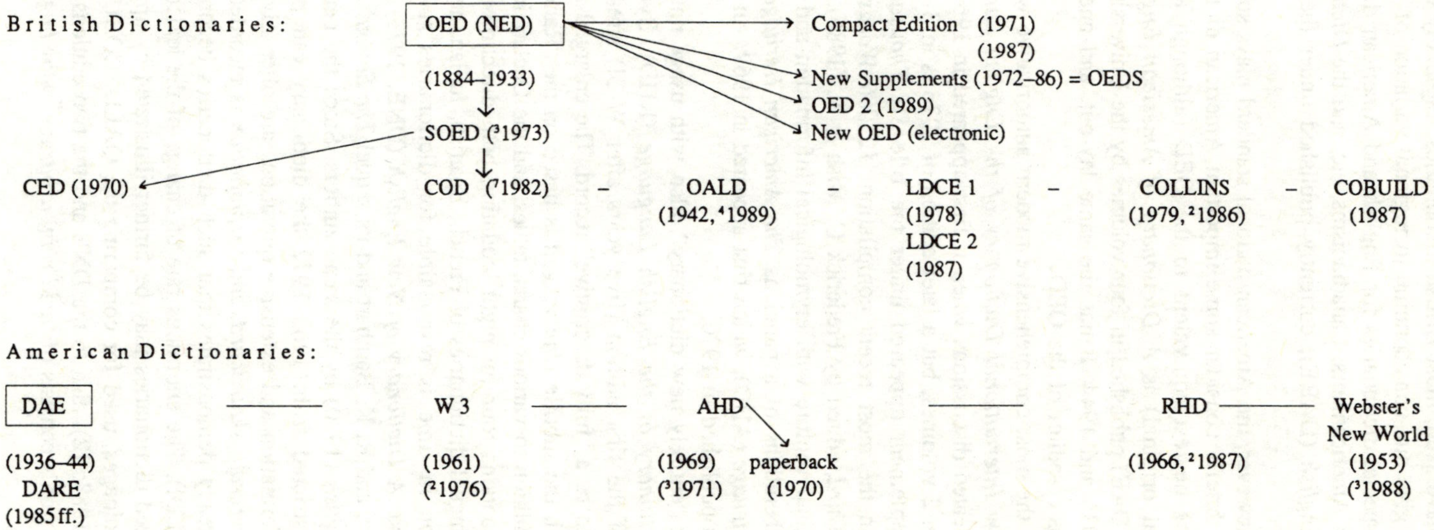
British Dictionaries:
OED (NED)
(1884–1933)
SOED (^{3}1973)
Compact Edition (1971)
(1987)
New Supplements (1972–86) = OEDS
OED 2 (1989)
New OED (electronic)
CED (1970)
COD (^{7}1982)
–
OALD
(1942, ^{4}1989)
–
LDCE 1
(1978)
LDCE 2
(1987)
–
COLLINS
(1979, ^{2}1986)
–
COBUILD
(1987)
American Dictionaries:
DAE
(1936–44)
DARE
(1985 ff.)
W 3
(1961)
(^{2}1976)
AHD
(1969)
(^{3}1971)
paperback
(1970)
RHD
(1966, ^{2}1987)
Webster's
New World
(1953)
(^{3}1988)

As we have seen, most British dictionaries, especially the recent medium-sized ones, give due consideration to regional variation of English. There are, of course, special dictionaries for English and American dialects, for Scottish English, for Americanisms, Canadianisms, etc. and the *Dictionary of American Regional English* (DARE), currently published under the direction of F.G. Cassidy.

Since, however, the American national standard plays such an extraordinary role, I will briefly consider some important American dictionaries mentioned in (10). The nearest equivalent to the OED (although a far cry from the monumental original) is *A Dictionary of American English on Historical Principles* (DAE) published in four volumes by the University of Chicago Press between 1936 and 1944. It has the same lay-out, and one of its editors, W. Craigie, was co-editor of the OED.

Perhaps the most comprehensive modern authoritative work is *WEBSTER's THIRD New International Dictionary of the English Language* (W 3) that provoked heated discussions when it first appeared in 1961. It was originally published in 2 volumes, but a later edition of 1976 is in 3 volumes. The same year, a supplement appeared under the title *Six Thousand Words*. This is contained in the most recent compilation: *12 000 Words: A Supplement to Webster's Third*, edited by Frederick C. Mish et al. (1986).

An original venture with etymological information and usage notes, based on the deliberations of a panel, is *The American Heritage Dictionary of the English Language* (AHD), which first appeared in 1969. An abridged paperback edition was published in 1970.

Another "entirely new dictionary", also with usage notes, is *The Random House Dictionary of the English Language* (RHD). Symptomatically, the foreword of the first edition (five years after W 3!) stresses the need for a dictionary to be a "fully descriptive" record. The enlarged and updated second edition, with the subtitle *Unabridged* is based on the "Random House citation files". In addition to various charts, tables, and the Declaration of Independence, it further contains four (or eight, counting both directions, e.g. E/F and F/E) concise bilingual dictionaries of French, Spanish, Italian, and German.

Variation in time is responsible for dictionaries specialized on "New English" like *A Dictionary of New English* (DNE, 1973) by C. L. Barnhart, S. Steinmetz, and R. K. Barnhart and its sequel *The Second Barnhart Dictionary of New English* (1980) by the same authors. Since the period covered by the DNE is restricted from 1963–1972 the dictionary can provide much more detailed information and extensive quotations are often given. The appearance of e.g. *Hovercraft, skateboard,* and *sexploitation* is recorded.

This already demonstrates that such dictionaries become old very rapidly (like the NED!). The enormous rate of change of the lexicon and its record in medium-sized dictionaries may be further illustrated by applying the checklist of recent coinages, used for comparing the OALD, COBUILD, and LDCE in Summers (1988: 12), also to the DNE and the two editions of COLLINS. This list of new words consists of: *acid rain, arbitrage, baby buggy, bag lady, expert system, hacker, insider trading, yuppie*. Of these the DNE only contains *acid rain* and *bag lady* and the COLLINS (1979) only *arbitrage* and *baby buggy*. The second edition of the latter (1986) records all the items of the list except *insider trading*, but gives *insider information* instead. Incidentally, of the parallel checklist of formal, historical, and literary words, all are contained in the COD. Summers (1988:13f.) concludes:

> The future for dictionaries must surely be electronic ... The dictionary could be partnered with a corpus of authentic written text ... paper dictionaries specially for ELT needs will no doubt exist for as long as there is a demand for them ...

As a third group, besides the major British and American dictionaries, those for specific purposes should be briefly discussed here. For the history of individual words, besides the OED, the *Oxford Dictionary of English Etymology* (ODEE, 1966) and its shortened version, the *Concise ODEE*, edited in 1986 by T. F. Hoad, must be mentioned.

There are countless dictionaries of English idioms, which cannot be dealt with individually here. More or less idiomatic fixed collocations (cf. Lipka 1972: 76 ff. and see also 3.2.5. and 4.3.5.) are listed in all good dictionaries. Two books specializing in contemporary English collocations are Friedrich/Canavan (1979), *Dictionary of English Words in Context*, and Benson/Benson/Ilson (1986), *The BBI Combinatory Dictionary of English*. A special type of British and American collocations and proverbial sayings (from the sixteenth century onwards) are to be found in Partridge/Beale (1985), *A Dictionary of Catch Phrases*, first edited in 1977 by E. Partridge alone. It is intended as a companion volume to his monumental work of reference *A Dictionary of Slang and Unconventional English* ([7]1970), in two volumes. The corresponding work across the Atlantic is the *Dictionary of American Slang* ([2]1967) by Wentworth/Flexner.

There is a related dictionary, of rather restricted scope, that deals with a unique phenomenon only found in one specific variety of English, namely Cockney, *A Dictionary of Rhyming Slang* ([2]1971) by J. Franklyn. Rhyming slang has some characteristics of a secret language, and consists of the replacement of a complex expression for a single word. Both are linked by rhyme, such as *apples and pears* for *stairs, trouble and strife* for *wife*. Often the expressions are abbreviated, which destroys the connection by rhyme. Thus, *daisy roots* for *boots* is shortened to *daisies* and *china plate*, for *mate*, according to Franklyn ([2]1961:50) is "invariably reduced to *China*". Some terms have gained wider currency, beyond Cockney, as e.g. *loaf (of bread)* for *head*, as in the expression *use your loaf* 'think!'.

As with idioms, there are many books on good current usage, especially for teaching purposes. I shall single out two here, which I believe to be most valuable for foreign users, particularly German ones. A balanced and objective look at contemporary vocabulary is given in Howard (1985), *A Guide to Good English in the 1980s*, with helpful advice about sexist, racist, and four-letter words. The same year, Pascoe/Pascoe (1985), *Sprachfallen im Englischen*, was published, an extremely useful small dictionary, functioning as an eye- and ear-opener, warning of false friends.

For the purposes of hearing and pronouncing correctly, the standard pronouncing dictionaries for the two most important national standard varieties of English are still Jones/Gimson ([14]1977), *Everyman's English Pronouncing Dictionary* (the EPD) and Kenyon/Knott ([4]1953), *A Pronouncing Dictionary of American English.* A most useful addition is the *BBC Pronouncing Dictionary of British Names* ([2]1983), with no American equivalent. In case of need the larger dictionaries must be consulted. For determining the frequency of words and their particular meanings, we have West ([3]1967) *A General Service List of English Words* (GSL) and Hofland/Johansson (1982), *Word Frequencies in British and American English.* The latter contains only word lists based on the LOB and Brown corpora, without differentiating senses and not even homonyms.[25]

In the fourth category, there are dictionaries of a very different kind, not organized according to the normal alphabetical principle and without any explanations or definitions. The *Reverse Dictionary of Present-Day English* by M. Lehnert (1971) is a list of words arranged according to the letters they end with. Such "dictionaries", which merely list words in reverse order, may be useful to the philologist for the emendation of mutilated texts, the intelligence expert for the deciphering of codes, as a rhyming dictionary, and for research in word-formation, in particular connected with suffixation.

The last type of non-alphabetical, thematical reference book is the thesaurus. In such a work, lexical items are arranged on a more or less intuitively determined basis of similarity of meaning and association. This principle of arrangement is more linguistic than a mere alphabetical listing. However, in practice, explicit semantic criteria are not used and normally modern linguistic research in the area is not drawn upon (but cf. McArthur 1986:esp. 119 ff., 148 ff.).

For the English-speaking world, ever since 1852 when the first edition appeared, ROGET's *Thesaurus of English Words and Phrases* has been a household name. It was devised by Peter Mark Roget, as his own personal instrument for improving his powers of expression. In 1805, as a young doctor, he started setting up a "classed catalogue of words". Since then the work has gone through many editions, and has been published by various editors and publishing houses. The latest edition was prepared by Betty Kirkpatrick, and published in 1987 by Longman.

According to the preface (1987 : vii):

---

[25] The GSL does consider "semantic frequencies", as mentioned in its subtitle. However, since it was originally produced in 1936 and revised in 1953 (with a number of subsequent impressions), it is questionable how far it represents good contemporary usage. Thus there seems to be a need for up-to-date frequency counts, which are of considerable importance for language learning (cf. Carter 1987: 43, 183 ff.).

> This new edition has been made necessary by the unprecedented rapid expansion of the English vocabulary in the 1980s, reflecting major scientific, cultural and social changes.

Examples given of such neologisms include *acid rain, AIDS, cellular radio, genetic fingerprint* etc. This strongly reminds us of the never-ending story of the OED.

The grouping of items in ROGET's *Thesaurus* is according to logical connection and semantic likeness (cf. McArthur 1986:120 f.). Sets are established by deduction and association and may be compared to our "lexical sets" (as opposed to "lexical fields", see 4.2.5.). The classification starts from 6 very general classes, which are then split up into larger categories, or "sections", and ultimately into roughly 990 "heads" oder "topics". These are intended to subsume practically the whole range of ideas expressed in the vocabulary. The six general classes are: 1. "Abstract Relations", 2. "Space", 3. "Matter", 4. "Intellect", 5. "Volition", and 6. "Affections". These are further split up into subclasses called "sections". Thus, e.g. *Class* 1: *Abstract Relations* consists of the 8 "Sections": "Existence, Relation, Quantity, Order, Number, Time, Change, Causation". These distinctions are not based on linguistic principles, such as paradigmatic or syntagmatic relations between words or their contents. It is therefore no strict semantic classification. However, since *ROGET's Thesaurus* groups together words related logically and by subject matter, it is an inexhaustible treasure house for finding the appropriate and "correct" word in the writing of texts. The most recent – and at the same time original – thesaurus of the English language was produced by Tom McArthur, at the end of nine years' work, published in 1981 as the *Longman Lexicon of Contemporary English* (LLCE), based on the material of the LDCE. Following ROGET's example, the *Lexicon* attempts a combination of: a) thematization, as in the work of compilers of human knowledge over the centuries, and b) semantic structuring, as proposed by linguists like John Lyons and certain anthropologists (cf. McArthur 1986:148 f.).

As stated in the preface, the LLCE (1981:vi) "has only fourteen 'semantic fields' of a pragmatic, everyday nature", e.g. A: "Life and Living Things", B: "The Body: its Functions and Welfare", C: "People and the Family", etc. As only explained in McArthur (1986: 149 f.), these "themes" represent the "macrostructure" of the *Lexicon*. They each contain a range of "sub-themes", or "supersets", like e.g. life and death, living creatures, animals/mammals, birds, etc. (of A "Life and Living Things"), or the universe, light and colour, weather and temperature, etc. (of L "Space and Time"). These, in turn, are further subdivided into "lexical sets" or "word sets", which form the "microstructure" of the *Lexicon*. The author openly admits the subjectivity of the method and labels its result "Tom McArthur's taxonomy of semantic fields". Thus, the LLCE is based on the view that language and the world cannot be interpreted independently of each other, and that our linguistic and encyclopedic knowledge is stored as a network of associations in a conceptual framework. This approach is clearly compatible with our discussion of association and "lexical sets" in 4.2.5.

Chapter II

THE LINGUISTIC SIGN. What's in a Word?

After discussing some problems of a general nature, we now turn to various aspects of the linguistic sign. First and foremost we have to look at some important models of the linguistic sign (2.1.) which derive from Saussure's ideas about it, although these views will be modified later (see 4.1.1.). Closely connected is the further question about the definition of the meaning of the linguistic sign (2.2.). In this context we may distinguish purely language-immanent approaches from those that take into account the extra-linguistic reality. If, following Saussure, we separate the language system (his *langue*) from its realization and application (his *parole*) we then must distinguish between 'denotation' and 'reference' (2.2.3.).

But the linguistic sign not only has a meaning, it also has a form. If we start from this aspect, we must distinguish between words, word-forms, morphemes (defined here as the smallest signs of a language), and lexemes (2.3.). The distinction between 'type' and 'token', is also relevant here.

2.1. Models of the Sign

In modern linguistics, Saussure was the first scholar to consider language as a structured system of signs. From this basic assumption he derived several further axioms, which we cannot discuss in detail here. His binary model of the sign, however, must be considered more closely. A second important concept is Ogden/Richards's *semiotic triangle*. It is crucial to realize that both models – Saussure's and Ogden/Richards's – abstract from certain facts that have been rediscovered in linguistics during the last twenty years or so (cf. Lipka 1975a). These are the users of signs, the context of use, and the function of the linguistic sign. All three have since been integrated into linguistics under the label "linguistic pragmatics". A model of the linguistic sign that does not only encompass extra-linguistic reality, but also speaker, hearer, and the functions of language, is the so-called "Organon Model" postulated in 1934 by Karl Bühler (cf. Bühler ^{2}1965 and Hörmann 1986 : esp. 79ff.). A closer inspection of this model, too, is indispensable in my opinion.

2.1.1. Saussure's Approach

In Saussure's view of language as a system of signs, sign and system are mutually conditioning, since a sign only derives its value from within the system on the basis of its relation to other signs. This structural insight is particularly relevant for the theory of lexical fields (*Wortfeld*, cf. Lyons 1977: 250–261, Lipka 1980). Although Saussure in his posthumously published work of 1916 explicitly deals with the concrete process of communication, as an exchange between a speaker and a hearer (Saussure [3]1965: 27–29), he later abstracts from this process and concentrates on the non-individual, social, abstract language system which he called *langue*.

For him the linguistic sign itself has two sides: a given notion ("concept") that is associated in the brain with a certain phonic image ("image acoustique"). Both are mutually conditioning and evoke, or call each other up, mutually. This is symbolized by the arrows in the following diagram (1) taken over in slightly modified form from Saussure ([3]1965: 99):

(1) Saussure's model:

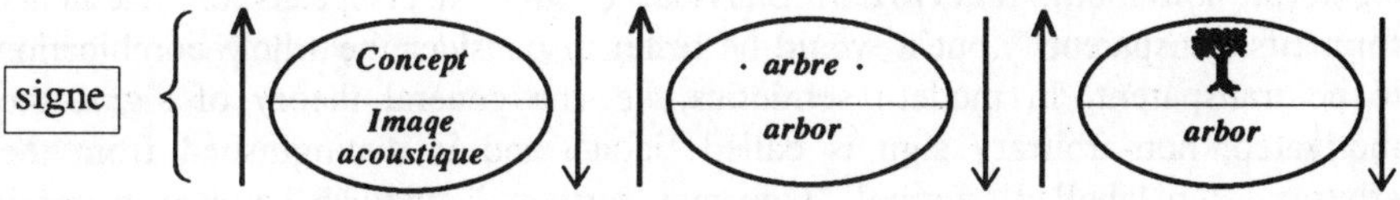

Saussure stresses repeatedly that the linguistic sign is a mental unit ("une entité psychique à deux faces"), and does not link a thing and a name, but a concept and a phonic image. This image is for him nothing material, physical, but a mental impression of a sound. The connection of *concept* and *image acoustique*, of concept and sound picture, for Saussure constitutes the *signe linguistique*, the linguistic sign. The notions "concept" and "image acoustique" are later replaced by him by the terms *signifié* and *signifiant*, which have since become internationally accepted technical terms, due to their precision and unambiguousness. It must be pointed out here, that *signe, signifié* and *signifiant* are all considered as discrete entities by Saussure. The model is therefore incapable of handling the fuzziness inherent in all languages (see 2.2.3.).

Saussure's psychological approach is essentially different from another linguistic school, which is also usually included under the comprehensive label "structuralism", namely American linguistics during the forties and fifties. The North American structuralists, who considered as their authority Bloomfield and his book *Language* (1933), tried to ban subjectivism and intuition from the description of language. A psychological view of language was therefore frowned upon in so-called "taxonomic structuralism" as the "deadly sin" of "mentalism". For this reason, most linguists regarded statements about the meaning of linguistic elements that were based on introspection as highly suspect. Semantic description, i.e. conclusions concerning the meaning side of language, was either postponed to a later period, when semantics could be captured with more objective means, or was identified with the results of the natural sciences. Thus, Bloomfield himself (1933:139) claimed that the meaning of the English word *salt* was 'sodium chloride (NaCl)'.

Saussure ([3]1965:100 ff.) postulates two principles: 1. the arbitrariness of the sign, and 2. the linear character of the *signifiant*. For him the relation between the two sides of the linguistic sign is fundamentally arbitrary ("arbitraire"), non-motivated, or conventional. There is no necessary connection between the *signifié* and the *signifiant*. Even onomatopoeic words (sound symbolism), like *cuckoo*, and interjections, like *ouch*, are for him basically not motivated and are acquired conventions of a specific language system. We may, however, object to this view. With some onomatopoeic formations, e.g. *crash, bang, ding-dong* etc., there exists nevertheless a non-arbitrary relation between *signifiant* and *signifié*. Furthermore, as Saussure ([3]1965: 180 ff.) himself points out, there are degrees of arbitrariness and transitions between arbitrary and motivated formations and vice versa. Thus, the principle of arbitrariness only holds for simple linguistic signs. Combinations of signs, such as complex lexemes, may be morphologically motivated by their constituents, as e.g. *twenty-four, sixty-eight*, or *houseboat, letterwriter*. Saussure ([3]1965: 181) speaks of "éléments formatifs transparents", but it would be better to consider the whole combination to be transparent. In modern semiotics, i.e. the general theory of signs, the motivated, non-arbitrary sign is called 'icon', and is distinguished from the arbitrary sign labelled 'symbol'. One may further distinguish between primary and secondary iconicity (cf. Lyons 1977:193 f.).

According to Saussure's second principle, of the linearity of the *signifiant*, this is made up of a chain of temporally successive elements. The principle is based in the last resort on the fact that one cannot produce several sounds simultaneously. The linearity corresponds to the syntagmatic dimension of language already treated, but on the phonetic and phonological level.

To sum up, for Saussure the linguistic sign is binary or bilateral, since it consists of two parts. Its meaning, its content, is defined as a concept and therefore as a psychological or mental entity. Saussure consequently uses a binary, mentalistic model of the sign abstracted from the users and the functions of the sign. In this binary model the extralinguistic object denoted by the linguistic sign is not included. This, however, plays a role in the triadic model developed by Ogden and Richards to which we will now turn.

2.1.2. Ogden/Richards's "Semiotic Triangle"

The model of the linguistic sign developed by Ogden and Richards is represented in (2) in modified form:

(2)

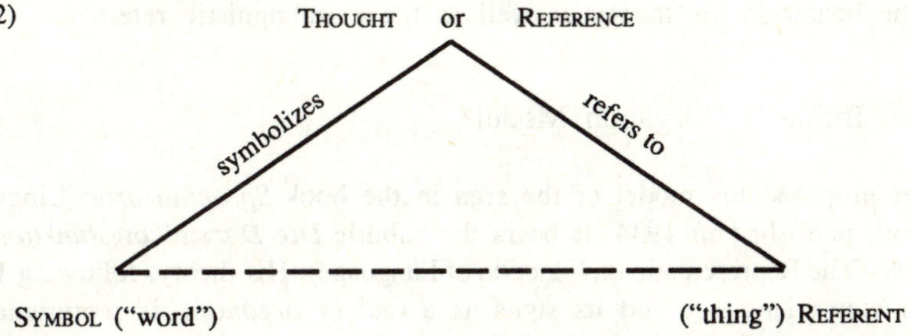

Besides the term 'semiotic triangle', the labels 'triangle of signification', and 'referential triangle' are also used in the literature. The last term is justified by the fact that the model includes the "referent". It has to be interpreted in the following way. There is no direct relationship between the word or 'symbol' and the extralinguistic thing or 'referent' denoted by it. This is symbolized by the broken line connecting the two, which Ogden/Richards characterize as "an imputed relation", saying that the 'symbol' "stands for" the 'referent'. The relationship between the two is indirect and mediated by a concept or "thought", which Ogden/Richards also label *reference*. Since in this schema a psychological or mental entity, namely *thought*, plays a role, we have a mentalistic model here too.

The term *reference*, identified with *thought*, is used in a different way by Ogden/Richards than in many recent linguistic theories. In the latter, *reference* is usually understood as a relational concept (see 2.2.3.).

The term is either used for the relation between the full linguistic sign and an extralinguistic referent, or the action of a speaker referring to an extralinguistic object by means of a linguistic sign. According to Ogden/Richards's semiotic triangle, there is then, for example, no direct relation between the *signifiant* (or symbol) *dog* and a certain class of living beings, or a specific element of this class. They stress the point that the meaning of a linguistic symbol (as a concept or thought) has to be clearly distinguished from the extralinguistic object (or referent) denoted by it. Words, as linguistic signs, are therefore indirectly related to extralinguistic referents.

For this relationship (besides *reference*) some linguists, such as Coseriu (1970:159) have used the term *designation* ("Bezeichnung"). Coseriu postulates that designation, as a relation between linguistic signs and extralinguistic referents, has to be clearly distinguished from *signification* ("Bedeutung"), i.e. the content of words or the relation between the contents of words. We will return to this problem.

Saussure's binary model of the sign is thus expanded in the semiotic triangle into a triadic model with the corners *symbol, thought*, and *referent* (cf. Lyons

1977: 96, where "sign", "concept", and "significatum" are used). However, this model still excludes the speaker and the hearer. Thus, both models, the "Saussurean egg" and the triangle, are non-pragmatic, in that they abstract from the users of the sign. It was as late as 1934, when Karl Bühler, in his organon theory of language ("Organonmodell der Sprache"), also included the speaker and the hearer in his theory as well as the extralinguistic referent.

2.1.3. Bühler's "Organon Model"

Bühler proposed his model of the sign in the book *Sprachtheorie* (Linguistic Theory), published in 1934. It bears the subtitle *Die Darstellungsfunktion der Sprache* (The Representational Function of Language). His theory, following Plato, which views language and its signs as a tool (= *organon*), is represented in somewhat simplified form in the following diagram (cf. Hörmann 1986:79ff.).

(3) Bühler's organon model:

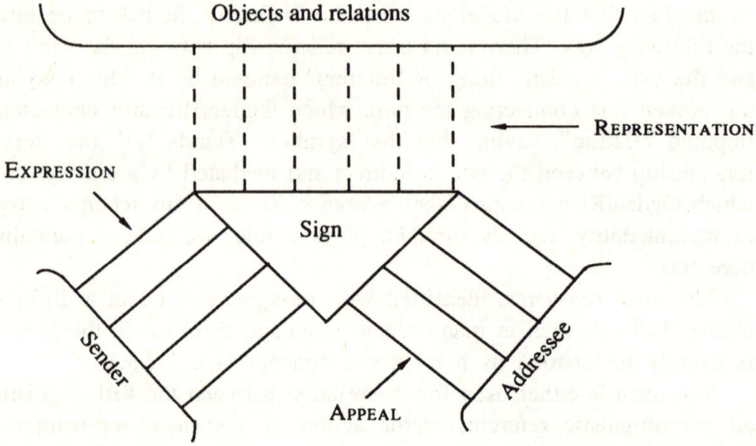

Diagram (3) has to be understood in the following way. The sign in the centre links a sender (normally the speaker) with an addressee (normally the hearer) and the represented objects and relations. The connecting lines between the sign and the three elements just mentioned symbolize the three most important functions of the complex sign, i.e. language, namely: *EXPRESSION* (also called '*emotive* function'), *REPRESENTATION* (also called '*referential* function'), and *APPEAL* (also called '*conative* or *vocative* function'). Language, as well as the individual linguistic sign, is an "organon", i.e. an instrument or tool for its users, hence the name of Bühler's linguistic model. The linguistic sign, as an instrument, is an expression of the sender who uses it, i.e. the speaker in the spoken and the writer in the written medium. At the same time it serves for the representation of objects, states of affairs, and relations, i.e. the extralinguistic referents. Thirdly the linguistic sign and language in general have the function of appeal to the addressee, i.e. the hearer or reader.

As an expression of the speaker or writer, i.e. due to its dependence on the sender, the linguistic sign is a *Symptom*. Because of its correlation with an extralinguistic referent, it is at the same time a *Symbol*. In view of its relation to an addressee, whose behaviour it is meant to direct and control, the sign, finally, is a *Signal*. These three types of sign, as well as functions of the complex linguistic sign (and therefore language in general) may be summarized as follows:

(4) 1. EXPRESSION (speaker, writer) ——— *Symptom*
2. REPRESENTATION (referent) ——— *Symbol*
3. APPEAL (hearer, reader) ——— *Signal*

Bühler's model has been expanded by others, e.g. by Jakobson (1960), who added three additional functions, namely the '*metalinguistic*', the '*phatic*' and the '*poetic function*' (see 2.2.4. for the connection with types of meaning). Jakobson does not dispute the domination of the representational function of language, but argues for a mixing of functions in the concrete realisation of a sign. Bühler is interested in the concrete speech situation and therefore in the problem of deixis. By this term one usually understands some kind of pointing, anchored in the speech situation, by means of gestures and words, to the people involved, in particular the speaker, as well as to the place and time of speaking. Deictic expressions, sometimes called "indexical" signs, relate utterances to the spatio-temporal co-ordinates of the act of speaking, namely to speaker, hearer, and their location. Traditionally, a distinction is made between person deixis, place deixis, and time deixis (cf. Lyons 1977:281f., 636ff.).

In Bühler's *Sprachtheorie* (^{2}1965:79ff.) the important second chapter deals with the field of pointing and the pointer words ("Zeigfeld der Sprache" and "Zeigwörter"). The origin of the field of pointing and of the orientational system is the speaker at a particular place and a particular time. This centre point can be represented by the pointer words *hier, jetzt, ich / here, now, I* (^{2}1965:102). Other linguists, e.g. Fillmore, have referred to this phenomen as deictic anchoring. For Bühler (^{2}1965:81, 90) pointer words ("Zeigwörter"), such as *here, there*, function primarily as Signals ("Signale"), whereas naming words ("Nennwörter, Gegenstandszeichen"), such as *table, tree, hat*, are Symbols ("Symbole") for extralinguistic objects. Pointer words are at the same time Symbols, since e.g. *here* denotes a location, *today* may denote any day, and *I, you* denote the sender and addressee.

In the following discussion of the structure of the English lexicon, we will largely neglect pointer words (although they are not exclusively signals) and pragmatic phenomena, such as deixis. We will rather concentrate on the other type of signs which Bühler calls symbols. These are often referred to also as "content words" or "contentives". The latter usually stand in opposition to the so-called "function words" or "grammatical words" (cf. Jackson 1988:15ff.), which are said to have grammatical function rather than lexical content. We will return to this distinction in 2.3. It has a long tradition and was made earlier, e.g. by Sweet, in terms of "full words" vs. "form words" (sometimes "empty words" is used). The term *function word* is mainly used in American structuralist linguistics and in language teaching. Both pointer words and function words have in common that they belong to relatively restricted grammatical systems, i.e. so-called closed classes (cf. Quirk et al. 1985:67ff., see also 2.3.1., 4.1.2.). These are more or less stable and do not change in a language except over a long period. Instead of looking at such closed sets, we will mostly concentrate on elements of open classes, such as nouns, adjectives, and verbs.

2.2. The Meaning of Signs and Kinds of 'Meaning'

That *meaning* is a notational term (like several others we have already discussed) becomes particularly apparent if we look at Ogden/Richards's book ([2]1949:186f.) entitled *The Meaning of Meaning* where a list of 22 definitions of *meaning* is given. There is certainly no single, correct explanation of *meaning*. Lyons (see 2.2.4.) distinguishes three kinds of meaning, or semantic information, namely 'descriptive meaning', 'social meaning', and 'expressive meaning'. For him, these are correlated with the descriptive, social, and expressive functions of language. In most chapters of his book, however, he is solely concerned with 'descriptive meaning'.

Leech ([2]1981:23) identifies *meaning* in the widest sense with *communicative value*. This comprehensive notion may be split up into three groups: 1. *sense*, 2. *associative meaning* and 3. *thematic meaning* (see 2.2.4.). The second category may itself be further divided into a number of subgroups (a-e), as shown in the following diagram:

(5)

MEANING = COMMUNICATIVE VALUE
- 1. *conceptual* m. (*sense*)
- 2. *associative* m.
  - a. connotative m.
  - b. stylistic m.
  - c. affective m.
  - d. reflected m.
  - e. collocative m.
- 3. *thematic* m.

According to Leech *sense*, or *conceptual meaning*, is the most important element in linguistic communication. This is probably the reason why he restricts himself, like Lyons, almost exclusively to this type of meaning. We will return to the other kinds later, as well as to the three levels of word meaning Leech introduced in the second edition of his book ([2]1981:121). A crucial point in any discussion of meaning is the relationship between language and the extralinguistic world (2.2.1.). This is closely connected with the question of the fuzzy nature of meaning. Both cannot be regarded independently of the general problem of which approach to semantics is chosen (2.2.2.). In this context Lyons (1977) convincingly introduces a useful distinction between *reference* and *denotation* (2.2.3.). Following a discussion of this distinction, we must have a look at the various kinds of nondescriptive meaning (2.2.4.). Finally, the opposition between denotation and connotation leads to a consideration of the notion of markedness (2.2.5.).

2.2.1. Language and Reality

We have already seen that Coseriu stresses the importance of the distinction between *signification* ("Bedeutung") and *designation* ("Bezeichnung"). *Designation*, for him, denotes the relationship between the full linguistic sign (combining *signifiant* and *signifié*) and the extralinguistic object or referent. Only *signification*, however, is purely linguistic and linguistically structured, and it alone is therefore relevant for structural semantics. Nevertheless, he does not deny the importance of *designation* for communication and actual speech. He distinguishes three types of designation (cf. Kastovsky 1982a:26f.): 1. Designation in speech, as when *pig* is used instead of *man*; 2. multiple designation, as when the same referent is classified as either *house, building, cottage*, etc. and 3. the coalescence or syncretism of classes of referents, as when in Greek the human species is classified as either *ánthrōpos* ('man as non-animal') or as *brotós* ('man as non-god').

According to Coseriu the distinction between 'signification' and 'designation' is necessary for two reasons. Firstly, it is possible to denote the same extralinguistic object with different linguistic means. Secondly, linguistic and extralinguistic relations must not be confused, since knowledge of the language is not to be identified with the knowledge of the world and of objects.

Coseriu, Lyons (1977:197ff.) and other linguists often quote famous examples from philosophers such as Frege and Husserl which demonstrate the need to distinguish between the meaning of a linguistic expression and its relationship to an extralinguistic object in reality. These are often treated in the context of a discussion of what to understand by *reference*. Thus, according to the logician Frege's classic example, the complex words *morning star* (*Morgenstern*) and *evening star* (*Abendstern*) both refer to the same extralinguistic referent, namely the planet *Venus*. They obviously have a different meaning. Similarly, as Husserl noted, the expressions *the victor at Jena* and *the loser at Waterloo* clearly differ in meaning (or 'sense' in Lyons's terminology), but have the same reference, or, as Coseriu would call it, *designation*. Although *victor* and *loser* are not only different in meaning, but opposites, they may be used for referring to an identical referent, to whom, for instance, the proper name *Napoleon* could also have been applied.

However, in this case – and strictly speaking also in the case of *the morning star* and *the evening star* – we do not have a single word for referring to an object, but a whole expression, a so-called '*definite description*'. Only in this case does Lyons (1977) use the term *reference* and speak of an extralinguistic *referent*. The relationship between a single word, or lexeme, and a class of objects (or a single element from this class) is called *denotation* by Lyons, while he calls the class, or set, or category of objects denoted by a lexeme *denotatum* (1977: 207). We will return to these distinctions presently. What is important at the moment is that both *reference* and *denotation*, as used by Lyons, fall together in Coseriu's *designation*, but are strictly separated by him from *signification*.

Coseriu's concept of *meaning* (*signification, Bedeutung*) excludes extralinguistic objects and relations, and is therefore restricted to language itself. His position can thus be characterized as a language-intrinsic or language-immanent approach to structural semantics. In his theory, lexical items are opposed to each other, and this opposition or contrast yields specific 'distinctive features' or semantic components. The methods or techniques of phonology, as a functional and language-immanent discipline, are carried over to lexical and semantic structures and applied in semantic analysis.

It must be pointed out that words are not simply names for pre-existing extralinguistic categories. Different languages do not capture reality in the same way. This becomes particularly evident in language comparison, as carried out by contrastive linguistics. Thus, e.g. Ger *Student* and *Lehrer* do not denote the same class of extralinguistic objects as *student* and *teacher*, since in German we also have *Studentin* and *Lehrerin*, which must be used if the referent is female.[1] The classes, or categories, denoted by the first two pairs of words, are therefore not identical. *Student* and *Studentin* taken together are equivalent to the category *student* in English.

The distinction that must be made in German, but is neutralized in English, is also relevant in English when a different word class is at stake, namely pronouns. In the singular, the linguistic distinction of gender between *he* and *she* largely coincides with the respective biological categories of sex.[2] On the other hand, *they* may refer to persons of any sex and also to things. The meaning of *they* therefore contains "less" than that of *he* or *she*. In more precise terms, adopted from the logic of classes, the 'intension' (in German *Begriffsinhalt*), i.e. the set of properties which determines the applicability of the term, is smaller. Conversely, the 'extension' (German *Begriffsumfang*) of *they* is larger, since the class of things to which it may be applied is larger, i.e. it may be used for denoting more referents (see diagram (8) p. 51).[3]

---

1 This is a simplification. The lexeme *student* consists of various lexical units (e.g. in *a student of human nature*, cf. the different entries in LDCE and LDCE 2 and the respective "usage notes"). In AmE the word is also used for children in schools (*pupils* in BrE). For the exact delimitation of the class of referents, the lexical set (see 4.2.5.) for the persons concerned must be considered, including at least *student, pupil,* and *scholar* (cf. I 136 in the LLCE).

2 A semantic change in the word *gender* seems to be under way, as witnessed by recent publications and the use of the word in TIME magazine, replacing *sex,* in the sense 'condition of being either male or female' (still the first definition in LDCE 2). This new use of *gender* is labelled *infml* in LDCE 1 and *euph* in LDCE 2. Cf. also OEDS s.v. *sex*.

3 The static, logical sense of *extension* ('class of objects' vs. *intension* 'set of essential properties') (cf. Lyons 1977:158f., 1981ff.) must not be confused with the traditional, dynamic, historical sense of *extension* (e.g. in *metaphorical extension*) characterizing a kind of semantic change or transfer. Thus, Ger *Abendstern* and *Morgenstern* have the same 'extension', since they both denote the planet Venus, but Ger *Ball* and E *ball* do not, a fact which is relevant for contrastive and applied linguistics. The extensions of AmE and BrE *student* also differ.

In general terms, the different categorization of the same extralinguistic reality by different languages may be represented as in the following diagram, adapted from Leisi ([2]1985: 5) (cf. also Lipka 1989a).

(6)

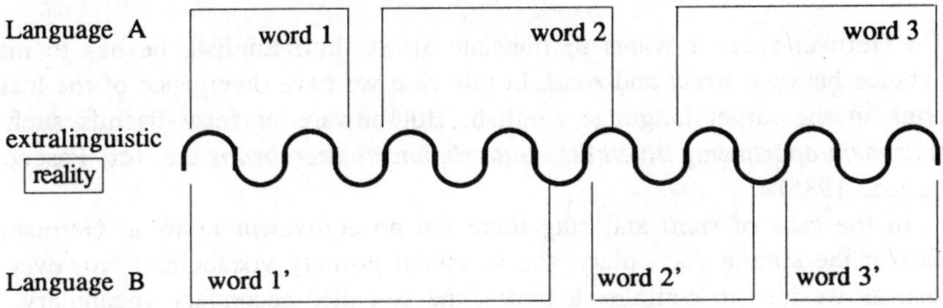

This may be interpreted as follows. In the extralinguistic world, there are no clear-cut borderlines or distinctions. The lines between certain categories are only drawn in a specific language. It is not the case, as is often believed, in a naive view of language, that pre-existing categories in nature simply have to be correlated with their respective names (cf. Lipka 1988b). There are no clearly distinct categories of things, processes and properties in reality. This is most obvious if we compare colour terms in different languages (cf. Bennet 1988). Although the physical spectrum of light, split up according to wave-lenght, is the same everywhere, different languages take a different choice. Thus, the extralinguistic continuum is articulated and categorized in a language-specific way. To apply (6) to our example: word 1 in the diagram (e.g. *Student*) and word 2 (e.g. *Studentin*) taken together are almost equivalent to word 1' in the schematic representation (*student*), but in the concrete example they cover exactly the same ground. We may say that two lexical items in one language (e.g. German) converge in a single lexical item in another (e.g. English), and thus, that there is 'convergence'. Looking at the same situation from the point of view of the other language, e.g. English, or, more concretely from the perspective of a native speaker of that language, we have 'divergence', i.e. the speaker has to make a choice between two (or more) items in the target language when he wants to render a single item of his own language (cf. Farrell [3]1977).

This non-coincidence of categories, even with very concrete everyday words, can be illustrated with the following examples (from Lipka 1981a: 376 f.). The German category *Schnecke* is split up in English into *snail* and *slug*. The category *Affe* corresponds to the two categories *ape* and *monkey* in English. This situation can be represented in the following way, where the extension of the English terms taken together is equivalent to the range or class of referents of the German lexeme:

(7a)

S c h n e c k e	
snail	slug

(7b)

A f f e	
ape	monkey

If a German speaker wants to translate *Straße* into English, he has to make a choice between *street* and *road.* In this case we have divergence of the lexical items in the target language English. But beware of false friends such as *Apartment/apartment, Blitz/blitz, Butterbohnen/butter beans* etc. (cf. Pascoe & Pascoe, 1985).

In the case of *snail* and *slug* there are no equivalent items in German, at least in the simple vocabulary, the so called primary vocabulary. However, as soon as we turn to complex lexemes, the so-called secondary vocabulary, the differences can be rendered in German as well, by using the compounds *Weinbergschnecke* and *Nacktschnecke.* Syntactic paraphrases could also be used, such as e.g. *Schnecke mit/ohne Haus.* This possibility is due to the interrelation of syntagmatic modification and paradigmatic lexical structuring in languages (cf. Lipka 1981a). The same holds for *Menschenaffe/ape* and *Äffchen/monkey.*

Cases of divergence in German, for native speakers of English, are *eat* vs. *essen/fressen* and *drink* vs. *trinken/saufen.* The English learner of German must discover under which conditions each word is used.[4] For the German learner of English, however, no problem arises, since there is convergence in *eat* and *drink.* On the other hand, he has a problem when he wants to translate the German category *Handschuh,* which is split up in English into *glove* and *mitten.* There are specific complex words for this in German, namely *Fingerhandschuh* and *Fausthandschuh,* or *Fäustling.* However, in English there is no superordinate term for *glove* and *mitten,* and so we have an obligatory distinction that must be drawn in the classification of extralinguistic reality.

To show that the situation may be even more complicated, let us look at the German equivalents for *paperweight* and *paperknife.* Here, the German lexical items *Briefbeschwerer* and *Brieföffner* may be considered as denoting practically the same class of extralinguistic objects.[5] Although the denotation

[4] Farrell (^{3}1977) is no help here since he does not treat either verb, but only gives Ger *Getränk, Trank, Trunk,* the paraphrase *etwas zu trinken, Alkohol,* and the nominalized verb *Trinken* as equivalents of the E noun *drink.* The informal verb *gobble* comes fairly close to Ger *fressen* when applied to humans, though it has the extra element 'quickly', not contained in *fressen.* By contrast, *eat* is not restricted to humans (see 4.3. for syntagmatic relations).

[5] AmE *letter opener* (equivalent to BrE *paper knife*) does not subsume the instrument under the category of knives (cf. LLCE: H 140). From the illustrations in LLCE and LDCE 2 (s.v. *knife*) the best English equivalent of Ger *Taschenmesser* is *penknife,* but *pocketknife* is also possible. Another most interesting contrastive example of language-specific categorization (E/Ger and BrE/AmE) is Ger *Nadel* vs. E *pin/needle* (cf. the illustrations in LDCE 2, s.v. *needle, pin*). It is also instructive for the usefulness of the notions of 'prototype' and 'visual

(Coseriu's *designation*) of the English and German linguistic signs is almost identical, the meaning of the complex words (e.g. 'knife for paper(s)', 'Öffner für Briefe') is clearly different.

If we confine ourselves to a single language, and return to the example *student* discussed above, we can see that the same referent may be designated, or referred to, by means of a variety of different words. The choice of words with a different meaning depends on the speaker and his intentions. Thus, instead of *student*, the following linguistic signs could be used: *beginner, candidate*, but also *son, uncle, husband*, or *daughter, aunt, wife*. This is another case of what has been called multiple designation above (p. 47). Consequently, the meaning of linguistic signs and their use for referring to extralinguistic objects or relations, in specific situations, must be distinguished in principle (see also 2.2.3.).[6]

In the previous discussion we have not been concerned with individual extralinguistic objects in the real world, but mainly with whole categories or classes of referents in reality. A class can be considered as a collection of individuals. In order to describe the relationship between classes, the logic of classes, or set theory, may be used (cf. Lyons 1977:154ff.). In the graphic representation of such relations so-called Venn diagrams are often used (Lyons 1977:158). Class-membership may be given either by means of an extensional definition, i.e. by listing its members, or by an intensional definition, i.e. by giving its identifiable, essential properties.

For our purposes the most important concept is that of the inclusion of classes, or class-inclusion (cf. Lyons 1977:156f.). Since linguistic signs have both meaning and denotation, two different types of inclusion are possible that must not be confused. Either the meaning (or 'sense' in Leech's use) of one item may be included in that of another, or the class of extralinguistic referents denoted by a sign may be included in the class of referents denoted by another sign. Thus, we may distinguish between *meaning* (or *sense*) *inclusion* and *referential* (or *denotational*) *inclusion* (derived from the noun *referent*). This is represented in the following diagram:

(8a)

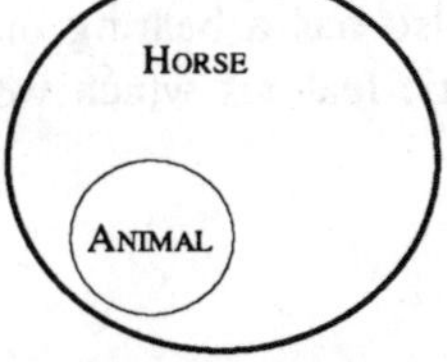

(8b)

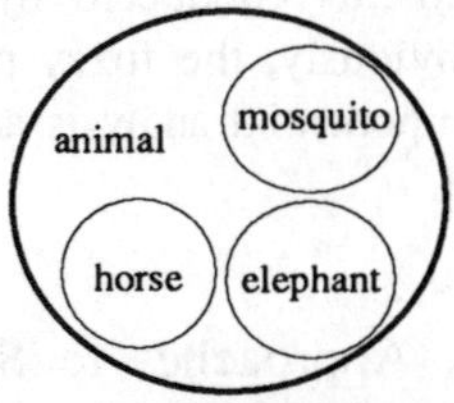

meaning (sense) inclusion — vs. — referential (denotational) inclusion

intension — extension

---

image' (cf. Lipka 1989b, Ilson 1987), metaphor, metonomy, and collocation (e.g. *to needle, pins and needles*) (see 3.3.3., 3.4., 4.3.5.).

[6] To be precise, referring is a matter of pragmatics (cf. Cruse 1977). Context-dependent 'reference' (in the sense of Lyons 1977:177) is not made by means of 'lexemes' (nouns, or verbs) but means of 'referring expressions' (e.g. the noun phrases: *that embittered old bachelor, the professor of linguistics, the postman*) containing them.

As pointed out by Leech (²1981:93) there is an inverse relationship between "meaning inclusion" and "referential inclusion". This is equivalent to the traditional logical relationship between the intension and the extension of a term. Thus, the meaning of *animal* is included in the meaning of *horse*, but the class of referents of *horse* is included in the class of referents of *animal*. Similarly, the meaning of *animal* is included in the meaning of *poodle*, but the class of referents of *poodle* is included in the category, class, or set of *dogs*, and is therefore a subclass or subset.

This brings us back to the vexing problem of the fuzzy nature of word meaning. The question of referential boundaries and the recognition of the fact that word meanings are not always precise, but rather essentially vague, have received growing interest in recent linguistics. As far back as 1960, the philosopher Quine (1960:125–156) discussed referential vagueness and opacity in chapter 4 of his book *Word and Object*, entitled "Vagaries of Reference". Quine talks about "fuzzy edges" and mentions that terms denoting physical objects may be vague in two ways. This is illustrated by his example *mountain* (1960: 126), which is:

> vague on the score of how much terrain to reckon into each of the indisputable mountains, and it is vague on the score of what lesser eminences to count as mountains at all.

Thus, the physical extent of the extralinguistic object denoted by *mountain* is not precisely delimited and it is also unclear where to draw the line between a *mountain* and a *hill*, as distinct categories.

Leech (²1981:120f.), in his discussion of "fuzzy meaning", points out that it is not at all easy to state what persons should be counted among the classes denoted by *girl* and *child*. He proposes to solve the problem by drawing on the notion of 'prototype', or "prototypic category", which is frequently used in recent psychological and linguistic research. We will return to this concept in our discussion of reference and denotation in 2.2.3., in connection with some experiments conducted by Labov on referential boundaries.

Obviously, the fuzzy nature of language also has a bearing on the method of componential analysis and the use of semantic features which we will discuss in 3.3.

2.2.2. Approaches to Semantics

Before we go on with our discussion of the meaning of linguistic signs, it will probably be helpful to have a look at some general differences between various approaches to semantics.

A broad distinction can be drawn between structural semantics and generative semantic theories (in the wider sense). Although such simplifying labels may be misleading, they are useful and necessary in giving a general survey. Structural semantics is mainly concerned with word semantics, while semantics in generative grammars often deals with sentence semantics. The former, however, is not confined to isolated items, but has focussed on lexical fields and paradigmatic semantic relations between words generally. Within generative grammar, two schools of thought can be distinguished, namely the so-called Interpret(at)ive Semantics and Generative Semantics. Scholars of the former group (Katz, Fodor, Chomsky, Jackendoff) focus on the syntagmatic semantic relations, while those of the latter (McCawley, Postal, Lakoff) argue for lexical decomposition and are thus largely limited to word semantics (cf. Lipka 1972: 30–83, 1976).[7]

In our context it is most appropriate to concentrate on word semantics, or lexical semantics. We may distinguish between a language-intrinsic or language-immanent approach to semantics on the one hand and a referential or denotational approach on the other. Coseriu's position can be characterized as a language-immanent one (see 2.2.1.). In his theory lexical items are opposed to each other and this opposition or contrast yields specific distinctive features or semantic components. The methods and techniques of phonology, as a functional and language-intrinsic discipline, are carried over to lexical and semantic structures and are applied in semantic analysis. Componential analysis in the tradition of Hjelmslev is a further example of a language-immanent approach to semantics (see 3.3. and cf. Lipka 1976).

Both the schools of Interpretive Semantics and Generative Semantics must be generally counted among the language-immanent approaches to semantics, since in their concepts of meaning they do not normally look beyond language. Finally, with some reservations, the work of Lyons and Leech also belongs here, although both differ fundamentally in their attitude towards componential analysis.[8]

Yet, many other linguists have concentrated on the properties of the referents denoted by linguistic signs, and can therefore be said to be doing referential, or denotational, semantics. Among those that have to be mentioned here are Nida, Lehrer, and Leisi. In Leisi's influential book *Der Wortinhalt*, published for the first time in 1952, the second chapter ([5]1974:25 ff.) bears the title: "Die Darstellung *des Bezeichneten*" (the representation of the referent, my italics, LL). In contrast to e.g. Coseriu, Leisi in his analysis of the content of words makes explicit reference to specific properties of extralinguistic referents. Thus,

---

7 See 3.3.4. p. 101 ff. and the reference to Cognitive Linguistics in the index of this book. George Lakoff has since become one of the leading figures of this discipline (besides Ronald Langacker and Gilles Fauconnier). He argues that the "new view of *experiental realism*", which uses 'cognitive models', prototypes, holistic gestalt properties, and imaginative mechanisms (like metaphor and metonymy) for the construction of categories should replace the traditional, atomistic, logical view of language which Lakoff labels *objectivism* and which "involves the manipulation of abstract symbols" (cf. Lakoff 1987: ix ff.). With reference to semantics, the latter, analytical approach has also been labelled "Aristotelian semantics" or the "checklist theory of semantics". See 3.3.3. and cf. also Rudzka-Ostyn (1988).

8 Cruse (1986) – but not (1977) – in which Lyons's theory is further elaborated, is another important example.

for him, the form, substance, thickness, or number of referents may for instance play a role in the determination of the content, or meaning, of words.

The following example (9) from Leisi's book *Praxis der englischen Semantik* ([2]1985: 37) may illustrate his referential approach to semantics. He points out that the two words *tower* and *Turm* in English and German are not at all equivalent, in spite of their etymological kinship. According to Leisi the conditions for the use of these words ("Gebrauchsbedingungen") are crucially different. He also argues that especially for the conditions of use of the English word *tower*, the form of the extralinguistic referent-type plays an essential role. The objects depicted in (9) can all, according to Leisi, be called *Turm*, but not all can be called *tower*. This he represents in the following way:

(9) *Turm* ≠ *tower*

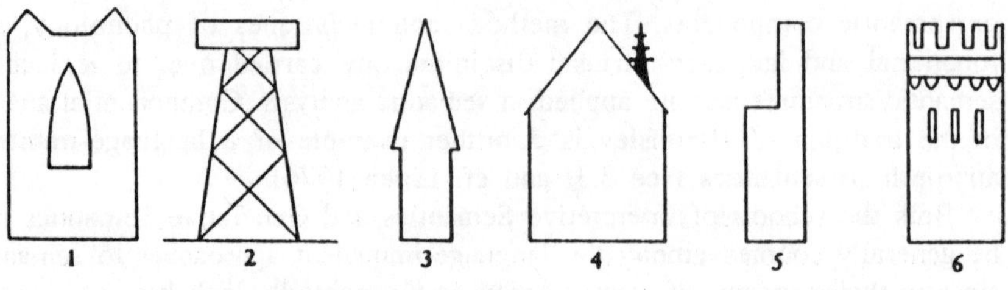

The German word *Turm* and the English word *tower* both denote a category or class of objects. These classes, however, are not identical. In English *tower* does not include objects of the type 3 and 4. Leisi generally defines the meaning of a word as the conditions under which its form may be used in connection with an ostensive definition, i.e. when pointing at an object while saying: "This is a ...".

For the appropriate use of *tower*, in contrast to German *Turm*, according to Leisi ([2]1985:45) two conditions must be fulfilled: a condition of form, and a condition of position. The referent must not be pointed and it must start out from the ground. For this reason, objects of the type 3 and 4 cannot in English be denoted by *tower* according to Leisi. The word is in opposition to *steeple, spire, turret, pinnacle*, which all taken together are equivalent to the extension of the German word *Turm*.[9]

A second definition of meaning ("Bedeutung") given by Leisi ([2]1985:38) identifies it with the relation ("Bezug") between the phonological form ("Lautgestalt") and all objects of a certain category. For the conditions of use for verbs, the states of matter of an extralinguistic object may be relevant. Leisi ([5]1975:66f.) points out that German *spritzen* requires a liquid extralinguistic

[9] Leisi does not give any evidence for specific 'conditions of use', and does not draw on tests with informants. It is true that some pointed tall structures may be called *tower*, e.g. the *Eiffel Tower*.

object, while *streuen* can only be used with a powdery, or granular referent. In contrast, the English verb *sprinkle* can be used with either type of referent.[10] The states of matter also play a role with verbs of cooking and with e.g. *eat* vs. *drink*. In Ger *setzen, stellen, legen* the form of the object is a relevant condition, which is neutralized in E *put*. Finally, the weight of the referent is essential for the use of both Ger *schleudern* and E *hurl*.

In many of his contrastive analyses of words in English and German Leisi is concerned with concrete extralinguistic referents. Here, a referential approach is certainly sensible and useful. It is further evident that insights for the explanation of child language acquisition and foreign language learning can be gained from such an approach. Leisi, however, does not claim that his theory can capture the meaning of all words in all languages. On the contrary, in his *Praxis der englischen Semantik* (^{2}1985 : 42) he explicitly points out that from a certain degree of abstractness onwards words can only be defined by means of other words (namely paraphrases).

As a last remark, his views must be related to the notions of prototype and gestalt in psychology and linguistics. His concept of meaning is basically holistic and nonanalytic. Thus, Leisi (^{2}1985 : 41, 45) repeatedly stresses that "Bedeutungen gestalthaft und nicht analytisch erfaßt werden", i.e. that meanings of words are perceived as wholes, and that the speaker-hearer possesses them as wholes.

2.2.3. Denotation and Reference

As we have seen, the categories of objects denoted by *tower* and *Turm* are not identical, and thus the denotation of the words is not the same. This can be explained by means of different conditions of use ("Gebrauchsbedingungen"), in this case the shape of the extralinguistic referents.

In an article entitled "Denotational Structure" Labov (1978) describes experiments he conducted to discover "the conditions for the denotative use of *cup, bowl, glass* and other container terms" (1978 : 221). This formulation reminds one strongly of Leisi's *Gebrauchsbedingungen*. Labov starts out by saying that linguistic analysis is the study of linguistic categories, and claims that the character of category boundaries has remained largely unexamined

---

[10] Leisi does not mention the verbs *spray* and *scatter*, which as G. Pascoe rightly points out, cover broadly the same field as *spritzen* and *streuen* and seem to have the same syntagmatic restrictions. *Schmieren* requires its object to be viscous, which is not the case with *spread*. There is partial convergence of both *spray* and *inject* in Ger *spritzen*, while, on the other hand, German lacks a superordinate term equivalent to E *sprinkle* (but cf. the more general words *Schnecke, Affe, Uhr, Straße, Stadt, Handschuh, Kissen, Nadel* and their (partial) English equivalents). Cf. Durrell (1988: esp. 233), for the non-congruence of lexical structures between the two languages and the problematic status of both *cutlery* and *Besteck* as superordinate terms.

within linguistics. The studies of container terms he reports on deal with denotata that form continuous series of increasing width or height. Informants were first asked to name the objects without any particular context. In a second experiment they had to imagine them filled with coffee, food, soup, or flowers. Besides diameter, height, and shape, Labov also introduced material (e.g. china or glass) as a variable. In the following diagram (10) (cf. Labov 1978:222) b) and c) show extreme cases of the varying ratio of height to width. (10a) shows the typical proportion for the use of *cup*, i.e. it can be considered the 'prototype' (in more recent terminology). Shape d) is the most favoured form for *mug*.[11]

(10)

a) b) c) d)

cup *mug*

Labov shows that the boundaries between *cup* and *bowl* are vague (or "fuzzy" in modern terms), and that context plays an important role, so that in spite of increasing width, an object like (10b) may still be called *cup* if it is filled with coffee. Presence and absence of a handle also has a decisive influence. Labov (1978:223) finds "two general properties of denotational boundaries: (1) vagueness and (2) interdependence". By the second term he means that variables (such as height, width, or function) are not independent of each other.

Labov (1978:226) distinguishes two kinds of semantic judgements, which he calls "categorical" and "weighted" judgements. Both are necessary in denotational structure. The former concern yes/no-decisions, or necessary conditions, such as the presence of a stem for using *goblet*, or the condition "female" for *mother*. The latter concern gradable properties, such that if a variable X is present, the use of a particular word is more or less likely. According to Labov (1978:226) "achieved statuses like 'adult' would require weighted judgements".

---

[11] This category does not exist in High German, but it does in other varieties (e.g. Bavarian *Haferl*). A *Becher* does not have a handle.

Labov also reports on experimental studies with drawings of bottle-shaped containers, where several dimensions such as neck opening, width, and overall height were varied. The results were that the object most likely to be called *bottle*, the "prototypical bottle", appeared to be "a glass object with a narrow opening and a neck one-third the width of the bottle" (Labov 1978: 231). Labov (1978: 232) also discusses properties of a "prototypical *mama*" and a prototypical *cat* in child language acquisition.

Both the experimental studies on container terms reported by Labov (1978) and the (originally purely psychological) research in Prototype Theory or Prototype Semantics (cf. Lipka 1986, 1987a) are concerned with the culture-dependent categorization of reality, of the extralinguistic world, in natural languages (cf. Lipka 1988b). While Labov is primarily interested in the fuzziness of category boundaries, Prototype Theory is concerned with their prototypical kernel. Language, or more specifically the lexicon of each natural language, is a means for interpreting our environment, for classifying or categorizing our experience. By such language-specific categorization we impose a certain structure on extralinguistic reality. In the view of the recent discipline of Cognitive Linguistics,[12] each language is equivalent to a particular conceptual system by means of which we perceive, structure, organize, and understand the infinite flow of impressions from the world we live in. Rosch (1977: 36) has pointed out that 'prototypes', as unitary gestalt-perceptions, relieve the human brain of laborious cognitive processes by providing an "efficient processing mechanism of matching to a prototype".

The notion of 'prototypic category' or 'prototype' derives from research in psychology, from which it has been argued that we recognize members of a category by matching them with a 'prototype'. It has recently been adopted into linguistics, e.g. in the work of Fillmore and Leech (^{2}1981 : 84–86, 120). Fillmore (1978 : 153) even opposes a "prototype semantics" to what he calls the "checklist theory of semantics", and argues that the former

> makes it possible to talk about a central or nuclear sense of a word, and ... about the various weightings of the individual criteria that go into specifying the prototype.

For him (1978 : 167) the "prototype definition" of *murder*

> involves killing somebody, intending to kill the person that got killed, and having a malignant heart about the whole thing.

A great deal of work in linguistics on the subject has been done in the meantime (cf. Lipka 1987, Aitchison 1987 : 51 ff., Hüllen/Schulze 1988). The concept of 'prototype' makes it possible to distinguish between the central or typical example of a category (e.g. *house, dog, fish*) and the periphery of the category, where a decision on membership is not so easy, and only a few conditions, properties, or criteria are present.

---

[12] For various approaches within this general framework cf. Rudzka-Ostyn (1988).

In my opinion, both the notions of 'prototype' and of 'semantic feature' (or 'semantic component', see 3.3.) are necessary and useful. It is unreasonable to impose a choice between them and set up a false alternative (cf. Lipka 1987a). The two approaches to lexical meaning are complementary and there is a division of labour (cf. Cuyckens 1984).

When talking about categories and categorization, we are concerned with classes of extralinguistic objects, not with single, individual referents. This important difference is most clearly brought out in the distinction made in Lyons (1977:174ff.) between 'denotation' and 'reference'. In order to clarify this distinction, we must make use of the concept of *lexeme*. By this concept, coined in analogy to *phoneme* and *morpheme*, Lyons understands an abstract linguistic unit (spelt in capitals) with different variants (e.g. *WRITE* as against *wrote, written*). We will return to this concept of *lexeme* in 2.3.

For Lyons the relation of *denotation* holds between a lexeme and a whole class of extralinguistic objects, as represented in the following schema:

(11a)	Denotation – Denotatum		
RELATION:	lexeme	→	class of objects
	DOG, COW, ANIMAL, MAMMAL;		
	TURM, TOWER, SNAIL, CITY.		

Lyons (1977: 207) defines the *denotation* of a lexeme as:

> the relationship that holds between that lexeme and persons, things, places, properties, processes and activities external to the language-system. We will use the term denotatum* for the class of objects, properties, etc., to which the expression correctly applies.

He characterizes the *denotatum* of e.g. *cow* as a particular class of animal, and adds that the individual animals also are its *denotata*. Lyons further points out that the denotation of a lexeme is independent of the concrete circumstances of an utterance. On the other hand, expressions such as *the cow, John's cow*, or *those three cows over there* may be used to establish a relationship of *reference* with specific individuals as *referents*. In this case the reference of these expressions containing *cow* is partly determined by the denotation of the lexeme *Cow* in the system of the English language.

This brings us to the notion of *reference* as defined by Lyons (1977) in *Semantics*. He discusses a fair number of uses of this term in philosophy and linguistics (1977:177ff.) and gives a preliminary definition of *reference* (1977: 174) as:

> the relationship which holds between an expression and what that expression stands for on particular occasions of its utterance.

This clearly is a relational conception, as is his view of *sense*. For Lyons *reference* depends on concrete utterances, not on abstract sentences. It cannot relate single lexemes to extralinguistic objects. He expresses this (1977:176) in the following way:

> reference … is an utterance-dependent notion. Furthermore, unlike sense and denotation, it is not generally applicable in English to single word-forms; and it is never applicable to lexemes.

His use of the term *reference* can be summarized and illustrated in the following way (but see below for his basic conception):

(11b) **Reference – Referent**

RELATION: expression / 'definite description' → specific object

the man over there, the cow, Napoleon, the queen, the king of France.

For Lyons (1977:206) both lexemes (i.e. single vocabulary words) and larger expressions have sense and denotation. Reference, however, is a property only of expressions, more specifically the subset of 'referring expressions'. The sense of an expression is a function of the senses of the lexemes it contains and of their occurrence in a particular grammatical construction. This compositional notion of the meaning of larger linguistic expressions is sometimes referred to as the Fregean principle of meaning. The first attempt in linguistics to apply the compositional idea to sentence semantics was made in Katz/Fodor (1963).

Although we will not often be concerned with *reference* here, in a book primarily discussing lexemes, it should be noted that Lyons distinguishes various kinds of reference, including "successful reference" (1977:180f.). This, obviously, is a pragmatic concept, no longer purely relational and language-immanent, but based on the concept of 'speech act' (cf. Searle 1969:72ff., Verschueren 1981). Lyons does not make use of it, but he abstracts from the speaker who refers by means of a referring expression to a referent, thus establishing the relationship of reference.

Closer inspection of Lyons's concept of *reference* reveals, however, that he is not really in disagreement with Searle. It is only on a single page in his monumental work (1977:177) that Lyons states explicitly that he too considers reference as an act performed by a speaker for a hearer by means of a linguistic expression (successfully or not). Although he believes that "it is the speaker who refers", namely in "the act of referring", he continues (1977: 177):

> It is terminologically convenient, however, to be able to say that an expression refers to its referent … and we will follow this practice.

So for purely external reasons of economy a shorthand way of speaking is introduced which creates the impression that Lyons had a relational notion of *reference.*

The clearest example of such a pragmatic use of the term *reference* is to be found in Searle's *Speech Acts* (1969). Chapter 4 of this book bears the title "Reference as a Speech Act". Here, the conditions and rules for this *illocutionary act*[13] are discussed in detail. For Searle (1969:95) – as for Lyons – reference is a linguistic act, by means of which a speaker may successfully "pick out or identify" an extralinguistic "object X", or *referent*, for a hearer.

According to Searle (1969:81) "definite reference" may be performed by means of the following linguistic categories:

1. Proper names, e.g. *Socrates, Russia*;
2. Complex noun phrases in the singular – often with a definite article – a category that is normally termed *definite descriptions* in philosophy, e.g. *the man who called, John's brother*;
3. Pronouns, e.g. *this, that, I, he, she, it;*
4. Titles, e.g. *the Prime Minister, the Pope.*

The concept of *reference* as used by Searle demonstrates again how important it is to distinguish between *reference* – or more clearly *referring* – as (establishing) a relation to a single extralinguistic object, and *denotation*, as the relationship between a class of objects and a lexeme. We will be specifically concerned with denotation in the following.

As we have seen, Lyons (1977:210f.) distinguishes between *denotation* and *sense*. For him, both are equally basic relations, and they are dependent on each other. According to him (1977:210) there are some words, such as *unicorn*, which have no denotation, but nevertheless have sense. This conclusion is based on the observation that a sentence such as *There is no such animal as a unicorn* is perfectly normal, while a sentence such as *There is no such book as a unicorn* is semantically odd. It further proves that both lexemes *unicorn* and *animal* are "related in sense".

2.2.4. Other Kinds of Meaning

In the following we will use the terms *denotation* and *reference* as illustrated in the diagrams (11a) and (11b) in spite of what has been said about the act of referring. There are, however, other types of meaning. They might be referred to as non-descriptive, non-conceptual, or non-denotative. As mentioned at the beginning of 2.2. (p. 46), Lyons distinguishes descriptive meaning from social and expressive meaning, while Leech separates conceptual meaning (or sense) from various types of associative meaning and from thematic meaning, as shown in diagram (5) (p. 46).

At this point it should also be mentioned that within 'descriptive meaning' Lyons (1977:247) makes a further distinction between the "central or focal, denotation of a lexeme" and its "total denotation". Languages may differ with respect to the denotational boundaries of words, but still be in agreement

---

[13] Cf. Searle (1969:23f.) where "complete speech acts" such as stating, questioning, commanding, promising etc. are labelled *illocutionary acts*, a term originally introduced by the founder of speech act theory J.L. Austin.

concerning the "focal denotation" of equivalent words. Thus, certain "focal types of colour, shape, texture, biological and social function" have to be recognized. For this, the notions of *biological* and *cultural salience* are introduced by Lyons (1977:247f.).

The different kinds of meaning are clearly related to different language functions (see 2.1.3.). Language does not only serve to transmit information (Bühler's 'representation'), although this function has been the main concern of traditional grammar and of structural as well as generative linguistics. Leech ([2]1981:40 ff., 42, 57) distinguishes five functions of language: the informational, expressive, directive, aesthetic, and phatic function. They correspond to those distinguished by Jakobson (1960:353ff.), but his 'metalinguistic function' is missing (see p. 45). The position adopted in Lyons (1977:50 ff.) can be summarized as follows:

(12) *language functions*:

1. descriptive
2. social } – interpersonal (emotive, "expressive" ...)
3. expressive }

According to Lyons (1977:51), whose main concern in the book is with descriptive meaning, the distinction between the expressive and social functions of language, and the respective expressive and social meanings is far from clear-cut. Both may be included under a single term, such as "interpersonal", "emotive", "expressive" etc., all of which have been used in publications. Lyons himself prefers "interpersonal" for the common aspects of the social and expressive functions of language. He further discusses in some detail the instrumental, metalinguistic, phatic and poetic functions of language (cf. also Jakobson 1960).

It should be obvious, if we compare this with Leech's approach, that *expressive function* is also a notational term. We can already see from (12) that there is a wider use of "expressive" (by other authors) than in Lyons's distinction of three functions of language. Leech's use is still narrower, since for him "expressive" is further distinguished from "directive", "aesthetic", and "phatic", which all concern social or interpersonal aspects of language.

Besides distinguishing between *denotation* and *reference*, Lyons – within *descriptive meaning* – further recognizes the existence of *sense*. Already in his *Introduction to Theoretical Linguistics* (1968:427) he had defined the *sense* of a word as:

> its place in a system of relationships which it contracts with other words in the vocabulary.

This, obviously, is another relational definition of meaning (cf. the discussion of "sense-relations" in 4.2.). Generally speaking, Lyons's approach as a whole can be characterized as relational semantics. In his later two-volume work on semantics, a clear, explicit definition of *sense* is not given. He remarks at one point (1977:202) that sameness or difference of *sense* depend on descriptive meaning and that expressions with the same *sense* must be regarded as synonymous. Clearly, his concept of *sense* is here again primarily seen from a relational point of view. This is also apparent in the following quotation (1977:206):

> Sense is here defined to hold between the words or expressions of a single language independently of the relationship, if any, which holds between those words or expressions and their referents* or denotata*.

It follows that *sense* is a purely language-immanent relationship. On the other hand, both *reference* and *denotation* are relations between linguistic units and the extralinguistic world. However, single lexemes, as well as larger expressions, have *sense* and *denotation*. But only expressions have *reference* (cf. 2.2.3.).

That *sense* also is not an absolute concept, but a notational term becomes quite clear if we compare its use by Leech. Both Lyons and Leech use the term quite differently. Incidentally, Lyons himself draws attention explicitly at various points (e.g. 1977:206) to the fact that other authors use *denotation* and *reference* differently, sometimes even the other way round.

As we have seen in diagram (5) (p. 46), Leech uses *sense* synonymously with *conceptual meaning*. For him, it is the most central aspect of *meaning* (in the wide sense), or "communicative value". As is clearly shown in (5), for him *connotative meaning* is only a subclass of *associative meaning*.

With regard to lexemes it has been customary in linguistics to distinguish between *denotation* and *connotation*. Lyons's *social* and *expressive meaning*, as well as Leech's *associative meaning* can all be regarded as various aspects of the same phenomenon that may be summarized under the term *connotation* (see below 2.2.5.). *Thematic meaning* is different in that it concerns the ordering of elements larger than lexemes, and is thus mainly relevant for sentence semantics. However, since lexical converses, such as *own* and *belong* are also involved, it may have some bearing on word semantics. This is illustrated by the following example (13), where the (a) and (b) sentences are identical in denotative or conceptual meaning, but differ in thematic meaning:

(13) (a) My father *owns* the Rolls Royce.
(b) The Rolls Royce *belongs* to my father.

Before we come to our wider notion of *connotation* let us look at one last recent proposal concerning word meaning. Leech ([2]1981: 121), in the revised version of his book on semantics, sets up a three-level approach to "word-meaning" which partly integrates some of the aspects of 'lexical meaning' discussed above. This approach – which is not entirely unproblematic – can be represented and summarized as follows:

(14) *levels of 'lexical meaning'*:

1. 'word-sense' = conceptual unit
2. features: f_1 f_2 f_3 ... prototypes
3. attributes (fuzzy sets of): a_1 a_2 a_3 ....

The "word-sense" as a whole may be regarded as a "conceptual unit", also referred to as "prepackaged experience" by Leech (^{2}1981): 32). According to him, this unit or category (in the sense of linguistic categorization discussed in 2.2.3.) may then be split up into features or components by componential analysis (cf. Lyons 1981:84). Finally both 'word-senses' and features, which represent prototypic categories, may be broken down into "fuzzy sets" of "attributes". It is probably more convincing to regard the 'attributes' of Prototype Semantics as equivalents of the 'components' or 'features' of componential analysis or Feature Semantics (cf. Lipka 1986a).

This new focus on concepts is quite in keeping with the theory of Cognitive Linguistics. Already in the first edition of his book, Leech had stressed "language as a conceptual system" and emphasized that it is not only an instrument of communication, but the means by which we "classify or 'conceptualize' our experience" (1974: 28). He also discussed lexical innovation as a technique for introducing new concepts, and the abbreviatory function of the word, as well as its "concept-defining role" and its "concept-forming power" (1974:36f.).

'Lexical meaning', i.e. the meaning of a lexeme or lexical unit, is a matter of *langue*, or the language-system. This may be modified when words are used in context (see 4.4.), a fact recognized by the distinction sometimes made (cf. Schmidt ^{2}1967) between 'lexical meaning' and 'actual meaning'.

2.2.5. Connotations and Markedness

In some treatments of lexical semantics, a binary distinction is made between *denotation* and *connotation*, or *denotative* vs. *connotative meaning* (cf. Kastovsky 1982a:37ff., Hansen et al. ^{2}1985:17ff., Ullmann 1962:74; but not in Cruse 1986). Other authors like Lyons (1977:287) and Leech (^{2}1981:12 ff.) use *connotation* and *connotative* in a specific sense. The latter regards this type of meaning as a subclass of his *associative meaning* see (5) (p. 46), which could be seen as a paraphrase of the more general sense of *connotation*. The concept is closely tied up with a widespread definition of *synonymy*. In this view, synonyms have the same *denotation*, i.e. cognitive, or conceptual meaning, but differ in connotations. Connotations must be regarded as an inherent property of lexical items. Synonyms may be specifically marked by connotations.

Such additional ("associative") aspects of meaning[14] – as opposed to the central denotational core – can be illustrated with the following examples of "stylistic" or "social and affective meaning" from Leech (^{2}1981:14f.):

(15)	(a)	steed	(poet.)	(b)	domicile	(leg.)	(c)	cast	(lit.)
		horse			residence	(fml.)		*throw*	
		nag	(sl.)		abode	(poet./old)			
		gee-gee	(baby l.)		*home*			chuck	(sl.).

The twofold distinction between *denotation* and *connotation* can be justified, in that the *denotative meaning* refers to the relation between a linguistic sign and its *denotatum. Connotations*, however, are additional properties of a lexeme. Leech marks *steed* as "poetic", *nag* as "slang", and *gee-gee* as "baby language". Dictionaries give further characterizations, such as "literary, rhetorical, humorous" for *steed*, "colloquial" for *nag*, and "(child's word for a) horse" for *gee-gee. Domicile* is labelled "very formal, official" by Leech, while dictionaries give "formal" and "legal". *Abode* is marked "poetic" by Leech and "old, literary, legal" by various dictionaries. Finally, Leech marks *cast* as "literary, biblical"[15] and *chuck* as "casual, slang".

The apparent discrepancies between the various dictionaries and Leech's characterization are explained by the fact that there are no clear-cut boundaries between the labels *colloquial, casual*, and *slang*. Also, dated and archaic words are often found in poetical, literary and legal usage. In other contexts, these connotations may be exploited for humorous effects. In figure (15) we have the same *denotation* in all three cases, i.e. the denotatum of the nouns in (a) and (b) and of the verbs in (c) is the same. But the synonymous words have different connotations – in other words, they are 'marked', or instances of 'marking' or 'markedness' (cf. Lyons 1977:305ff.). This is why the italicized lexemes are characterized as "general" by Leech.

The notion of *marking* or *markedness* is derived from phonology, where the marked item of a pair of phonemes is distinguished by a specific feature. Thus, of the phonemes /t/ and /d/, the /d/ is marked because it exhibits the additional feature of voice. In analogy to this we can say that *horse, home* and *throw* are unmarked, while the other lexemes are 'marked' in one way or another. It is obvious – in particular from (15a) and (15b) – that markedness is not only a matter of binary opposition, as Leech (^{2}1981:113) claims and

---

14 As already mentioned in 1.3., in connection with variety class 5 "attitude", it is sometimes difficult to draw a line between 'connotation' (or stylistic marking) and 'denotation'. Lyons (1977:618f.) argues that Scots English *loch* (vs. *lake*) can be regarded either as a dialectally marked variant of the Standard English word or as a different lexeme, with a specific "descriptive meaning", or 'denotation'.

15 Alternatively, as with the marking of *nag* as (sl.) discussed in 1.3., one could hold that *cast* should be labelled *fig.*, as in *cast aspersions* on, or also *tech.*, as in *cast a fishing line*. The LDCE 2 gives "lit or old use" (for *fishermen cast their nets*) and *fig.* (for *The witch cast a spell*).

derivation of the concept from phonology suggests. There may be a number of marked lexemes related to a single concept or neutral word. The unmarked lexemes are neutral and not restricted to specific contexts in their use.

In his magnum opus, Lyons (1977 : 307 ff.) introduces the concept of *semantic marking*. For him, a semantically marked lexeme is more specific than an unmarked one. For this reason he labels *bitch* – as opposed to *dog* – as well as *lioness* (as opposed to *lion*) "semantically marked". Furthermore, *lioness* is also "formally marked" by the suffix *-ess* and therefore a case of *formal marking*. In this connection, Lyons (1977 : 308) discusses the problem of whether we can distinguish two distinct lexemes DOG. If *dog* is used in opposition to *bitch*, we could speak of a different lexeme dog_2 , which is distinct from dog_1 in the wider sense.[16] I would like to illustrate this hypothesis with the following diagram:

(16)

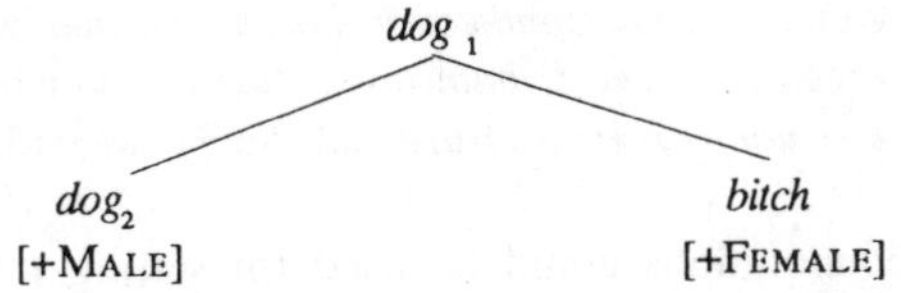

According to Lyons it may make sense to ask a question like: *Is that dog a dog or a bitch*? Such a question would then contain both lexemes (or 'lexical units') dog_1 and dog_2.[17] However, Lyons decides against such a solution, as could be expected. He argues that the phenomenon of semantic marking is widespread and that it is necessary only in exceptional cases to refer to sex by a marked lexeme like *bitch*. Since for him polysemy has to be distinguished from semantic marking, he is against treating *dog* as an instance of polysemy.

Lyons's notion of (formal, distributional, semantic) 'marking' is not identical with my use of *markedness* in connection with connotation. There is a certain amount of overlap, however, since semantically marked lexemes as well as words with additional connotations have a more specific meaning than the unmarked, neutral lexeme.

We can further subcategorize, if required, the class of connotatively marked lexemes of a language. This will depend on the specific purpose of a description and the relative delicacy of the semantic analysis. Such a finer classification could also result in a particular structuring of the vocabulary (cf. Hansen et al. ²1985 : 19 ff.). Certain aspects of linguistic variation (cf. figure (8) in ch. I) may serve to distinguish between regional, temporal, and social connotations.

---

[16] Cf. Rohdenburg (1985). Obviously, there is also a connection between the notions of 'marking' and 'extension'. The marked item has a narrower extension, but its 'intension' is greater. If we draw on the notion of 'lexical unit' (see 4.1.1.), we could claim that the lexeme DOG contains two lexical units dog_1 and dog_2, with different (although largely overlapping) 'senses'.

[17] See 4.1.1. for the notion of lexical unit which I adopted from Cruse (1986). The term is used in a similar way in Chafe (1970: 44, 105 ff.).

Besides stylistically, affectively, or emotionally marked lexemes, we could furthermore group lexical items according to regional or dialectal, archaic or neologistic, and sociolinguistic variation (cf. Lipka 1988a). We could draw on parameters like 'medium', or 'field, mode, tenor', or like Leech (who follows Crystal and Davy) on 'province, status, modality'. Furthermore, we could set up a comparison between Leech's subclassification of *associative meaning* and the labels used in dictionaries, for example the LDCE (cf. diagrams (8), (9) in ch. I). However, all this would lead too far here.

Let us therefore look at another possible system of connotations, namely the one proposed in Hansen et al. ([2]1985 : 19 ff.). I shall try to represent its most important points in diagrammatic form below, illustrating only with a fraction of their wealth of examples. The three main classes of connotations are the following:

(17) A. stylistic: eg. *edifice, swain, apothecary, baksheesh, buddy, bloke, bugger;*
B. expressive: *niggard, bastard, bathroom, bugrake* 'comb', *dolly bird;*
C. regional: *elevator, streetcar, truck* (all AmE), *wee* (Scottish E).

These three classes of connotations could be used for setting up three distinct groups of lexemes. The unmarked lexical items will then form a fourth large category. According to Hansen et al. (who speak of zero-connotation in this case) neutral lexemes make up the vast mass of common vocabulary. The authors further state that connotations can affect either the complete meaning of a lexeme or only specific senses of it, i.e. in their terminology only single 'sememes' of a polysemous lexeme.

The major categories of connotations are further subclassified in the book as represented in my following diagrams:

(17a)

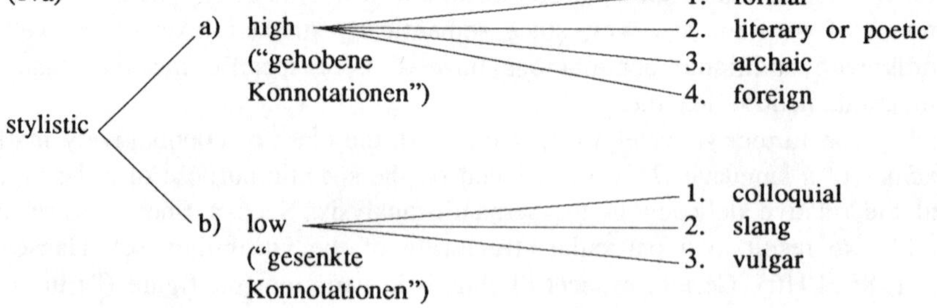

(17b)

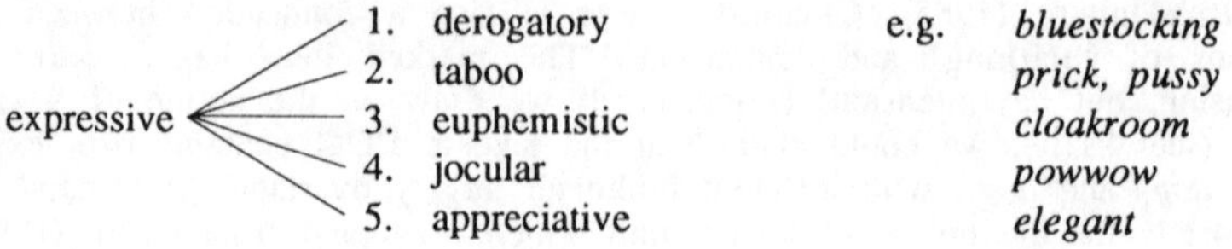

Regional variation is not further subclassified in Hansen et al. (^{2}1985). The authors mention varieties such as British, American, Scottish, Irish, Canadian, Australian, New Zealand, South African, Indian English and also point to further interior differentiation (e.g. Northern English). They only give examples of Americanisms, correctly stating that there is considerable American influence on British English as well as fluctuation.

It has to be stressed here that this is one possible taxonomy of connotations and connotatively marked lexemes in English. It is certainly one of the most detailed descriptions available but other systems are also possible. The classification sketched here deserves a few comments. Social variation is clearly neglected, e.g. the much talked-about distinction between *U* and *non-U* in Britain (cf. also Trudgill 1983, Lipka 1988a). Within temporal variation neologisms are also relevant (cf. the dictionaries discussed in 1.4.). Within expressive connotations, the distinction derogatory/appreciative belongs together, since approval/ disapproval is a binary distinction of attitude. It is quite systematic in at least part of the lexicon, and may be expressed by specific word-formation processes. Thus, for example, appreciative *manly, womanly* is opposed to derogatory *mannish, womanish, effeminate.* In this connection it may be of interest that according to Quirk (1986: 129) and the introduction of the COBUILD dictionary (1987:xx) terms of racist abuse and sexist language are today considered very offensive and are far more dangerous than sexual or religious taboo and swear-words.[18] Furthermore, approval and disapproval seem to be distinct from affectionate connotations of lexemes, as e.g. when *town* is used for a large city, as in *Chicago my home town*! (cf. Lipka 1986:137).

Technical language and register are mentioned by Hansen et al. (^{2}1985: 22) as "funktional-stilistische Merkmale" and they stress the possible combination of connotations and the corresponding combination of labels in dictionaries. Situationally determined variation is of course closely connected with the problem of the definition of the terms *stylistic* and *style* (cf. Lipka 1988a).

In sum I would like to stress again that the binary distinction between *denotation* and *connotation* is a useful and necessary one but that a further subcategorization of connotations to a greater or lesser degree may be necessary, depending on the purpose of the description. Dictionaries may legitimately use different labelling systems, depending on whether they have the foreign learner in mind or an educated native speaker.

---

[18] G. Pascoe suggests the following taxonomy of taboo words, with three classes: 1. "becoming weaker": a) swearwords (*damn, bloody*), b) sexual words (*prick, pussy*); 2. "slowly becoming stronger": sexist words (*man* 'species', *broad* 'girl'); 3. "rapidly becoming much stronger": a) human pejorative (*mongol, cretin, lunatic*), b) racist (*nigger, Jewess, yid*).

2.3. Morpheme, Word, Lexeme

The notion of *word* is not as simple as it seems at first sight. We will return to the ambiguity of the term presently. Even a superficial look at the simple example (18) will show immediately that the word and the linguistic sign can not be equated. Words are certainly linguistic signs, but the reverse is not the case, since not every linguist sign is necessarily a word. The smallest linguistic sign is the *morpheme*.

2.3.1. The classification of morphemes

In classical American structuralism, the most important procedures for discovering morphemes were segmentation and classification. Linguistic utterances produced by so-called informants were first segmented, i.e. broken down into possible constituents. The elements resulting from this, the *phones* on the level of sound and the *morphs* on the level of form, were then grouped into classes. This grouping was made on the basis of the function and distribution of the elements. Thus, the *phoneme* comprises a class of variants called *allophones*. Likewise, the *morpheme* can be defined as a class of variants, namely its *allomorphs*.

If we now apply the method of segmentation and classification to the English word *farmers*, we get the following smaller units (cf. Matthews 1970: 98):

(18)	*farmers*:	FARM	-ER	PLURAL
		farm	*-er*	*s*
		free	bound	bound
		lexical	lexical	grammatical
		morpheme	morpheme	morpheme

Such a morphological analysis reveals several linguistic signs in one word. It describes several elements (*items*) in a particular sequence (*arrangement*). Such a morphological model has therefore been labelled *Item and Arrangement* (abbreviated as *IA*). This simple example, however, does not show the following two kinds of difficulties which may arise for classical morpheme analysis:

1. For words like *took* and *ran* such a simple segmentation is not possible even in a morphologically simple language like English (cf. Matthews 1970:107ff. for It *canterebbero*). To solve this difficulty, the notion of *replacive allomorph* was introduced by some linguists (cf. Gleason ²1961).
2. In certain inflecting languages, like Latin or Russian, another method of morphological description will be more appropriate. Charles Hockett, one of the most important representatives of American structuralism, has called this the *Word and Paradigm model* (abbreviated *WP*). Here, words

like *amo, amas, amat* etc., or *gallus, galli, gallō* etc., are described and learnt in an inflectional paradigm. For such languages the *IA* model is less adequate. The difficulties of segmenting some words in English were solved elegantly in early generative grammar by a third model: *Item and Process* (*IP*). I cannot discuss this here.[19]

In the history of linguistic thinking the development of the notion of morpheme in descriptive structuralism can be understood as a counter-reaction in two ways: 1. In opposition to traditional grammar, which was word-based and mistakenly projected the situation in the classical languages onto modern English; 2. As a counter-reaction against the vagueness of the notion of *word* and the manifold difficulties in defining it.

However, the new basic unit of *morpheme* was not completely immune against such difficulties. In my opinion, the structuralist notion of 'morpheme' can only be captured adequately by conjoining three different definitions:

1. The morpheme is the smallest meaningful linguistic unit and therefore the smallest linguistic sign.
2. The morpheme consists of a class of variants, the allomorphs, which are either phonologically or morphologically conditioned.
3. The morpheme is an abstract unit of the system of a language, for example the plural morpheme or the past tense morpheme in English, symbolized by $\{Z_1\}$ and $\{D_1\}$.[20]

Thus, for example, the English past tense morpheme in *hit* is realized as a *zero-morpheme*, symbolized by Ø. In the case of *took* it is realized by a special type of element called a *replacive morph*, namely /u/← /(ei)/. Only the three definitions taken together completely capture the classical concept of 'morpheme'.

I now propose a classification of morphemes which is language-independent, but will be illustrated with English examples. This classification is not strictly hierarchically ordered, but the classes partly overlap. In linguistics, such a phenomenon is termed a *cross-classification.*

As a first step, the elements found by segmentation and classified as allomorphs on the basis of their distribution may be divided into two great classes: 1. *Lexical morphemes*, (also called 'semantic morphemes') and 2. *grammatical* (functional) *morphemes*.[21] In spite of the fact that there are difficulties with

[19] Cf. Matthews (1970: 103–107). E.g. *sank* or *men* are described as the result of morphological and morphophonemic processes triggered by abstract morphemes ('Past Tense', 'Plural') which are combined with basic representations (*sink, man*).

[20] Cf. Lipka (1969) where the plural morpheme $\{Z_1\}$ and the past tense morpheme $\{D_1\}$ are discussed in detail (as well as $\{Z_2\}$ = genitive, $\{Z_3\}$ = 3rd person singular present, $\{D_2\}$ = past participle). The notation is adopted from Gleason (^{2}1961: cf. 75), who prefers, however, the term *"zero-allomorph"* to the (lexicalized) *zero-morpheme* (see fn. 3 ch. I).

[21] Cf. Jackson (1988: 15–17) for the parallel distinction between 'lexical' and 'grammatical words', regarded as a gradation between the two extremes: "completely lexical" (nouns) and "completely grammatical" (articles, auxiliary verbs).

definition and overlap in some areas, the two large classes can be characterized on the basis of certain features or attributes in the following way:

(19)

lexical morphemes	*grammatical morphemes*
denote (particular) extralinguistic objects & states of affairs: e.g. actions, events, situations, relations.	denote (general) grammatical functions: e.g. plural, tense. syntactic relations: e.g. concord of gender, number.
open class (set).	closed class (inventory).
precede grammatical morphemes (in Germanic languages).	follow lexical morphemes (in Germanic languages).
combination (with other lex. m.) often restricted.	combination (with lex. m.) relatively unrestricted.
result of combination: new *lexemes*.	result of combination: *word-forms*.

It is customary to refer to the combination of lexical and grammatical morphemes with the terms *inflection*, or *morphology* (in the narrow sense, cf. Lipka 1969). On the other hand the combination of lexical morphemes with each other is usually labelled *word-formation*. Since it results in new (complex) words, or more precisely units of the lexicon, i.e. lexemes, it ought to be called "lexeme-formation" (cf. Bauer 1983:13). However, we will stick to the lexicalized, or institutionalized, term *word-formation*.

It is sometimes difficult to draw the distinction between lexical and grammatical morphemes, because there are borderline cases and the limits of an individual morpheme may be vague or fuzzy (e.g. *-ic/al*, *-er*). Furthermore, it may be hard to assign a single specific meaning to a particular constant form (see below for the concept of *formative*). But basically, the distinction is sound and useful and can be easily made in most cases.

The two large groups of morphemes can be further subclassified on the basis of other criteria. First and foremost, morphemes may occur either alone and independently, or only in conjunction with others. This leads to the distinction between *free* and *bound morphemes*. A further aspect of their distribution is position. With bound lexical morphemes it is relevant whether they are added in front or behind, i.e. as a *prefix* or *suffix*. Finally, it is important to know whether a morpheme only occurs once, as a so-called *unique* or *blocked morpheme*, or repeatedly.

Examples, such as *Fri* in *Friday* or *cran* in *cranberry* are called *blocked morphemes* by Marchand and those who follow him. They could be subsumed under the class of *formatives*, as done in Kastovsky (1982a:70). I will here use the term in the same way, for minimal formal units without identifiable meaning, which are only relevant on the phonological or syntactic level. It is not a comprehensive term (as in Bauer 1983: 16, 124) which includes both such formal units as well as morphemes. Thus for me the term denotes the formal segments of words like *understand* (with past tense *understood*) and idiomatic verb-particle constructions like *make up* (one's face), *set off* (the alarm). It includes blocked morphemes, but not full linguistic signs. Formatives could also be called *pseudo-morphemes* (cf. Tournier 1985:85f.).

The criteria just discussed for defining and distinguishing morphemes lead to the following classification (or rather cross-classification, cf. Kastovsky 1982a:73) of *morphemes*:

Diagram Outline

(20)

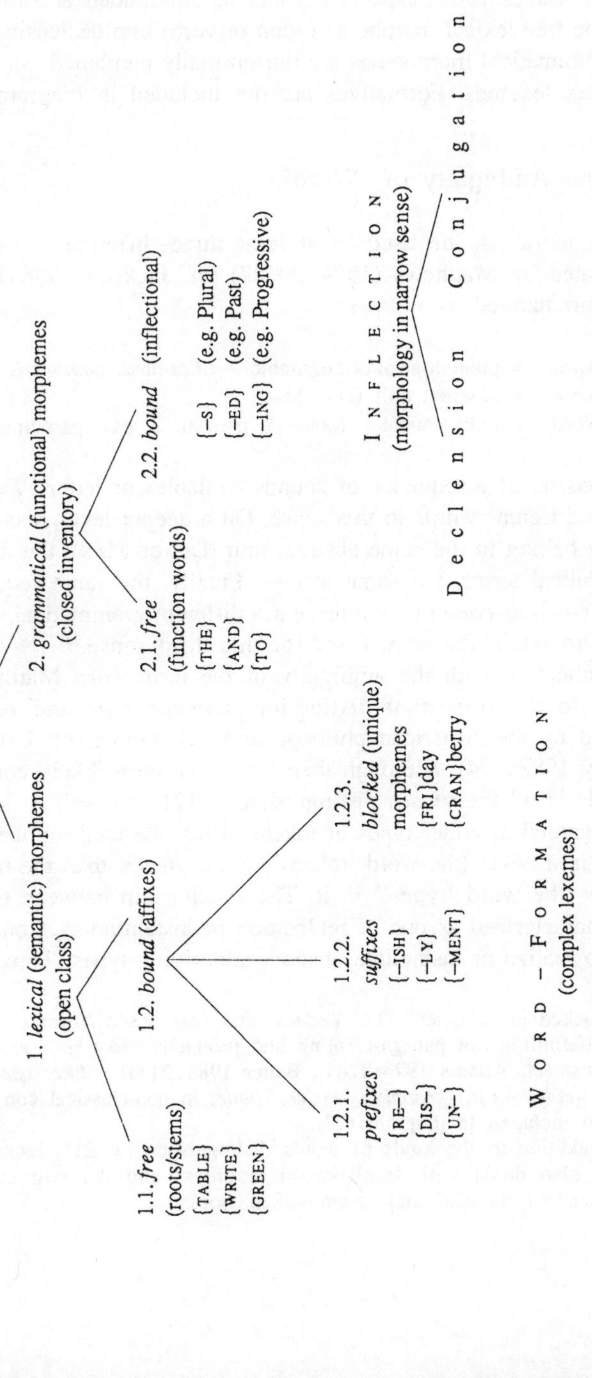

A few comments must be added to figure (20). Word-formation is not restricted to the addition of affixes (sometimes called *derivation*), but includes the combination of free lexical morphemes, i.e. *compounding*, (*tablecloth, greenhouse, writing-table*). Examples of *affixation* include: *rewrite, unclean, greenish, writer, Wednesday, raspberry*.[22] The combination of free grammatical and lexical morphemes belongs in *syntax*. Inflection (or *morphology* in the narrow sense) (cf. Bauer 1988: esp. 73 ff.) can be subdivided according to the word class of the free lexical morpheme (noun or verb) into declension or conjugation. Bound grammatical morphemes are not normally combined but added to simple or complex lexemes. Formatives are not included in diagram (20).

2.3.2. The Ambiguity of 'Word'

The term *word* can be used in at least three different senses, as has been demonstrated by Matthews (1974: 20–27) (cf. Jackson 1988: 1 ff.). His views can be summarized as follows:

(21)	*word*$_1$	= phonological/orthographic ~ (*dies/died, man/men*)	= WORD-FORM
	word$_2$	= abstract unit (DIE, MAN)	= LEXEME
	word$_3$	= grammatical ~ (*come* 1. present, 2. past participle)	= WORD.

Word$_1$ consists of a sequence of sounds, syllables or letters. *Dies* and *died* are obviously different words in this sense. On a deeper level, such different forms obviously belong to the same abstract unit (DIE or MAN), the dictionary *word*$_2$, or in technical terms, the same *lexeme*. Finally, the same sequence of sounds or letters (such as *come*) may represent a different grammatical *word*$_3$. Matthews proposes to retain the term *word* for this third sense.[23]

In connection with the ambiguity of the term *word* Matthews also draws attention to the important distinction between *type* and *token*, originally introduced by the American philosopher C. S. Peirce (cf. Lyons 1977: 13 ff., Kastovsky 1982a: 74). Although there are some more likely correlations, basically words in all the senses distinguished in (21), as well as letters or sounds, can be regarded as either types or tokens. Thus, the total number of occurrences of words in a novel (the word 'tokens') is far greater than the number of different words (the word 'types') in it. The relationship between tokens and types can be characterized as one of realization or instantiation. Concrete tokens can be said to realize or instantiate abstract underlying types. Thus, the same letter

---

[22] 'Blocked morphemes' like *Wednes-* and *rasp-* (and 'formatives' generally) are by definition not pattern-forming and productive like *re-, -er, -ize*. 'Combining forms' (cf. Adams 1973: 128 f., Bauer 1983: 213 ff.), like *astro-, disco-, hydro-* and *-cide, -crat, -graph(y), -meter, -phile,* in neo-classical compounds, have not been included in diagram (20).

[23] In addition to the kinds of words distinguished in (21), Jackson (1988: 8, 11, 15) also deals with 'multi-word lexemes' and the two classes (open and closed) of 'lexical' and 'grammatical words'.

type *e* may occur several times in one word (e.g. *reference*) or in different shape (different tokens of the same letter type) in the hand-writing of different people.

The 'types' of words (lexemes), sounds, and letters belong to the lexical, phonological, and orthographic system of a language (Saussure's *langue*), while the 'tokens' belong to its concrete realization (*parole*).

As we have seen in 2.3.1., words are not the smallest linguistic signs. The word, in the traditional sense, consists of at least one free lexical morpheme. But it can also be made up of a whole series of lexical morphemes, like *beer-drinker, theatregoer, segregationist,* or *denationalization.* Leech ([2]1981: 222) gives the examples *drum-majorettishly* and *railway-station refreshment room.* The fact that lexical morphemes can be combined again and again in principle is an instance of the phenomenon called *recursiveness* in linguistics. That the resulting new word is one lexeme is apparent from the possibility of assigning it to a specific word class. Even very complex words can be inflected, i.e. grammatical morphemes can be added to such a combination of lexical morphemes. These inflected words are then cases of word-forms, not instances of new words. i.e. new lexemes.

2.3.3. Lexemes, lexical items, and word-forms

Before we continue with our discussion, some terminological clarification will not be out of place. As in (11a) (p. 58) we will henceforth use the terms *lexeme* for the abstract unit of the lexicon and *word-form* for the (inflectional or other) variants of the lexeme on the morphological, phonological, or graphemic level. In contrast to Matthews's usage represented in (21), I will use *word* in a general sense when there is no need for the specific technical terms and no ambiguity arises. I will continue to use the established term *word-formation,* although it should really be *lexeme-formation,* because it has a long tradition in linguistics and is lexicalized and institutionalized.

Some books (e.g. Quirk et al. 1985) prefer the term *lexical item* to *lexeme.* I will occasionally use both terms as synonyms, for stylistic variation, but will normally prefer *lexeme* for various reasons. It is shorter, seems to be more current in English and general linguistics (especially for Romance languages), and furthermore stresses the parallel with the concept of *morpheme.* Like the latter, the lexeme is:

1. A complete sign on a particular linguistic level, namely the lexicon;
2. A class of variants, namely word-forms;
3. An abstract unit of the language system.

Unlike the morpheme, the lexeme is not the smallest unit and may be a simple, a complex, or a *phrasal lexeme.* Let us look again at some examples which illustrate the necessity of the distinctions introduced. The lexemes FIND and TAKE are realized (amongst others) by the word-forms *find, found* and *take, took, taken*. On the other hand *singer* does not belong to the lexeme SING despite its close phonological and morphological connection with *sing, singing*. The last two word-forms, however, are related to the phonologically more different forms *sang* and *sung*. The lexeme, as a unit, therefore comprises a group of word-forms, in analogy to the morpheme and its variants, the allomorphs. Thus, the complex lexeme SINGER also includes, besides the unmarked form *singer*, the genitive *singer's* and the plural *singers*. It is itself composed of the morphemes {SING} and {-ER}.

But there are also complex lexemes whose constituents are not morphemes. Examples are *hold up* (a bank), *put up with* (something), *do out of* 'cheat' (in *He did me out of five pounds*) which can be characterized as discontinuous lexical items or *phrasal lexemes* (cf. Lipka 1971:215, Lyons 1977:23). These verbal lexemes cannot be decomposed into meaningful units, i.e. morphemes. The formal segments cannot be correlated with an invariant content which also occurs in other combinations. Consequently they are not morphemes but *formatives*.

Such formatives of a single lexeme can often be interrupted by other morphemes or strings of morphemes. This is frequently the case in idiomatic and non-idiomatic verb-particle constructions (cf. Lipka 1972), where interruption by a pronominal object is the rule. But it is also possible with noun phrases, as for example in *She beat the dust out, We woke the man up*. In these non-idiomatic verb-particle constructions, however, the constituents are morphemes, not formatives. In spite of the discontinuity, we must recognize here a single lexeme.

Other formally complex lexemes which cannot be broken down into morphemes are normally labelled *idioms* (cf. 3.2.5.). With some idioms the formal constituents never occur independently or in other combinations, e.g. *eke* in *eke out*, *peter* in *peter out*. With other idioms, the constituents are homonymous with independently occurring free lexical morphemes, e.g. in *understand, pull someone's leg*, AmE *shoot the breeze* 'talk idly', *blow a raspberry* 'make a vulgar noise with lips to, express contempt, dislike, disapproval'. In the past tense the formatives *shoot* and *stand* behave exactly like the homonymous morphemes. In order to capture such phonological regularities, a concept like the 'formative' is absolutely necessary.

As a result of the preceding remarks, we can now give a further twofold definition of the *lexeme*, namely from a syntagmatic and a paradigmatic point of view. A lexeme can therefore consist of:

1. One morpheme or two or more formatives or morphemes (syntagmatically);
2. A set of mutually substitutable word-forms (paradigmatically).

Chapter III

The Internal Structure of Words. Word-Formation, Features, and Componential Analysis

Lexemes may have internal structure, but their relationship to other lexical items is also structured in various ways. Both kinds of structuring are neutralized in the ambiguous noun phrase *lexical structure*, which refers: 1. to the structure of lexemes and 2. to the structure of the lexicon. We will discuss both in turn in chapters III and IV.

If 'lexemes' are defined as consisting of 'lexical units' (related to the various 'senses' of a polysemous word, see 4.1.1. p. 130 ff.), they clearly have internal semantic structure. 'Word-formation' (or, more precisely 'lexeme-formation') then produces new 'lexemes', while the productive semantic processes of metaphor and metonymy (or 'semantic transfer', see 3.4.) produce new 'lexical units'. Both, lexemes and lexical units, may then be affected by 'lexicalization', and 'institutionalization' (cf. Bauer 1988 and see 3.2.5.).

The internal formal structure of words can furthermore be analysed on the graphemic and phonological level (possible sequences of letters, consonants and vowels, phoneme clusters, syllable structure), but this is clearly not the business of an outline of English lexicology. In the following, we will first look at polysemy and the morphological structure and then investigate the semantic structure of lexemes, also from a dynamic point of view. Consequently, word-formation processes and semantic processes will play a role here.

3.1. Polysemy, Lexical Entries, and Sememes

Before looking more closely at the internal morphological structure of words, we must raise the question of the unity of the word. This has always been a knotty problem for both linguistic theory and lexicographic practice. It is often not easy to decide whether in a specific instance we have a single lexical item with several meanings, i.e. a case of *polysemy*, or several lexemes which are formally identical, i.e. *homonymy* (cf. Lipka 1986b). We will return to this problem in greater detail in 4.2.1. after adopting the new notion of *lexical unit* in 4.1.1.

Let me mention here, however, that the problem of polysemy has received a great deal of attention recently, and also that I have modified my position on this since 1986. The rediscovery of polysemy (cf. Lipka 1975a) must be seen in connection with two central issues of Cognitive Linguistics: the fuzziness of word meaning and the ubiquity of metaphor (cf. Paprotté/Dirven 1985).

Like so many other words in the language of linguists, *polysemy* is a 'notational term'. Lehrer (1989:1) explicitly states that she is "not using it in the standard way". She adopts a very wide notion of polysemy (including metonymic pairs of material and product, e.g. *nylon, nickel, paper, glass* and even "nominalizations" of movement verbs, e.g. *a walk, a swim, a fly*, cf. 1989: 11, 24f.). Rohdenburg (1985) discusses it in the context of the markedness or hyponymy of items such as *dog* (see 2.2.5. p. 65). The most comprehensive theoretical treatment of the subject, combined with an extensive computer-aided corpus study, is Schneider (1988).

Spatial metaphor and "localist approaches to semantics" are not new, as King (1988:555) points out (cf. also Leech/Svartvik 1975:82–90). However, a cognitive point of view may open up new perspectives to a fuller understanding of originally locative relations, which include visual images and representations which are banned from purely language-immanent structural semantics (cf. Rudzka-Ostyn 1985).

At the moment we will introduce the following convention. We start out from the assumption that a word of a specific spoken or written form and particular syntactic properties (especially belonging to a specific word class) is a single lexeme. The possible different senses of this lexeme, like those of *word* discussed in 2.3.2., will be labelled *sememes* following Hansen et al. (^{2}1985:14, 179ff.). *Sememe* is here defined as a specific meaning, or 'sense' of a lexeme made up of a complex of semantic components. The term *sememe* is not used by many linguists, in particular it will not be found in Kastovsky (1982a), Leech (^{2}1981), Lyons (1977) and in the work of Coseriu (but cf. Lipka 1972:33 f., 43f.). Kastovsky (1982a:84f., 90, 92) only introduces the term *archisememe* to denote the features common to all lexemes of a word-field, which may be realized materially as an *archilexeme*.

The following examples may illustrate the need for introducing such a concept and my use of the term *sememe*:

(1)

(a) BULB
- sememe 1 'round root of plant'
- sememe 2 'sth. like *bulb*$_1$ in shape'

(b) HOUSE
- sememe 1 'building'
- sememe 2 'people in *house*$_1$'

The second illustration draws on an example introduced into linguistic research in 1963 by Katz & Fodor (cf. Kastovsky 1982a:247ff.) which has been extremely influential. Originally, it served to introduce so-called *lexical entries* with different types of semantic components (cf. Lipka 1972:37ff.). We will return to this question in 4.1.

(2) BACHELOR
- animal — 1 'young fur seal without mate'
- human — 2 'so. with first academic degree'
- human — 3 'young knight serving a great noble'
- human — 4 'so. who has never married'

Note that *bachelor* consists of a rather specific sequence of sounds or letters, especially if compared for example with *cup*. Surprisingly, this property has never played a role in the long discussion of the distinction between polysemy and homonymy.

The following example is a modified and simplified version of the representation of various senses of the noun *cup* given in Dirven (1985:102). As in many other cases discussed here, definitions from various dictionaries are integrated in my diagram. Diagram (3) can be regarded as illustrating either a possible lexical entry for an English noun, or eight different sememes of the polysemous lexeme *cup*.

(3) see page 78

Obviously, metaphor and metonymy play an important role in (1) and (3). It can be clearly seen that the word definitely has internal structure (cf. Hansen et al. [2]1985: 208 f.), which can be brought out more or less clearly by an appropriate analysis and representation. I will not give any further detailed comments on my proposal in (3), since alternative representations are certainly possible. We will now discuss the morphological structure of lexemes.

3.2. Morphological Structure: Simple vs. Complex Lexemes

We now turn to the distinction between simple and complex lexemes, like *cup* or *table* vs. *decentralization*. Clearly, the latter has a complex morphological structure, in that it consists of a number of lexical morphemes (see 2.3.1.). We are thus concerned with analytic, synchronic word-formation in the sense of Bauer (1983), Adams (1973), and Marchand ([2]1969). Basically, the combination of lexical morphemes may be regarded either from 1. a synchronic or a diachronic and 2. an analytic or synthetic point of view. In this outline we have to restrict ourselves, for practical reasons, normally to a synchronic perspective. Furthermore, the main focus here will be on the analytic aspect of word-formation, i.e. the perspective of the hearer or reader who encounters already existing complex lexemes. In other passages (see 3.4.) we will stress the complementary synthetic aspect, namely the perspective of the speaker/writer who creatively produces a new lexeme. The productive nature of word-formation, in particular of certain patterns and processes, has been emphasized by many linguists, notably by Hans Marchand.

The clear distinction between analytic and synthetic word-formation is relatively recent (Lipka 1971:222f., Kastovsky 1982a:16f., 151ff., Hansen et al. [2]1985:28, 32f.). Analysis in word-formation can be linked to a structuralist

(3)

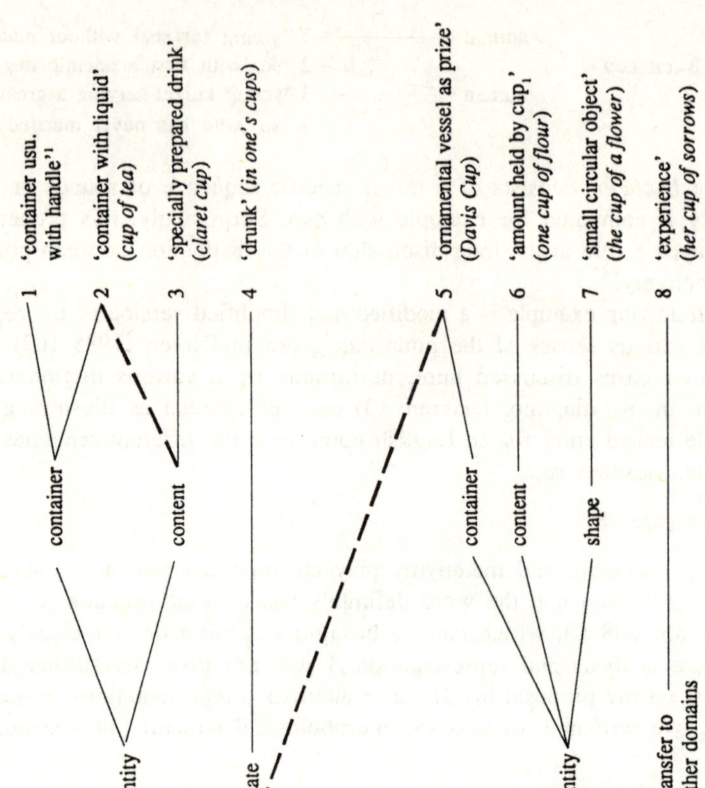

[1] It is well known in the discussion of 'prototypes' that there are *cups* (for example Chinese ones) without a handle. However, they do not invalidate the statement that the prototypical *cups* have a handle (cf. Lipka 1987a:287f.). In German the attribute is criterial for the distinction between *Tasse* and *Schale*.

approach while the synthetic perspective is inherent in the various models of generative grammar, whose starting point is the sentence (cf. Kastovsky 1982a: 216 ff.).

A complex lexeme may be synchronically analysable but no longer motivated, like *blackboard* or *watchmaker*. If its complete meaning is not derivable from its morphological structure and the pattern exhibited in parallel formations, as in *callgirl, highwayman, streetwalker, pushchair, wheelchair,* we say that such lexical items are idiomatic. We will return to such questions of *lexicalization* and *idioms* in 3.2.5. For the moment we will concentrate on the question whether lexemes are analysable, i.e. decomposable into linguistic signs, namely morphemes. Word-forms, i.e. the inflected variants of a lexeme (see 2.3.2.), are irrelevant for the description of lexical structure. Although they can be segmented into signs, such combinations of grammatical and lexical morphemes do not belong in lexicology. They are the object of morphology in the narrow sense.

Formatives (in our sense), i.e. pseudo-morphemes (see 2.3.1., 2.3.3.) are also of marginal interest for word-formation. They do, however, play a considerable role in the discipline of *phraseology* which is concerned with idiomatic *phrasal lexemes* (cf. Gläser 1986:15). There are also other properties, besides idiomaticity, which distinguish phrasal lexemes from the results of word-formation and speak for not regarding phraseology as a sub-discipline of lexicology (cf. Gläser 1986:15–25). Thus there are relatively close connections with syntax, and phrasal lexemes shade off into complex idiomatic phrases, proverbs, quotations, and routine formulas. Practical reasons, of course, also favour a separation of lexicology proper from phraseology.

The result of the combination of lexical morphemes can be labelled a *syntagma*, more precisely a word-formation syntagma. Such a morphological syntagma can be regarded as the reduced form of an explicit syntagma, the sentence (cf. Lipka 1971:218 f.). This idea, as well as the concept of syntagma itself, taken over from Charles Bally, belongs to the foundations of Marchand's theory of word-formation (cf. Lipka 1976 : 119, Marchand ^{2}1969 : 2 f.). For Marchand as well as those who follow him (cf. Kastovsky 1982a : 22, 152 f.) including myself, a *syntagma* is a combination of full linguistic signs, which are in a determinant/determinatum relationship to each other. Thus, the sentence is a full grammatical syntagma, with the subject considered as determinatum and the predicate as determinant. In a word-formation syntagma, in English and other Germanic languages, the determinant (dt) normally precedes the determinatum (dm, in the following in capitals): *space/SHIP*, *re/WRITE*, *writ/ER* The determinatum furthermore denotes the identified element, which is already known, while the determinant represents the differentiating element, the new information.

The combination of formatives (pseudo-morphemes) and lexical morphemes can be represented in schematic form as in (4), a diagram, which also shows certain general *categories* of word-formation. I here make a terminological distinction between such *categories*, as general procedures (like compounding, affixation etc.) and specific types (in Marchand's sense), as subclasses, for example within compounding (e.g. *steamboat, blackbird, watchmaker, colour-blind, waterproof, easygoing, highborn*). These types are not to be identified with Marchand's *types of reference* (e.g. the Subject-type, Adverbial Complement-type etc.). As general, neutral terms for the combination of lexical morphemes I will use *combination* or *composite* in the following:

(4)

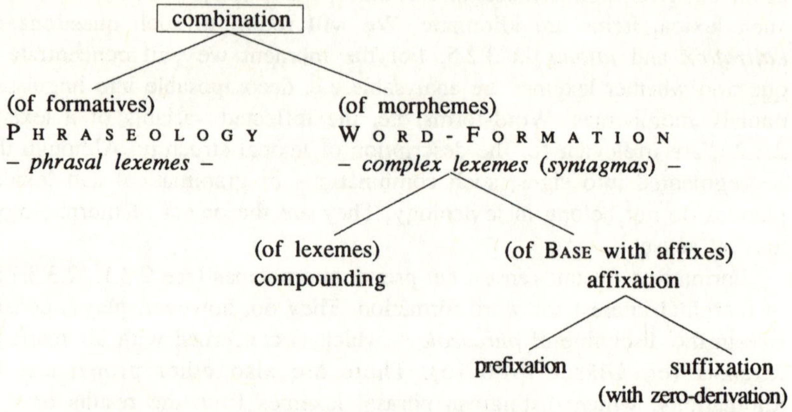

As can be seen from the diagram (4), I prefer the term *affixation* to the ambiguous term *derivation*, except in the special case of *zero-derivation* (cf. Tournier 1985: 48, Quirk et al. 1985: 1539 ff.). Prefixes and suffixes are said to be attached to a *base*, which may be simple or complex, and in this case has its own internal structure (cf. Quirk et al. 1985: 1519). This can be illustrated in the following way:

(5)

polarize	=	POLAR + ize
depolarize	=	de + POLARIZE
disgracefulness	=	DISGRACEFUL + ness

The segmentation into base and affix reveals the *Immediate Constituents* (or ICs) of the complex lexeme. This notion was introduced into linguistics in classical structuralist syntax, where the analysis into ICs, starting from the sentence, was often performed down to the level of morphemes. An illustration of the IC-structure of *decentralization* is found in Kastovsky (1982a: 170).[2]

[2] His analysis is *decentraliz/ation* but *de/centralize*, which shows that 'base' and 'determinatum' are not identical. For reversative verbs in English and German generally (e.g. also *unload, entladen, desensibilisieren*) cf. Funk (1988). IC-analysis presupposes a semantic analysis and thus we have Ger *Straßen/wettervorhersage*, E *un/gentlemanly* but *old maid/ish*. Spelling and hyphens may indicate the closeness of ICs, as e.g. in *lighthouse-keeper* vs. the noun phrase (NP) *light housekeeper*. Cf. also the improbability of *guaranteed used/cars* and the possibility of both *selfconscious/ness* and *self/consciousness* (cf. Ger *Selbstbewußt/sein* which is lexicalized in a different way).

The ICs of a word-formation syntagma are the determinant and determinatum, with the latter usually in second position in English, as e.g. in *houseboat* vs. *boat-house*. Each can internally be complex and analysed into constituents on a deeper level. Thus, e.g. *selfconsciousness* has a complex determinant, while *letter-writer* has a complex determinatum.

I will not normally use the term *stem*, which Quirk et al. (1985:1518f.) illustrate with *jeal-, pie-* in *jealous, pious.* Like Marchand (^{2}1969:5f.) I consider these cases, as well as *conceive, deceive, receive*, and *horrify* as not analysable into full linguistic signs, and therefore consisting of formatives. These are relevant for phonological regularities, but not for word-formation.

Tournier (1985:72) gives the following general formula for affixation in English, which is not a theoretical postulate but based on the observation of a large corpus (cf. also Stein 1971 for recursive affixation in English and French adjectives).

(6) $P_2 \quad P_1 \quad (B) \quad S_1 \quad S_2 \quad S_3$

As can be seen from (6) the base in English complex lexemes, which forms a sort of nucleus or kernel, can be combined with up to two prefixes and three suffixes.

In the following, I shall discuss compounds, derivatives, and nominalizations in some detail. Although I prefer the action noun *affixation* to *derivation*, I shall employ, for the result of this process, the useful cover term (*prefixal, suffixal, zero-*) *derivatives.* The three groups will serve to show in an exemplary way the problems which arise in the analysis and description of complex lexemes. For an extensive description of the productive patterns of English word-formation I refer the reader to Tournier (1985), who calls these *matrices lexicogéniques* (including also productive semantic processes), to chapter 2 in Hansen et al. (^{2}1985), and to the *Appendix* I in Quirk et al. (1985). Before we come to the survey of the three groups, three general remarks are necessary.

The first one concerns so-called *nominalizations* (see 3.2.3.). The criterion for setting up this category of lexemes is the result of the word-formation process of nominalization. This class provides the most obvious justification for a syntactic level in word-formation. Thus, both Marchand (^{2}1969) – but not the first edition of his book – and generative grammarians start from an underlying sentence, which is converted into a nominalization by transformations. In our short survey it is impossible to take up the controversy which has arisen within generative grammar over the treatment of nominalizations. Two competing hypotheses have been proposed, the so-called transformationalist hypothesis (or TH) and the lexicalist hypothesis (or LH) (cf. Kastovsky 1982a: 220ff.).

Secondly, I would like to emphasize again that complex lexemes constitute a separate area within the lexicon, as opposed to simple lexemes. As already illustrated in diagram (3) in 1.2. (p. 11), Coseriu distinguishes word-formation, as secondary lexical structures, from primary structures like “word fields”. This distinction within paradigmatic lexical structures has led him to distinguish the *primary vocabulary* from the *secondary vocabulary* in a number of publications. It corresponds to the opposition between arbitrary and motivated linguistic signs and is particularly relevant for foreign language learning and teaching. Simple lexemes have to be learnt in isolation, while complex lexemes are internally structured and can thus be related to other lexemes in the mental lexicon (cf. Aitchison 1987).[3]

As to my third remark, it must be stressed, however, that the same kind of distinctions which can be made by specific simple lexemes like *drive*, can in principle also be expressed through syntagmatic modification of a general lexeme, as in *go by car* (cf. Lyons 1968:452). This general principle also holds for complex lexemes, in which the determinatum is syntagmatically modified by the determinant. I have discussed this interrelation between syntagmatic modification and paradigmatic lexical structuring in English in great detail in Lipka (1981a). Thus, for example the simple lexeme *settle* (noun) necessarily contains the semantic components 'without legs' and 'made of wood', which are not specified in e.g. *armchair*. On the other hand, this complex lexeme necessarily contains 'with arms', which is explicitly expressed morphologically, as well as the facultative *inferential features* (see 3.3.2.) 'upholstered' and 'comfortable' (cf. Lipka 1985). These, in turn, are obligatory, inherent components of *easy chair*.

From a contrastive point of view the principle of interrelation also holds, as demonstrated in Lipka (1981a) by comparing *ape* and *Menschenaffe, monkey* and the suffixal derivative *Äffchen*. For simple lexemes Cruse (1977) discusses the question of the degree of lexical specificity chosen by a speaker in a specific situation, when he has at his disposal e.g. *dog, animal*, and *alsatian*. Cruse argues that *dog* here represents the neutral level of "lexical specificity". He claims that "under-specification" *animal* (in this case) is chosen when the speaker is either unwilling or unable to give further information. According to Cruse this suggests either compassion (e.g. *The poor creature! The way they treat that wretched animal is disgraceful!*) or that he is an expert in a particular field (e.g. using *stone* and *instrument* for a diamond or a violin).[4]

Although the problem of lexical specificity is related to the choice between simple and complex lexemes, it must be maintained that this concerns reference in a particular situation and is therefore a matter of pragmatics.

---

[3] However, sometimes it may be easier to learn simple, unrelated lexemes than a series of compounds, especially if irregularity and lexicalization are involved. G. Pascoe argues that German beginners learn *dead/kill* faster than English ones learn *tot/töten*.

[4] But cf. Lehrer (1989:7), for another aspect of technical language and expertise, where it is argued that "the polysemous use of *dog* is used mostly by dog breeders, for whom a word denoting 'male dog' would be desirable" (see p. 65). The equivalent 'specification gap' in the German 'word-field' *Pferd* (see 4.2.4.) is filled with the compounds *Hengstfohlen* and *Stutfohlen* in the language of horse breeders.

3.2.1. Compounds

We have mentioned already that traditionally the essential criterion for a combination to be a *compound* is that it is made up of at least two free lexical morphemes. According to our terminological conventions (see diagram (4) p. 80) we must now specify that a compound consists of at least two lexemes. This means that on the highest level of analysis, it is made up of at least two constituents which occur (or can in principle occur) in isolation. These ICs may themselves be complex, as e.g. *writer* in the compound *letter-writer*. This is true for the morphological level, which may be in conflict with the IC-analysis on the syntactic level. If we keep the two levels apart, there is no conflict but two complementary analyses. Thus, e.g. *bloodsucker* is a compound on the morphological level (with the determinatum *sucker*) but a suffixal derivative on the syntactic level (*bloodsuck/ER)* as illustrated in Kastovsky (1982a:170).

For Marchand (^{2}1969:21) there is an additional necessary criterion for the definition of a compound: "The compound must be morphologically isolated from a parallel syntactic group". This criterion is not based on the internal structure of the complex lexeme, but serves to distinguish the lexeme from syntactic syntagmas. It has to be understood as the result of Marchand's originally structuralist approach, which is more obvious in the first edition of his book. The morphological isolation of the compound from parallel syntactic groups or phrases, according to him, can result from different causes, which may be strictly speaking not morphological. Thus, for Marchand, the compound *bláckbòard* is distinguished from the parallel syntactic group *bláck bóard* by a different stress pattern. Most compounds in English have a single main stress on the first element. However, there are also compounds which have two heavy stresses in isolation (so-called 'level stress') e.g. *bóttle-gréen*. In such cases, for Marchand, "morphological isolation" results from the different word order of parallel syntactic groups, as in *gréen bóttle*.[5]

In inflecting languages such as German, the presence or absence of an inflectional morpheme may, in addition to the stress pattern, serve as a criterion for morphological isolation. Here, the compound *Hóchschùle* is clearly morphologically distinct from the syntactic group *hóhe Schúle*. The same holds for *Gróßstàdt*, as opposed to the syntactic group of adjective plus noun *gróße Stádt*.

For Marchand, because of the missing morphological differentiation in English, *bláck márket* is not a compound, as opposed to *bláckbìrd*. For him, spelling and hyphenation are no criterion, because of their irregularity and inconsistency. The same holds for semantic specificity or the unity of a concept. It must be mentioned, however, that many linguists do not accept Marchand's criterion of stress, inter alia because it is difficult to apply (cf. Levi 1978:41f.).

---

[5] The compound *gréenbòttle*, just like the more common *blúebòttle* (both denoting a kind of fly), is again isolated from the syntactic group by the stress pattern ('forestress').

Compounds may be further subcategorized according to word class and other criteria on various levels (cf. Lipka 1983, Hansen et al. [2]1985: 43–64, Quirk et al. 1985:1567–1578). Thus, according to the word class of the resulting word-formation syntagma (in this case identical with that of the determinatum) we can distinguish between: 1. nominal or noun compounds like *steamboat, blackboard, writing desk*, and *watchmaker* on the one hand and 2. adjectival or adjective compounds, like *colourblind, ice-cold, easy-going* on the other. In Marchand ([2]1969: 60ff.) a very fine subclassification of further "types" of compounds is made, like e.g. 1. *blackbird, craftsman, whetstone, all-soul, he-goat, self-determination* and 2. *colour-blind, grass-green, heart-breaking, man-made, high-born.* The latest and most comprehensive semantic analysis of English noun-noun compounds is Warren (1978).

Another important type of subclassification introduced by Marchand is made according to the presence or absence of a verb in the compound. This leads him to distinguish between "verbal nexus combinations" and "non-verbal nexus compounds". Within the subclass of noun-compounds we can therefore distinguish between *crybaby, drawbridge, letterwriter* on the one hand and *steamboat, oil well*, and *oaktree* on the other. This distinction is particularly relevant if one tries to correlate complex lexemes (as reduced syntagmas) with complete sentences (as full syntagmas), or rather tries to derive the former from the latter synchronically.

3.2.2. Suffixal and Zero-Derivatives

The hypothesis that complex lexemes can be derived from sentences is particularly plausible with those derivatives and nominalizations which contain a verbal element. Thus, e.g. *bullfighter, theatregoer*, and *grave-digger* are obviously closely related to sentences like *Someone fights bulls, Someone goes to some theatre*, and *Someone digs graves.*

In an article published in 1966 Marchand (1966:133) first explicitly postulates:

> A morphologic syntagma is nothing but the reduced form of an explicit syntagma, the sentence.

As already mentioned, Marchand took over this idea, which is closely related to the transformationalist hypothesis first postulated in print in 1960 by the generative grammarian Robert B. Lees, from Charles Bally. The first edition of Bally's book *Linguistique générale et linguistique française* appeared in 1932. The notion and the term syntagma ultimately derives from Saussure (1916:133), who calls complex lexemes, groups of words, and sentences *syntagmas.*

In the second edition of Marchand's book ([2]1969: 31) this hypothesis is reformulated in the following way:

> Morphologic composites (= compounds, suffixal derivatives, prefixal combinations) are 'reduced' sentences in substantival, adjectival, or verbal form and as such explainable from 'full' sentences.

As already mentioned (p. 83), *bullFIGHTER, theatre-GOER, grave-DIGGER* can be analyzed in a twofold manner: 1. As compounds with a complex determinatum (*fighter, goer, digger*) and 2. As nominalizations with the determinatum *-er*, which corresponds to the subject in an underlying sentence (on the syntactic level). These competing analyses are not mutually exclusive alternatives, although they are based on different ICs. It is essential, however, for the group of suffixal derivatives which we are now discussing that the determinatum, i.e. the derivative suffix, determines the word class of the whole complex lexeme.

Whether we have deverbal derivatives like *arrival, guidance, payment, writing*, or deadjectival ones like *illness, warmth*, the suffix is always responsible for the affixation resulting in a noun. Also, the so-called *nomina agentis* can be derived from various word classes as bases with the help of different suffixes (e.g. *novel/ist, bak/er, cook/ø*). Similarly verbs can be derived with a variety of suffixes, as in *modern/ize, hyphen/ate, dark/en*, and *clean/ø*.

I mentioned the verb *clean* and the noun *cook* in the same breath with suffixal derivatives. This needs an explanation and justification, since this assumption is by no means uncontroversial. If we assume the presence of a so-called *zero-morpheme*, symbolized by ø, this is in contrast with many traditional opinions. To my mind, *zero-derivation* is an extremely productive process in contemporary English by which many new lexemes are formed. An alternative, pragmatic approach to the same phenomena is used in Clark/Clark (1979) (see 3.2.5., but cf. also Lipka 1982).

The term and concept *zero-derivation* is used in Adams (1973) and many publications by Marchand, Kastovsky, and myself, while *conversion* is preferred in Bauer (1983) and Quirk et al. (1985: 1558 ff.). It is sometimes claimed that the term *conversion* should be avoided in synchronic treatments, since word class in many English words is neutralized or latent and derivable from context. In Lipka (1971) I have argued against this notion, which has been revived recently in a number of generative proposals. Quirk et al. (1985: 1558) openly admit that:

> Conversion is the derivational process whereby an item is adapted or converted to a new word class without the addition of an affix. In this way, conversion is closely analogous to suffixation (as distinct from prefixation).

The authors treat it

> not as a historical process, but rather as a process now available for extending the lexical resources of the language.

Admittedly, it is sometimes difficult to determine the direction of the synchronic derivation, which may be contrary to the actual diachronic development. Marchand (1964) has proposed a set of criteria for doing this. Generally, we can assume that that lexeme is derived in whose paraphrase the other lexeme is used. This means for example that the verb *to nailØ* 'make fast with a nail, fasten with a nail' is derived from the noun. In contrast to this the noun *a cheatØ* 'someone who cheats' must be considered as derived from the verb. Leech (^{2}1981:224f.) proposed to give up the distinction and replace it by "bi-directionality", i.e. to regard such cases of derivation "as a two-directional process". According to him, this disposes of "the chicken-and-egg problem". The theoretical concept of *zero-morpheme* (see p. 69), however, is not exclusively based on semantic relationships expressed in paraphrases. It is furthermore supported by the parallel to derivational patterns in which the same derivative relationship is expressed morphologically by a suffix. Thus we can set up the following proportional equations:

(7)	*legal*	:	*legal/ize*	::	*clean*	:	*clean/Ø*	'make Adj'
	atom	:	*atom/ize*	::	*cash*	:	*cash/Ø*	'convert into N'.

Besides such deadjectival and denominal verbs, there are also obvious parallels with deverbal nouns. Examples are the following *nomina agentis*: *cheatØ*, corresponding to *swindl/er, cookØ* to *bak/er, spyØ* to *observ/er*. Other deverbal nouns are e.g. *drink, cover, dump* 'place where something is dumped', *attack*. Conversely, the following zero-derivatives are denominal verbs: *to hammer, to bomb, to pilot*, and *to slice*.

The notion of zero-morpheme was not introduced arbitrarily in order to complicate matters. It accounts for the fact that two homonymous lexemes, which are superficially identical, are in a synchronically directed relationship. One lexeme is the base, while the other one is derived from it by means of a zero-suffix. Nevertheless, the two distinct lexemes are very closely related semantically and morphologically (cf. Lipka 1986b).

To sum up: the zero-morpheme as a theoretical construct can be justified in two ways, namely 1. by a semantic inclusion relation, and 2. by parallel derivational patterns as in (7), where the suffix is overtly expressed. Zero-derivatives are therefore only superficially simple. On a deeper level of analysis, they are syntagmas, consisting of a determinant and a determinatum, like overt suffixal derivatives. As with all word-formation syntagmas, the determinatum is in principle semantically and grammatically dominant. This means in particular that it determines the word class of the entire syntagma and that it precedes grammatical morphemes, as in e.g. *the clean/er/s, he modern/iz/ed, he clean/Ø/s*. In languages like German, the determinatum also determines grammatical gender, as in *die Frau*, but *das Frauchen/Fräulein*.

3.2.3. Nominalizations

This third group of complex lexemes has been characterized above as determined by the result of the word-formation process. In this case it is a *nominal*, i.e. a nominal expression (cf. Levi 1978). The second criterion for the definition of nominalizations is their transformational derivation from a sentence. In linguistic research the term *nominalization* is used both for the transformational process as well as for the concrete result of this process, as in the title of R. B. Lees's most influential book *The Grammar of English Nominalizations*, originally published in 1960. Thus the term is used for a linguistic expression. However, terminological usage is far from being uniform. For example the term may also be used for complex noun phrases which function as subject or object, as e.g. *His continual drumming on the table with his knife and fork* (irritated me).

Alternatively, the term can be used in the narrow sense only for those noun phrases which have the structure of a noun itself. Exemples are: *watchmaker, bird-watcher, beer-drinker, cave-dweller, writing-desk, washing machine, housekeeping*, and *closing-time*. In the following, I will only deal with such nominalizations.

From the point of view of morphology, nominalizations may be either compounds or suffixal derivatives. The latter include zero-derivatives, like *chimney sweepØ*, which parallel overt derivatives, like *deer huntER* Obviously, many of the complex lexemes just mentioned are clearly related to full sentences and can therefore be considered nominalized sentences, like *bullfighter, theatregoer, grave-digger*. The synchronic derivation of such nominalizations from sentences has considerable explanatory power.

Marchand ([2]1969:32ff.) therefore postulates that the determinatum in such nominalizations corresponds to a particular constituent of an underlying sentence. He distinguishes the following *types of reference* (in his terminology):

(8)	S(ubject)-type:	*apple-eat/ER, cry/BABY*
	O(bject)-type:	*eating/APPLE, draw/BRIDGE*
	Pr(edication)-type:	*apple-eat/ING, arriv/AL*
	Ad(verbial Complement)-type:	*oil refin/ERY, carving/KNIFE*

Marchand labels these types according to the syntactic function of the element which corresponds to the determinatum in the complex lexeme. This classification is thus based on syntactic criteria. The principle can be illustrated with the examples *bullfighter* and *oil refinery*, with the help of the following diagrams (9) and (10) from Kastovsky (cf. Lipka/Günther 1981:378). *Bullfighter* (like *theatregoer, grave-digger*) is obviously a Subject-type:

(9)

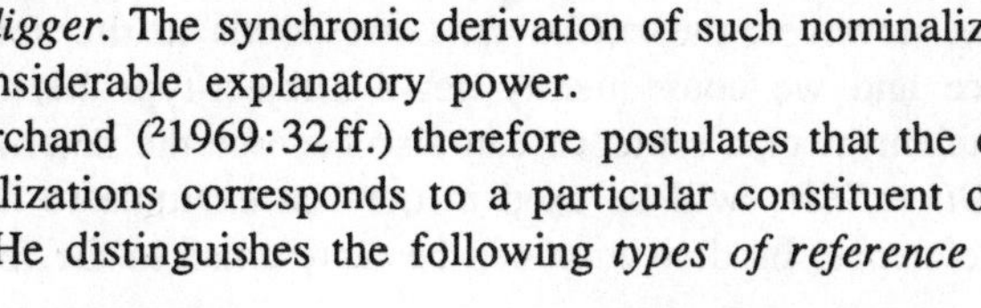

The determinatum in Subject-types is not necessarily the suffix *-er*, as can be seen from *chimney sweepØ*.

The Subject-type can also be represented by a compound, like *crybaby* 'person, esp. a child, who cries too often'. This can be derived from an underlying sentence like 'the baby cries' or 'some baby cries' with additional lexicalization (see 3.2.5.; but cf. also the derivation of "complex nominals (CNs)" in Levi (1978) by means of 'Predicate Deletion' and 'Predicate Nominalization').

Complex lexemes without a verbal element are more difficult to correlate with an underlying sentence. In this case one can either introduce a specific, concrete verb in the underlying sentence, or postulate an abstract semantic element. The second proposal was first made in Lees (1970). His notion of "generalized verb" only contains a minimal set of semantic features which characterize variants like *energize, drive, power, propel* in compounds like *motorcar, steamboat, windmill.* This suggestion corresponds to the later theoretical construct of "Recoverably Deletable Predicates (RDPs)" such as CAUSE, HAVE, MAKE, USE etc. used in Levi (1978). The most recent approaches to nominal compounds and adjective-noun combinations (Warren 1978, 1984) also start out from abstract semantic relations (cf. Leitzke 1989b).

Another illustration of the derivation of types of reference can be given for the suffixal derivative *novelist.* We can either start from an underlying sentence such as 'someone writes novels' or introduce a generalized verb like *make, produce* (or an RDP MAKE), which gives the sentence 'someone produces novels'. In either case, however, the suffix *-ist* corresponds to the subject in an underlying sentence and we consequently get a Subject-type here too.

The adverbial complement of a sentence can also become the determinatum in a nominalization. *Oil refinery* will be used in our last example to illustrate Marchand's types of reference. Its derivation can be represented in the following way:

(10) O *oil* — P *refine* — AdP *-ERY*

'(someone) refines oil at some place'
(S) P O AdP

The subject of the underlying sentence is not contained in the complex lexeme. The predicate, direct object, and adverbial complement, however, are clearly recognizable constituents of the nominalization. Since the locative adverbial has become the determinatum, we must classify *oil refinery* as an Adverbial Complement-type of Place (AdP).

For action nouns and other types of nominalization denoting a fact, process, event, or state, a more recent theoretical proposal is the so-called "head-noun analysis" (cf. Kastovsky 1982a:189 f., 200, 228 f.). Without going into detail, we can state that there is a close parallel to Levis's (1978) approach to 'complex nominals' (e.g. *viral infection, feminine intuition, urban riot,* cf. Leitzke 1989a:106 ff.), in that abstract antecedent "head nouns", like ACTION, FACT, PROCESS, EVENT, STATE etc., are postulated in the underlying structure from which such nominalizations are derived. Thus, on a deeper level, e.g. *cockfighting, bloodshedØ, boatrideØ, dancing, arrival* etc. contain ACTION, while the head noun for *departure* may be either ACTION or FACT. The interpretation depends on the context (e.g. *John's departure was odd*) and on the nature of the verb serving as base for the nominalization. Clearly, this proposal amounts to a more refined analysis of Marchand's Predication-type (cf. Kastovsky 1982a:189 f.).

This fourfold classification of nominalizations in (8) (namely the 'types of reference') has considerable explanatory power for disambiguating identical or similar surface structures. Thus, *dishwashER* can either be a S-type or an Ad-type of Instrument. In German both are clearly kept apart as *Tellerwäscher*, on the one hand and *Geschirrspüler* or *Geschirrspülmaschine* on the other. *Draftee* 'someone who has been drafted' is obviously an O-type. The same suffix in *escapee* 'prisoner who has escaped', however, corresponds to the subject of the underlying sentence and is therefore a S-type. The complex lexeme *payment,* like its German equivalent *Zahlung,* can either be used for the process or the sum paid. This ambiguity can be resolved by distinguishing the P-type from the O-type (cf. Lipka 1976: 134).

Marchand's 'types of reference', however, cannot only be used for the disambiguation and classification of nominalizations. In addition to this, they have a more far-reaching explanatory function. They can be used to explain the information selection and condensation which takes place in complex lexemes. Thus, if we look at diagram (8), we can see that different nominalizations can be derived from the same underlying sentence. *Apple-eater, eating apple, apple-eating* all go back to the sentence 'someone eats some apple'.

The question now arises why such different reduced syntagmas are derived from the same complete syntagma, the sentence. Marchand's explanation is based on the observation that the distinction between old and new information plays an important role here. According to his theory, the determinatum of the complex lexeme always corresponds to that constituent of the sentence which is presupposed as known information. Marchand ([2]1969: 32) characterizes this process in the following way:

> One grammatical part of the sentence is taken to be known: the Subject, the Object, the Predicate, the Predicate Complement, or the Adverbial Complement, and it is this part of the sentence that becomes the determinatum of the composite.

This process is often referred to as *topicalization* in linguistics. Marchand consequently also denotes his 'types of reference' as "selectional patterns of information". He points out that the distinction between old and new information was captured in the Prague school of linguistics by the terms *theme* (Thema) and *rheme* (Rhema). A number of American linguists have preferred the terms *topic* and *comment* for this distinction, hence the term topicalization. In Prague linguistic theory, the phenomena involved are usually discussed under the term *functional sentence perspective* (FSP). Today the terms *theme/rheme-structure, thematic structure* and *thematization* are often used for the phenomena involved. Obviously, the context of situation may be relevant here and topicalization is also determined by the textual functions of word-formation (cf. Lipka 1987b, Wotjak 1987 and see also 5.1.).

In this connection, I would like to take up again the distinction between denotation and reference as introduced in 2.2.3. If we apply this to Marchand's 'types of reference', we have to modify some of his statements. It is not a grammatical part of the sentence which is known or given, but the relationship between this constituent and an extralinguistic referent or denotatum. This relationship corresponds to the one between the determinatum of the complex lexeme and the identical referent or denotatum. For example the subject in the underlying sentence *Someone eats some apple* denotes the same extralinguistic referent as the suffix *-er* in the agent nominalization. This referent, the agent, as well as its existence are presumed to be known or given.

The given information does not only contain the relation of reference and the existence of the referent; it also includes the denotation of the linguistic sign used for referring. It is known that a *crybaby* is a kind of baby, a *drawbridge* is a bridge, and a *carving-knife* a knife. The syntagma belongs to a subclass and is therefore a hyponym (see 4.2.3.) of its determinatum (cf. Kastovsky 1982a:185f., Bauer 1983:30).

This fact is also expressed by the stress pattern of complex lexemes. As a rule, the determinatum only bears secondary stress or no stress at all. The determinant, which is more important from the point of view of given versus new information, normally bears the main stress. This pattern is found e.g. in *crýbàby, dráwbrìdge, cárving-knìfe, stéambòat, bláckbìrd, nóvelìst.* The determinant syntagmatically modifies the given determinatum and makes the category denoted by the syntagma more specific. Complex lexemes therefore have a higher degree of semantic specificity compared to the simple words that constitute their determinatum.

Up to now we have left aside an important point relevant for the classification of 'types of reference'. Marchand's basis for the classification is obviously a purely syntactic one. However, the distinction for example between the S-type and the Ad-type in the nominalization *dishwashER* also touches semantic questions. In one case we have an agent, in the other an instrument expressed by an adverbial complement. Yet the relation between the verb *wash* and an agent or an instrument is clearly of a different nature. This difference is therefore not only a matter of syntax, but also of semantics.

There is a linguistic theory which understands the relationship between the verb and other elements of the sentence as syntactic-semantic relations, namely Charles Fillmore's Case Grammar. In the framework of this linguistic theory, the relations just mentioned are labelled *deep cases* or *case roles*. These cases must not be confused with the surface cases of traditional grammar. In the latest model relevant here (an article published in 1971), Fillmore gives the following list of deep cases: Agent, Experiencer, Instrument, Object, Source, Goal, Location, Time. The grammatical subject and object, as syntactic functions, are understood as purely surface relations in the classical version of Fillmore's Case Grammar (see 3.3.1. p. 105).

If we now replace the syntactic categories in Marchand's 'types of reference' by deep cases, we can achieve a finer and semantically more appropriate differentiation of types. At the same time, this is more consistent and less heterogeneous. For details of such a proposal I refer the reader to Lipka (1976).

Some further remarks on the analysis of nominalizations, as a subgroup of complex lexemes, based on Case Grammar, may be appropriate. Thus, *bullfighter* is no longer a S-type, but an Agent-Type. The referent of the American word *draftee* is the goal of the action denoted by the verb. In Case Grammar this category is labelled *Goal*. Consequently *draftee* is, like most suffixal derivatives in *-ee*, a Goal-Type. The superficially similar *escapee*, however, is an Agent-Type. *Drawer* may be either an Agent-Type or an Object-Type depending on whether we refer to a person or a box-like container in a chest.

The traditional classification of adverbial complements on the basis of content is also captured by Case Grammar and leads to a more appropriate description of the Ad-types. Therefore *hunting season* is described as a Time-Type, *oil refinery* as a Location-Type, and *printing-ink* as an Instrument-Type.

We can now maintain that the application of Fillmore's deep cases to Marchand's 'types of reference' throws a new light upon the structure of complex lexemes and leads to a better understanding of the functioning of word-formation. With this theory we can capture fundamental differences between superficially and morphologically parallel words and explain them better. Thus, the lexemes listed in (11a) are all derivatives in *-er*, but represent different 'types of reference'. Conversely, morphologically distinct complex lexemes as for example those in (11b) can be explained and described as realizations of the same underlying type.

(11a)	*-ER*	(11b)	*AGENT-TYPE:*
	payer (Agent-)		*grave-digg/er*
	cooker (Instrument-)		*cut-throat/Ø*
	diner (Location-)[6]		*novel/ist*
	mourner (Experiencer-)		*cook/Ø.*
	container (Object-TYPE)		

To sum up, word-formation, in particular the device of nominalization, can be understood – on the basis of a revised theory of 'types of reference' – as a productive process for the economical expression of the communicative needs of the speaker of a language. Complete sentences can be transformed in a rule-governed way into nominalizations, i.e. complex lexemes. By this process, information-condensation is achieved, one of the most important functions of word-formation (cf. Lipka 1983, 1987b, Kastovsky 1982b). The complex lexemes thus formed can then fill the position of a simple lexeme in a sentence. The determinatum of a complex lexeme denotes given information; the simple or complex determinant contains the new information added to it. The various kinds of nominalization processes (Agent-, Action-, Fact-, Result- etc.

[6] Of course, *diner* may also be an Agent-Type.

nominalizations) in English and German belong to the most productive devices of word-formation and are relatively unrestricted.

3.2.4. Word-Formation Processes and Productivity

For Marchand (^{2}1969 : 2) word-formation is fundamentally a matter of productive processes, since he defines it as:

> that branch of the science of language which studies the patterns on which a language forms new lexical units, i.e. words.

For him, productivity is a matter of more or less productive types. In Bauer (1983 : 62–199) a whole chapter is devoted to problems of productivity (cf. Tournier 1988). He adopts a distinction originally drawn by Lyons (1977 : 549) between *productivity* and *creativity*. The former is a rule-governed feature of the language system, the latter concerns the unpredictable (non-rule-governed) innovations, i.e. the language-users' ability to extend the language system. Bauer illustrates the former with the literal meaning of the complex lexeme *headhunter* and the latter with the metaphorical extension of this lexeme to mean 'one who recruits executives for a large corporation'. For Lyons, metaphorical creativity is a matter of strategies, not of rules. Although Bauer recognizes that both productivity and creativity give rise to many neologisms, he restricts himself to the rule-governed innovations, i.e. productivity of word-formation.

Finally, Tournier (1985 : 21) criticizes Marchand and Adams for doing precisely this and claims that both semantic neologism and the external process of adopting loanwords have to be included in a comprehensive description in order to capture "la *totalité* des *processus* lexicogéniques de l'anglais" (his emphasis). He repeatedly stresses that the dynamic nature of lexical processes ("la dynamique lexicale") must be captured in an adequate description, and to do this proposes various lexeme-producing matrices, or moulds (1985 : 47 ff., 50; cf. Tournier 1988 : 18–24). He distinguishes three large categories, or macro-mechanisms, of such productive patterns, namely according to which elements of Saussure's linguistic sign are concerned: 1. Both *signifiant* and *signifié* (morpho-semantic neologism), 2. only the *signifié* (semantic neologism), and 3. only the *signifiant* (morphological neologism). The external process of adopting loanwords remains outside these three categories. Word-formation proper, for Tournier, falls within category 1 (compounding and affixation) and 3 (clipping and the production of acronyms).

His schema (1985:51) can be summarized in simplified form in the following way (see also diagram (4) p. 80):

(12)

1. Morpho-Semantic Neologism	Construction	Affixation	Prefixation Suffixation Backderivation
		Composition	Juxtaposition (e.g. *statesman*) Amalgamation (e.g. *sexploitation*)
	Phonetic Motivation		
2. Semantic Neologism	Class Transfer		Conversion
	Metasemantic Processes ("Métasémie")		Metaphor Metonymy
3. Morphological Neologism	Reduction of 'signifiant'		Aphaeresis (Fore-Clipping) Apocope (Back-Clipping) Acronymy ("Siglaison")
4. EXTERNAL	Loan-Processes		

In Tournier (1988: 18–24) twelfe types of mould (or "matrices lexicogéniques") are distinguished which correspond to the subclassification on the right in (12), together with onomatopoeia and loan-words, with 'clipping' forming a single type.

We will return to productive semantic processes for extending the lexicon after discussing the internal semantic structure of lexemes (see 3.3.). At this point, however, we must already have a look at the concept of motivation in lexicology. Ultimately, this concept goes back to Saussure, for whom the linguistic sign is basically arbitrary or non-motivated. He admits that sound-imitation, or onomatopoeia exists, but claims that onomatopoeic words are rare and of secondary importance. Further on Saussure (1916: 181) argues that signs like *dix-neuf, Handwerk* may be relatively motivated. Taking up this argument, Bally (1944: 129) claims that the sign may be motivated by: 1. the *signifié* (e.g. *dix-neuf, poir-ier*), 2. by its *signifiant* (e.g. the verb *croquer*), and 3. by both of them together (e.g. *croque-mort* 'gravedigger'). He thus claims that sound-imitating words and interjections are motivated "par le signifiant". Ullmann (1962: 81 ff.) introduces another threefold distinction, namely between 1. phonetic (onomatopoeia), 2. morphological (word-formation) and 3. semantic motivation (through metaphor and metonymy). He claims (1962: 92) that "in many cases, a word is motivated both morphologically and semantically". As examples of such "mixed motivation" he gives *bluebell* and *redbreast*.

Returning to word-formation proper, we must state with Marchand ([2]1969: 2 f.) that the combination of full linguistic signs (i.e. morphological motivation) is not the only kind of motivation that occurs in the coining of new words. He distinguishes two groups and consequently two kinds of process: 1. the combination of full signs (resulting in "grammatical syntagmas") namely Compounding, Prefixation, Suffixation, Derivation by a Zero-Morpheme, Back-derivation, and 2. the combination of other elements (not resulting in syntagmas), namely Expressive Symbolism, Blending, Clipping, Rime and Ablaut Gemination, Word-Manufacturing. The second group of processes, which may also be very productive, he sometimes labels non-grammatical word-formation.

In a book on English lexicology it does not seem out of place to have a short look at these devices for forming new words. It must be emphasized again that new lexical items belonging to the second group are not complex lexemes, because they are not syntagmas made up of morphemes. Nevertheless, they are not arbitrary words either, since they are partially motivated by their linguistic form. Marchand ([2]1969: 397 ff.) discusses them in the last four chapters of his book: VII. Phonetic Symbolism, VIII. Motivation by Linguistic Form: Ablaut and Rime Combinations, IX. Clipping, and X. Blending and Word-Manufacturing. I will just give a few examples of the phenomena described. *Hiss, click, bang, crash, spit, spew, chitchat, pingpong* are instances of expressive symbolism. In *motel, smog, brunch* two words are blended together. In word-manufacturing more or less arbitrary parts of words are combined to denote new scientific discoveries, organizations, etc. resulting in various subtypes of letter-words or acronyms, like *radar, Salt, Nato*. Recent *SDI* and *AIDS* testify to the enormous productivity of this process. In all these cases, the productivity is not rule-governed and pattern-based as with "grammatical word-formation", the result of the process is not a syntagma, and the partially motivated constituents are not morphemes.

3.2.5. Lexicalization and Idioms

Traditional studies of word-formation, including Marchand's, were almost exclusively concerned with established complex lexemes recorded in dictionaries. Although productive patterns and regularities of word-formation were studied, so-called *ad hoc-formations*, or *nonce-formations*, were excluded. In recent research, beginning perhaps with an article on English compound nouns by Pamela Downing published in 1977, non-established complex lexemes, their function, and the actual process of coining came into focus. Such 'innovations' may depend heavily on context, and were therefore termed *contextuals* by Eve and Herbert Clark in 1979 in a study on innovative verbs such as *to porch a newspaper, to Houdini out of a closet*. Although the Clarks argue against this, they may be interpreted as zero-derived denominal verbs. In my opinion both studies show that noun-noun compounding and zero-derivation of denominal verbs in English are almost unrestricted productive processes (cf. Lipka 1982). In spite of this enormous productivity and the regularity of certain word-formation processes, an adequate theory of word-formation must not disregard a certain phenomenon which affects complex lexemes, once they have been coined, to greater or lesser degree. I am referring to the process of *lexicalization*, which in my opinion particularly influences and changes frequently used complex lexemes (cf. Lipka 1981b). This phenomenon interferes with regular word-formation processes and overlaps their result. If the resulting irregularity is only slight, we can speak of *systematic lexicalization*, as Kastovsky (1982a:166f., 196ff.) does. If the semantic changes are so extreme that the meaning of the whole lexeme can no longer be derived from its parts, we speak of an *idiom* (cf. Lipka 1972:75ff., 1974).

I would like to define *lexicalization* as the phenomenon that a complex lexeme once coined tends to become a single complete lexical unit, a simple lexeme. Through this process it loses the character of a syntagma to a greater or lesser degree (cf. Lipka 1981b:120). In my definition an essential condition and a prerequisite for this gradual diachronic process is the fact that a particular complex lexeme is used frequently. For Kastovsky (1982a:164f.), whose definition of lexicalization is similar to mine, frequency of usage is not an essential criterion. He stresses the fact that lexicalization causes the integration of a syntactic or word-formation syntagma into the lexicon, with semantic and/or formal properties which are not completely derivable from either the constituents or the word-formation pattern. Both definitions are legitimate and to a large extent compatible, since *lexicalization*, in my view, is a *notational term*. This means that there is no single, correct definition of the term. This fact becomes particularly obvious if we look at the use of the term in Generative Semantics. Within this theoretical framework, *lexicalization* denotes a process in which a configuration of semantic elements in an abstract representation is replaced by a lexeme. In earlier generative models *lexical insertion* was used for this transformational process. The word *lexicalization* itself may thus exemplify the process it traditionally denotes within the discipline of word-formation. This sense, as well as the one current in Generative Semantics, can both be explained (according to Marchand's theory) if we derive the nominalization from the same underlying sentence 'Something becomes (a) lexical (item)' (cf. Lipka 1975a:205).

Other definitions of *lexicalization* are possible, thus demonstrating its nature as a notational term, as a look at chapter 3 in Bauer (1983:42–61) will reveal. His subtype of syntactic lexicalization is problematic, to my mind. More convincing is Kastovsky's (1982a:166f., 196 ff.) *systematic lexicalization*, which affects whole types of word-formation and adds very general semantic features.

Quirk et al. (1985:1522 ff.) distinguish lexicalization from *institutionalization*, by which they understand the integration of a lexical item, with a particular form and meaning, into the existing stock of words as a generally acceptable and current lexeme. This use of *institutionalization* is identical with the one found in Bauer (1983:48) and I will adopt it whenever I want to stress the sociolinguistic aspects of a word. A complex lexeme is institutionalized when the original nonce-formation is accepted by other speakers as a known lexical item. In this connection it is important to draw a distinction introduced into linguistics by W. J. Meys in 1975 between *item-familiarity* and *type-familiarity* (cf. Kastovsky 1982a:151, 164ff.). For example *family man* and *family tree* are both item-familiar and type-familiar, as instances of the productive compound type 'Noun+Noun'. Although *cow tree* is formed according to the same familiar type, it is not *item-familiar* because it has never been institutionalized. Finally *highwayman* meaning 'robber' is not only item-familiar but semantically lexicalized and therefore idiomatized.

Institutionalized and lexicalized complex lexemes clearly do neither belong to the level of the *langue* (with its systematic word-formation types) nor to the level of *parole* (with specific, concrete realizations of the underlying language system). Obviously, a level in between the two is needed. As early as 1951, Eugenio Coseriu (1967:11) proposed such an intermediate level and called it the *norm* of a language. It is not restricted to the lexicon, but also responsible for the conventional, unsystematic realization of certain sounds and for irregular inflections like *oxen, brethren, sang,* and *took.* It is particularly useful, however, to apply the concept of 'norm', as the traditional, collective realization of the language system to lexicology and word-formation. This has been done repeatedly in the past (cf. Lipka 1971b, 1972:85, 129f., Kastovsky 1982a:33, 205). The norm accounts for the choice between alternative word-formation types (*to nationalize, to clean*, but not **to nationalify*, **to national*), for lexical gaps, and for the habitual disambiguation, e.g. of *sleeping tablet* and *headache tablet*, or Ger *Schweinebraten* and *Jägerbraten.*

The results of the process of *idiomatization*, i.e. *idioms* of various kinds, also belong to the norm of a particular language (cf. Lipka 1972:75ff.). A survey of research in this field including a discussion of the work of Mel'čuk, Amosova, Hockett, Bugarski, Fraser, Chafe, and Weinreich can be found in Lipka (1974). Idioms are defined there as formally complex linguistic expressions whose meaning is not derivable from that of their constituents. They may be relatively simple compounds, like *callgirl*, and *holiday*, fixed collocations like *red herring* or *black market*, or complex expressions like *make up once's face, kick the bucket, blow a raspberry at.*

Idioms are not a simple, homogeneous category and syntagmas of various kinds are more or less affected by idiomaticity in the process of lexicalization. Idiomaticity is a matter of degress, and the phenomenon is of the more-or-less kind rather than the all-or-none kind. There is a continuous scale ranging from a simple conjunction of morphemes to the creation of completely new formal and semantic units, both from a historical and synchronic point of view. With regard to the use of competing terms like *idiomatization, lexicalization*, and *demotivation* there is a great deal of terminological variation in linguistics (cf. Kastovsky 1982a:164, Bauer 1983:48f., Bauer 1988:246f.).

In my opinion (cf. Lipka 1983:927) *lexicalization* is a gradual, historical process, involving phonological and semantic changes and the loss of motivation. These changes may be combined in a single word. Semantic changes, i.e. idiomatization, may be formalized as the addition or loss of semantic features. Synchronically, the result of this process, various degrees of idiomaticity, form a continuous scale. The process of lexicalization in general, as well as its result, namely the irregularity of the lexicon, can only be explained historically. In sum, I define lexicalization as the phenomenon that complex lexical items, through frequent usage, may lose their syntagmatic nature and tend to become formal units with specific content. Here, the border between complex and simple lexemes becomes fuzzy.

Let us look briefly at some examples of the various changes possible within the general, comprehensive notion of lexicalization. First, formal changes may involve either the spoken or the written medium or both. They are obvious symptoms for the lexicalization of a syntagma. Examples on the phonological level are the reduced final vowel in *postman, Sunday* and the more open first vowel in Ger *Hochzeit. Forecastle* 'part under the bows where the seamen have their living and sleeping accommodation' can serve as an illustration of both phonological and graphemic changes. The syntagmatic character is completely lost in the usual pronunciation ['fəʊksl]. In the alternative graphemic variant *fo'c'sle* the word has also become an unanalysable simple lexeme in the written medium (cf. also *boatswain/bo'sun, bosun*).

The second kind of change, the loss of morphological motivation, can be seen in *blackboard* (often green today), *watchmaker*, and "lipstick in a pot" (cf. Downing 1977:819). Demotivation may also be signalled by the addition of a second determinant, if a first one is no longer motivated. Some German examples are *Handtuch* 'towel' which is clearly analysable but has lost its motivation for many speakers, since it can also be used for the feet. Thus, a specific kind of small towel, which is exclusively used for the hands, may be referred to today by *Händehandtuch* or *Gästehandtuch.* Another case in point is *Ostwestfalen*, the area around Paderborn in Northern Germany. There is no contradiction, since *Westfalen* has become a single lexeme, where the first constituent is no longer motivated. Demotivation may result from either linguistic or extralinguistic developments. *Blackboard* and *watchmaker* (who today normally only repairs watches), and the zero-derived verbs *to sailØ*, and *to shipØ* show the results of such extralinguistic developments. And clearly, we can sail by steamboat or hovercraft and ship goods by train.

The third type of development, semantic changes, may be either slight or considerable. A very small degree of idiomatization is caused by very general additional features like [+HABITUAL] in *crybaby, sleepwalker, rattlesnake,* or [+PROFESSIONAL] in *baker, writer* (in *John is a writer*) and *chimneysweep.* These are instances of Kastovsky's "systematic lexicalization".

Rather specific, unpredictable semantic features are added in the following examples for what Leech (^{2}1981:225–227) called "petrification": *wheelchair, pushchair, trousersuit.* According to him they contain the additional meaning elements: 'for invalids, for infants, for women'. *Highwayman, streetwalker*, and *callgirl* are unpredictable idioms. In contrast to the latter, *callboy* is defined in dictionaries as 'a boy who tells actors when it is time for them to go onto the stage' but is now also used parallel to *callgirl*.

Examples of a combination of various changes in one lexeme are *holiday* and Ger *Hochzeit*. They combine phonological deviation and semantic changes, both the addition and loss of meaning elements. I have discussed the case of *holiday* in great detail in Lipka (1985:342–344). The sememe of its second constituent *day* has lost all its components except for [PERIOD OF TIME]. An inferential feature (see 3.3.2.) of the first constituent, namely [NO WORK] has become an obligatory feature of the whole lexeme. These examples shall suffice to illustrate the complexity of lexicalization in word-formation.

3.3. The Semantic Structure of Words: Componential Analysis and Semantic Features

Before we try to structure the content, *signifié*, or sememes of a lexeme, we must return to some problems already touched on in 2.2.2. and 2.2.5., namely different approaches to semantics and the distinction between denotation and connotation. To start with the latter distinction first, let me emphasize here that – like Lyons (1977) and Leech ([2]1981) – I will concentrate in this book on denotation, in spite of the extensive discussion of other kinds of meaning in 2.2. Reference will be made in passing to other aspects, but my main focus will be on denotative or conceptual meaning, both for practical reasons and because most research so far has been done in this area.

As regards the different approaches to semantics in linguistic research we can distinguish, in my opinion, two large groups or categories, namely language-immanent and referential ones. For the moment we can illustrate the two directions – within the field of word semantics – with the names Coseriu and Leisi. I derive the term *referential semantics* from the extralinguistic *referent*. As a synonymous expression we may also use *denotative semantics*.

Of course there are other possibilities of classifying directions of research in linguistic semantics. Another pair of alternatives would be *Feature Semantics* vs. *Prototype Semantics*. Semantic *features*, often used synonymously with semantic *components*, are understood as a specific kind of meaning elements. Not all linguists who subscribe to language-immanent semantics consider the postulation of semantic components useful and justified. This statement holds e.g. for John Lyons, whose language-immanent semantic theory is non-componential.

Within primarily logically oriented semantics, there are a variety of other subclasses, with which we will not be concerned in this book. More about them can be found in Lyons (1977) and Lutzeier (1985). I will just mention the names of such approaches, especially *truth-conditional semantics*, and a variety of more recent and specific models like *situation semantics, interval semantics, possible-world semantics*, and *game-theoretical semantics*.

Before discussing various methods of semantic decomposition in language-immanent theories, let me make an observation concerning Leisi and the concept of *metalanguage*. His denotational approach is closely related to Prototype Semantics (cf. Lipka 1987a). When Leisi (^{2}1985:37) compares *tower* with Ger *Turm*, he discusses the different categorization in the two languages. Both languages create similar, but not identical categories of extralinguistic objects. Although Leisi does not use the term, he is really concerned with the different prototypes for *tower* and *Turm*. The two languages divide up the same extralinguistic reality differently, by drawing boundaries between the respective classes of objects in a different way. Leisi tries to capture this distinct categorization of reality with the concept of *Gebrauchsbedingungen*, i.e. different 'conditions of use' for the respective lexemes. In doing this, Leisi obviously does not use a metalanguage for the analysis and description of lexical meaning; in other words, he does not resort to semantic features or components, or other formal meaning elements.

Let us briefly look at the distinction between *metalanguage* and *object-language* (cf. Lyons 1977:10ff.). This distinction has a long tradition in logic and philosophy. Metalanguage means "language used to describe language", the object language. Thus we might use English to describe French, as in Lyons's example: *The French word 'homme' is a noun.* Here, one natural language serves as a metalanguage for another. It is more common though, to restrict *metalanguage* (in a rather narrow sense) to specially constructed and formalized systems of representation. In a less technical sense, the terminology of grammar is a metalanguage. So are certain theoretical constructs and terms of specific linguistic theories, usually signalled as such by a specific notational convention or formalization.

Thus for example *phonemes* are metalinguistic constructs, written between slants (/ /), as opposed to square brackets for a phonetic notation. *Morphemes* are often marked as such by braces ({ }). In contrast to both, syntactic and semantic features were often signalled in generative grammar by square brackets ([ ]) as metalinguistic elements. An alternative notation for meaning components was introduced in the later framework of Generative Semantics, by linguists like McCawley and Lakoff. They conventionally symbolized what they called *atomic predicates* by using capital letters. For example the verb *kill* was decomposed into and paraphrased by CAUSE, BECOME, and NOT ALIVE – we will return to this so-called theory of *lexical decomposition* later. By this notation the metalinguistic construct CAUSE is clearly distinguished from the English word *cause* of the object-language. In spite of this clever device, a confusion between object-language and metalanguage occurred more than once in the publications of Generative Semanticists.

Metalinguistic elements like distinctive *semantic features* or *semantic components* can basically be derived in two ways: 1. by purely language-immanent procedures from the opposition of lexical items (cf. Coseriu/Geckeler

1981:34 f.), or 2. from properties of the extralinguistic referent or denotatum in a referential approach to semantics (cf. Coseriu/Geckeler 1981:41 ff.). In the latter case – as opposed to Leisi's *Gebrauchsbedingungen* – such features have to be standardized and formalized to some extent in order to be of general use. This can be done in many cases but not all, with the help of a binary feature notation using + and -. The advantage of such a notation is that it achieves a clearer and more economical description. Also, the results of a specific analysis can be verified and checked more easily. Such a simple formalization further reveals mistakes and inadequacies, which may be hidden by a merely verbal characterization of the conditions of use of a lexeme.

Examples of a purely language-immanent semantic approach can be found in Coseriu's position and the so-called *componential analysis*, which goes back to Hjelmslev. We will discuss this presently. The method of implicit or explicit paraphrase evaluation, practised e.g. by Generative Semanticists like Lakoff and McCawley, must also be discussed in this context.

3.3.1. Semantic Decomposition and its Justification

The decomposition of lexemes into semantic elements or components has a long tradition both in European structuralism and American anthropology. In the 1950s anthropologists like W. H. Goodenough applied the componential analysis of meaning to kinship terminology. As far back as 1943, the Danish linguist Louis Hjelmslev argued that words can be analysed into what he called *content figurae*. Some of the examples he gave for such a componential analysis are: *ram* = 'he-sheep', *ewe* = 'she-sheep', *man* = 'he-human being' etc. (cf. Lyons 1968:470–480; 1977:317–335; Coseriu/Geckeler 1981:34). It has often been noticed that such series of words have certain meaning components in common. These can be made visible by setting up proportional equations and applying the mathematical process of factorizing a number. The following English words are particularly suitable for such a procedure:

(13)	man	woman	child
	bull	cow	calf
	stallion	mare	foal
	... etc.		

To illustrate the process of factorizing a number and its parallel with lexical items, I will use an example given in Leech (²1981:91) in slightly modified and simplified form. Just as we can pick out a common factor from a set of numbers, we can extract certain semantic components from words.

(14)

		4	is to	10
(a)	as	6	is to	15
	as	8	is to	20
		(2x)		(5x)

		man	is to	*woman*
(b)	as	*boy*	is to	*girl*
	as	*gander*	is to	*goose*
		(male x)		(female x)

We can easily see the analogy of linguistic and arithmetical proportions. In (14a) the common factors 2 and 5 are picked out, just as in (14b) the components (male) and (female) are extracted. Returning to (13) it is evident that there are common components in both the horizontal and the vertical directions. Represented as a proportional equation (with :: symbolizing the equation) we can say that *man* is to *woman* is to *child* as *bull* is to *cow* is to *calf*. But *man* and *woman* as well as *bull* and *cow* also have something in common, as opposed to *child* and *calf*. From these equations we can extract the following factors, components, or features (spelt in capital letters) represented in diagrammatic form:

(15) HUMAN BOVINE

Man : woman : child :: bull : cow : calf

MALE FEMALE NON-ADULT MALE FEMALE NON-ADULT

ADULT ADULT

A considerable number of terms have been used in semantic research for various kinds of semantic elements, such as: *content figurae, semes, sememes, components, semantic markers/distinguishers/features,* and *atomic predicates* (cf. Sprengel 1980: 150). We will have a closer look at the concepts of *atomic predicates* vs. *semantic features* in order to show that these distinctions are not merely matters of terminology. We will see that not only the labels for the different theoretical constructs differ, but also the range of empirical facts covered by the respective theories. Consequently it can be claimed that traditional componential analysis and Generative Semantics are complementary (cf. Lyons 1981: 75 ff.). The former has almost exclusively been applied to nouns (but cf. Lipka 1972 for verb-particle constructions), while lexical decomposition into atomic predicates is practically restricted to verbs, in particular causative verbs (cf. Kastovsky 1973, Lipka 1982). In the following I shall try to characterize the main assumptions of Generative Semantics, especially its theory of *lexical decomposition* (cf. Lipka 1976; 1982:7 ff.).

The main proponents of this theory, namely McCawley, Lakoff, and Postal started out in the late 60s, at first only implicitly, from a paraphrase relationship between simple words and their definition. Some particularly suitable lexemes were decomposed into semantic elements as follows (cf. McCawley 1968: 73):

(16) *die* = (Become) (Not) (Alive)

These meaning elements were considered predicates in the sense of predicate logic (cf. Lyons 1981; 80f.) and labelled *atomic predicates*, because it was held that they could not be analysed any further. The so-called Recoverably Deletable Predicates (RDPs) later used by Levi were claimed to be possibly universal primitives, but not necessarily atomic (1978: 50 f.). Predicates were regarded as abstract units, not to be identified with the concrete words of the object language (Lipka 1972: 61 ff.). It is particularly important in our context that these meaning elements were supposed to represent the internal structure of lexemes not in a linear sequence, but as a hierarchic configuration. The analyses of specific English lexemes carried out in the various publications were not identical. There was also a development within the theory with some modifications, such as the introduction of an additional predicate DO (cf. Lipka 1976). Disregarding for the moment the hierarchic tree-structure postulated, the following examples of the decomposition of lexemes in Generative Semantics can be given:

(17)	*kill*	=	(DO) CAUSE BECOME NOT ALIVE
	break	=	(CAUSE) BECOME NOT WHOLE
	remind	=	STRIKE as SIMILAR, STRIKE LIKE/MAKE THINK
	apologize	=	REQUEST FORGIVE
	persuade	=	CAUSE BELIEVE, (DO) CAUSE BECOME INTEND.

One of the most important results of work in this field is the insight that many lexemes contain very general, possibly universal, semantic elements. Although these allegedly atomic elements of the metalanguage are derived from paraphrases in specific natural languages, they can be said to be transformed from object-language elements and raised to the status of metalinguistic semantic components (cf. Lipka 1972: 42). Thus, many causative verbs contain an element which can be symbolized either by BEWIRKEN or VERURSACHEN (derived from paraphrases in German for *töten, säubern, wärmen* etc.) or by CAUSE (contained in *kill, clean, persuade, legalize*). The same predicate can be postulated to underlie the object-language verb *make*.

The theory of Generative Semantics provides a mechanism and a principled way of relating explicit periphrastic causative constructions with *make, cause, have* (e.g. *make legal* or 'The goverment *caused* the zone to *become not military*') to complex lexemes like *legalize* and *demilitarize*, and simple lexemes like *kill, break, remind* (e.g. CAUSE, BECOME, NOT ALIVE). It postulates so-called *prelexical transformations*, which can be applied repeatedly, combining atomic predicates in various ways, before substituting concrete lexemes for such combinations. This process is called *lexical insertion*, or *lexicalization*. The theory can thus explain, for example, that the following two sentences (18a) and (18b) have the same meaning and an identical underlying abstract structure:

(18a) The court *legalized* bussing
(18b) The court *made* bussing *legal*
} CAUSE + BECOME

In (18a) CAUSE is contained in *legalize* together with the second predicate BECOME, which symbolizes a transition or change of state into a process or another state. In (18b), however, both abstract meaning elements have only to be combined with each other and realized in English *make*. In some publications by Lakoff the predicate BECOME is symbolized as Incho (from the traditional term *inchoative verbs*, i.e. "change of state verbs"). It can be justified by paraphrasing e.g. *harden* as 'become hard' and *liquefy* as 'become liquid'. In many English lexemes both inchoative and causative verbs are realized as a single surface form (cf. Lipka 1982). Kastovsky (1973: esp. 290 ff.) discusses explicit and implicit causative constructions in English in great detail and with much ingenuity, as well as derived causative verbs like *de/militar/ize* (the zone), *de/frost/Ø* (the icebox), *un/saddle/Ø* (the horse).

The much discussed stock example of Generative Semantics is *kill*. As opposed to Ger *töten* it is not a deadjectival derivative, but a simple lexeme. According to McCawley (1968: 73) it can be decomposed into *cause to die*. Although he does not say so, this claim is ultimately based on the observation that the paraphrase can replace *kill* in most contexts. *Die* itself can in turn be decomposed into BECOME, NOT, ALIVE. Both decompositions, however, do not consist of a simple linear sequence of atomic predicates, but must be understood as hierarchic configurations. Since the adjective *dead* itself can be decomposed into NOT ALIVE, the sentence, or rather proposition, *x killed y* can be represented in the following form:

(19) = x killed y

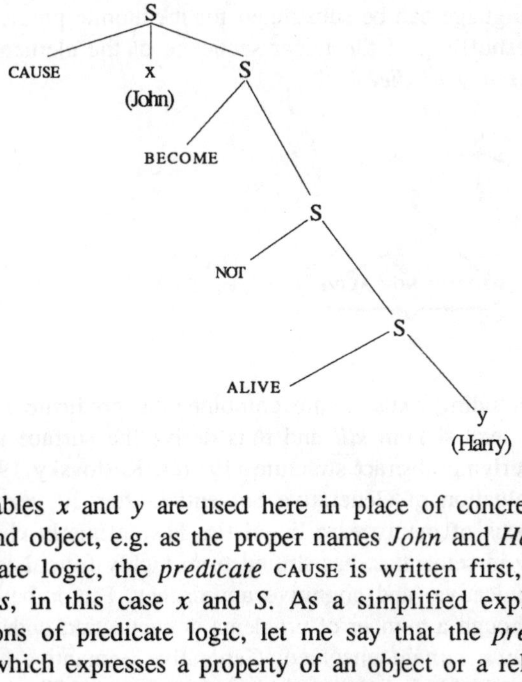

The variables *x* and *y* are used here in place of concrete realizations of the subject and object, e.g. as the proper names *John* and *Harry*. As is customary in predicate logic, the *predicate* CAUSE is written first, followed by its two *arguments*, in this case *x* and *S*. As a simplified explanation of the basic assumptions of predicate logic, let me say that the *predicate* is an abstract element which expresses a property of an object or a relation between two or more objects. Sometimes the less ambiguous term *predicator* is used instead. The objects to which a predicate applies are called the *arguments* in logic.

Thus e.g. in the sentences *John is tall* and *John is sleeping*, the adjective *tall* as well as the verb *sleep* can both be understood as predicates. Obviously, predicates are not necessarily verbs, but may be realized as adjectives, nouns, prepositions or conjunctions.

In '*x* killed *y*' the two variables are the arguments of the two-place predicate *kill* on the surface level. On a deeper, more abstract, underlying level or structure, the second argument of the predicate CAUSE and the only argument of the one-place predicates BECOME is the symbol or node S. The only argument of the predicate ALIVE is *y*.

This hierarchic structure is postulated as the abstract representation underlying a concrete linguistic utterance. Starting from this configuration of atomic predicates, we can now reverse the process of lexical decomposition in order to arrive at concrete linguistic material, i.e. lexemes.

Thus, to arrive at alternative verbal realizations of the underlying structure (19), which are paraphrases of each other, we have to apply so-called 'prelexical transformations'. The most important one is called *predicate raising*. It can be applied once or repeatedly and then combines two or more atomic predicates with each other. If for the result of the combination a lexeme exists in the language, it can replace the configuration and vice versa. Thus if predicate raising is applied twice to the structure (19), this may result in the following derived structure (20). The linear combination of the predicates BECOME NOT ALIVE can now be replaced by the lexical item *die*. Similarly, the English verb *cause* of the object language can be substituted for the atomic predicate CAUSE. With an additional reshuffling of the linear sequence of the elements, we get the paraphrase *x caused y to die*.

(20)

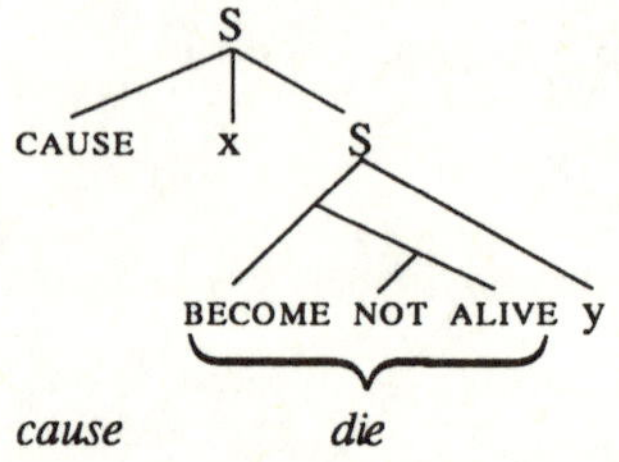

If all predicates – including CAUSE – are combined by predicate raising, we can insert the simple lexical item *kill* and thus derive the surface structure *x killed y* from the underlying abstract structure (19) (cf. Kastovsky 1982a:268).

Perhaps some evaluation of Generative Semantics after 20 years will not be premature. The focus of mainstream linguistics has definitely changed and the interest, especially in semantics, has shifted from highly formalized theories to pragmatic, communicative, and cognitive approaches. Prototype Semantics is a case in point. Although a number of problems in connection with the theory of *lexical decomposition* remain unsolved, Generative Semantics has clearly brought a number of valuable insights which are here to stay. The perspective has changed. The limitations of the theory are obvious and it must be seen, in my opinion, as a specific variant of componential analysis and at the same time as a complementary analytical counterpart to the holistic approach of Prototype Semantics.

The range of the theory is restricted – it concentrated almost exclusively on verbs. Consequently, it must be seen as complementary to those approaches in which nouns and noun phrases are more prominent. The method of lexical decomposition can reveal relationships between superficially very different structures like (18a) and (18b) and paraphrases such as *x killed y* and *x caused y to die*. The distinction between the object-language and the metalanguage was often confused in the publications of the Generative Semanticists, and the explicit discussion of the justification of atomic predicates by paraphrasing is only found in relatively recent articles (cf. Lipka 1972, 1976).

The claim of generality for predicates like CAUSE, BECOME, HAVE, NOT has proved most fruitful and stimulating in contrastive linguistics. Here, parallel semantic structures have been discovered in quite distinct surface structures. The abstract representations postulated for specific lexical decompositions usually contain the variables *x* and *y*. This explicitly demonstrates that predicates are in a syntagmatic relationship with certain arguments.

It shows, too, that the analysis of lexemes into an unordered set of semantic features does not yield an adequate description, which becomes particularly evident in the case of lexemes functioning as predicates, but less so when they function as arguments. This observation is easily compatible with the distinction Uriel Weinreich (1972) first made in 1966 between an unordered set of semantic features, which he called a *cluster*, and an ordered, directed set of features, which he labelled *configuration* (see 3.3.4.). The configuration was supposed to account for the relationship between a transitive verb and its object.

There are close connections with Case Grammar here.[7] This linguistic model also uses the basic notions of predicate logic and applies them to syntactic and semantic relationships. The predicate-argument relation is to my mind more adequately captured by *deep cases* than in the framework of Generative Semantics. The model of Case Grammar therefore is of considerable relevance to sentence semantics.

The lexical semantics studies published by Generative Semanticists and by Fillmore around 1970 almost invariably concentrated on a handful of lexical items, which were used as test cases or illustrative material to support or attack a certain theoretical point. An extreme case in point is Postal (1970) who

---

[7] See 3.2.3. p. 90f. The theory of Case Grammar was first proposed in Fillmore (1968b) and later developed in various publications. By 'case' Fillmore did not mean the inflectional variations in nouns, as in the traditional sense of the term (today also labelled 'surface cases'). He rather postulated some underlying deeper relationships (today called 'deep cases' or 'case roles') between verbs and nouns (or more precisely NPs) which are independent of their surface realizations. Thus e.g. the 'deep cases' relating the verb *open* and the NPs *John* ('Agent'), *the key* ('Instrument'), *the door* ('Object') remain the same in *John opened the door with the key, The key opened the door, The door opened, It was John who opened the door,* in spite of different surface subjects. Cf. Lipka (1976: 125–128) for a comparison of Case Grammar and Generative Semantics, and Lipka (1982: 7–9) for a survey of the latter theory.

discussed, on almost a hundred pages, various aspects of the single "surface verb" *remind*. Weinreich's complaint in 1966 that "the most urgent need in semantics is for fresh empirical evidence obtained by painstaking study of concrete lexical data" (1972: 120) had very little effect. More than 20 years later the situation is not radically different. Only now, with the advent of personal computers and the availability of a number of machine-readable corpora of the English language, have a number of large-scale projects got under way.

At the risk of seeming immodest, I would like to sketch briefly my own contribution to the field in Lipka (1972). The basis of this study of verb-particle constructions was an open-ended corpus with a collection of material that attempted to incorporate as many currently used collocations with *out* and *up* as possible (cf. Lipka 1972 :14 f., 154–162). In the semantic analysis of these verb-particle constructions the methods of the study of word-formation were combined with semantic feature analysis and complemented by a classification according to archilexemes representing certain word-fields. The constructions with *out* and *up*, functioning as transitive and intransitive verbs, were regarded as one-place or many-place predicates in the sense of symbolic logic. They were broken up into semantic components with the help of specific formulas for their semantic structure, consisting of *formators* and *designators*, as represented in (21):

(21)

$$\left\{\begin{array}{l} \text{BE} + \left\{\begin{array}{l}\text{LOC}\\ \text{POSITION}\\ \text{STATE}\end{array}\right\} \\[2ex] \text{BECOME} + \left\{\begin{array}{l}\text{LOC}\\ \text{POSITION}\\ \text{STATE}\end{array}\right\} \\[2ex] \text{CAUSE} + \text{BECOME} + \left\{\begin{array}{l}\text{LOC}\\ \text{POSITION}\\ \text{STATE}\end{array}\right\} \\ \text{CAUSE} + \text{HAVE} \end{array}\right. \quad \left\{\begin{array}{l} \pm\ \text{Apparent}\\ \pm\ \text{Awake}\\ \pm\ \text{Blocked}\\ \pm\ \text{Confused}\\ \pm\ \text{Covered}\\ \pm\ \text{Empty}\\ \pm\ \text{Exist}\\ \pm\ \text{Fastened}\\ \pm\ \text{Inflated}\\ \pm\ \text{Inside}\\ \pm\ \text{Process}\\ \pm\ \text{Proximate}\\ \pm\ \text{Vertical} \end{array}\right\}$$

Semantic components such as BE, BECOME, CAUSE, and HAVE were regarded in the study as 'connectives' or 'formators' which relate certain variables either to a certain place, position, or state, or to other variables. These variables, as well as PLACE, POSITION, STATE were represented by 'designators' which consist of semantic features. Those features which were found relevant in the analysis of the comprehensive corpus are listed on the right hand side of (21), beginning with [± Apparent] and finishing with [±Vertical].

In addition, the more general features [Degree], [Dynamic], [Negative Evaluation] were also found relevant in the study of verb-particle constructions.

The application of the formulas is illustrated as follows in (22). In the examples in which the feature [±Apparent] is seen functioning as a designator, the second argument of the two-place predicate is listed in brackets. The agent, as the first argument of the verb-particle construction is left unspecified.

(22) CAUSE + BE + POSITION:

hold out	(arms, hand, baby)
bend up	(wire, piece of metal, edge of a book)

CAUSE + BE + [± Apparent]:

blurt out	(secret)
bring out	(meaning of a passage, young lady, book)
call up	(scenes from childhood)
conjure up	(spirits, visions of the past).

The postulation of the binary semantic features functioning as designators was based on the use of semantic tests (cf. Lipka 1972:55 ff., Kastovsky 1982a:111 ff.). I cannot go into detail here. Suffice is to say that I first took up the subject in my book on *Semantic Structure and Word-Formation*, in which I further developed existing tests and applied them to verb-particle constructions. The most important discovery procedure suitable for the subject was the combination of the BUT-test and the SO-test. In the first edition of Leech's book on semantics he introduced the *Entailment and Inconsistency Test* and the *Tautology and Contradiction Test*. Kastovsky (1982a:111ff.) extensively discusses criteria and tests for the establishment of semantic features. Leech ([2]1981 : 73) uses so-called *basic statements* for the control of intuition and is generally concerned with "means by which intuitive data can be more securely backed up". In an article on the justification of specific components for English nouns and verbs I have come to the conclusion that there are at least three types of evidence and three methods of justification for the postulation of underlying semantic elements, namely: 1. morphological evidence from complex lexemes, i.e. compounds and affixations, 2. the postulation of components on the basis of acceptable paraphrase relationships, and 3. the evaluation of semantic tests and logical relationships such as implication, tautology and contradiction.

3.3.2. A Typology of Features

Before we come to a specific proposal for a typology of semantic features, we must first have a look at the concept of feature itself, which has been transferred from the discipline of phonology to the syntactic and semantic levels of language. It originated in the functional approach to phonology of the Prague school of linguistics around 1940. In this approach phonemes were no longer regarded as the smallest, indivisible units of language, but were regarded as representing bundles of phonological features. Only one of these features may be responsible for the functional opposition of two phonemes. Thus, for example, the distinction between the bilabial stops or plosives /b/ and /p/ in English and German can be accounted for by the single distinctive phonological feature [VOICE]. Such features have been labelled *distinctive features* (or DFs). A number of other consonant pairs in both languages are also distinguished only by an opposition concerning this dimension of voice (Kastovsky 1982a: 80 f.).

Conversely, phonemes can also be represented as the sum of distinctive features, as in the following example:

(23) /p/ = voiceless, bilabial, plosive
/b/ = voiced, bilabial, plosive
/d/ = voiced, alveolar, plosive

The binary feature [VOICE], where the + symbolizes the presence and the – symbolizes the absence of the feature, can be seen to conflate the two feature labels 'voiced' and 'voiceless'. This notation obviously provides a more economical way of representing phonological features. It is, however, only appropriate for characterizing so-called privative oppositions, in which one member of the pair lacks the feature in question. The Prague school also recognized other types of opposition in phonology, especially gradual and so-called equipollent oppositions. In the former, the members have various degrees of the same property in question, with extremes at either end of the scale. In equipollent oppositions the members are equal, or equivalent, i.e. they have the same power or status. All three opposition-types can also be found in semantics (cf. Kastovsky 1982a: 93, 99 f.).

It was already recognized by Hjelmslev, one of the founders of structural semantics, that generally speaking we can establish parallels between the phonological and semantic levels of languages. This parallelism therefore allows us to describe both levels with the same type of distinctive feature. Chomsky later transferred the concept of feature to the level of syntax as well. In my opinion semantic features must be empirically justified. In a purely language-immanent framework as in structural semantics, this can be done on the basis of the opposition of lexemes. We can then state, as in example (15), that *man, woman, child* have a feature [+HUMAN] in common and that *bull* and *cow* differ in a feature [MALE] or equivalently, [∓FEMALE]. This, however, leaves out of consideration that such distinctions along the dimension SEX (or in more recent wording GENDER) are not privative oppositions. We can also derive meta-linguistic elements, such as semantic features, in a referential approach to meaning, from properties or attributes of the referent or denotatum. Thus, we can say that the distinction between *snail* and *slug* can be captured by the binary feature notation [SHELL]. In this case, the +sign symbolizes the presence and the – the absence of a shell on the extralinguistic referent. In this way properties of the extralinguistic object, if they have a distinctive function, can be raised to the status of metalinguistic elements.

A survey of recent developments and an extensive discussion of the status of semantic features is to be found in Lipka (1972: 30–71). Features, basically, are theoretical units of the metalanguage and as such may be used for analysis and description on the phonetic, phonological, morphological, syntactic, and semantic level. Using the same theoretical construct on different levels undoubtedly makes linguistic theory more unified.

There are, however, also a number of difficulties and problems related to the concept of semantic feature (cf. Lipka 1986a: 87 f., 91). In my opinion, Feature Semantics and Prototype Semantics are complementary and we have a division of labour between both theories (cf. Lipka 1987a). The most detailed and comprehensive analysis of the problems of semantic features I know of is given in Sprengel (1980). He discusses the questions of discovery procedures and circular definitions, metalinguistic status, linguistic vagueness, the distinction between linguistic and encyclopedic knowledge, hierarchies and concatenation of features, and their universality and psychological reality. Some of his arguments do not carry the same weight as others, but on the whole, his approach is quite balanced and by no means a condemnation of feature analysis. Such a verdict would indeed have been surprising in the face of the many successful applications of the theory to a variety of languages, including English. Many of the allegedly insurmountable difficulties for Feature Semantics can be solved to a large extent by using a specific type of semantic feature which I have proposed in Lipka (1985), namely the *inferential feature*.

Obviously, the concept of semantic feature itself is not completely uniform and inseparable, as is often alleged. Nothing prevents us from distinguishing various types for different phenomena and purposes. I now come to my own proposal for a possible typology or classification of semantic features. This has been developed over the years in a number of publications (cf. Lipka 1985: 87, 1987a: 296). I do not claim that this is the one and only correct way of dividing up the category of semantic feature. Alternative taxonomies are possible and legitimate and have been proposed recently (cf. Schneider 1988 : 64 ff.). A comparison and evaluation of competing typologies must be based on their applicability, their descriptive adequacy, and the purpose of the classification. As with all classifications, the delicacy depends on the number and weighting of the criteria used for setting up subcategories. Ultimately, this runs up against the law of diminishing returns (see 4.2.3.4.). The criteria used in my classification are obviously heterogeneous. This is particularly evident for the seventh comprehensive "super-class" of *distinctive features*, which includes all others with the exception of *inferential features* (IFs). IFs are exceptional in other respects also. I would like to summarize and illustrate my classification in schema (24). On the basis of various criteria we can distinguish the following types of semantic feature:

(24) 1. denotative	e.g. [±HUMAN]	in *girl*	vs. *filly*
2. connotative	[±ARCHAIC]	*steed*	vs. *horse*
3. relational	[→PARENT][←PARENT]	*father*	vs. *son*
4. transfer	<–SOLID> or <2 PENETRABLE>	*to drink*	
5. deictic	[±PROXIMATE]	*now*	vs. *then*
		come	vs. *go*
6. inferential (IFs)	{STICK}	*to beat*	
	{TO GET ATTENTION}	*to nudge*	
7. *distinctive* (DFs):	all except 6.		

As already mentioned, except for IFs, all others function as distinctive features, a seventh, general, comprehensive type. IFs also have a special status in that they enable the linguist to capture synchronic and diachronic variation. A Feature Semantics which restricts itself to obligatory features cannot explain change of meaning, because in such a framework features cannot disappear or be added. This variable type of feature (IF) is furthermore exceptional in that it does not refer to a specific dimension, like sex, age, colour, heat, or physical state (SOLID, LIQUID, GASEOUS). It therefore does not have a particular value assigned to it (like +, –, 2, →).

In the following, I shall use the term (semantic) *feature* for a subclass of (semantic) *components*. Many linguists (e.g. Leech) use the terms interchangeably as synonyms. In my terminology, however, *features* are characterized by having a specific value (+, 2, →) assigned to them. Again, *inferential features* (as a lexicalized term) have an exceptional status in this respect. I do not claim that semantic *features* are indivisible or atomic and that they are absolutely universal units. However, as opposed to *components* (which can often be broken down into features) they have a tendency to be finer and more likely universal.

I would now like to comment on the notation and symbols used, before explaining my classification in detail. Both the arrows e.g. in [←PARENT] for *son* and the numbers, e.g. in <2PENETRABLE> for *to drink*, have been adopted from Leech (^{2}1981) as notational conventions. The former symbolizes the direction of the relation, which in Leech's terminology (^{2}1981:102f.) is a "relative opposition". Leech (^{2}1981:112) treats 1, 2, 3 PENETRABLE, which corresponds to the physical states 'solid', 'liquid', 'gaseous' as a scalar opposition or "hierarchy". In this case a binary feature notation (with + and -) is obviously not appropriate. This is also the case for his "multiple taxonomies", like primary colour terms, species of animal, or types of metal like *gold, copper, iron, mercury*. The angled brackets < > are used for *transfer features*, which I have adopted from Weinreich (1972). Finally, the braces or curly brackets { } for *inferential features* are taken from Lehrer (1974:84f.). However, she does not use the term, which I have coined under the influence of Nida (1975). It denotes optional meaning components which may be inferred from the use of an expression. There are close relationships with the concept of *inferential processes* in text linguistics and the Gricean notion of *implicature*.

A final, general remark. The symbols used for the feature notation are basically arbitrary but can be of considerable use in relieving the memory. Leech (^{2}1981 : 95), who also stresses the arbitrariness of a semantic notation, labels his metalanguage as *signese*. Obviously this name, which evokes *Chinese*, is coined in analogy to *journalese* and *officialese*. Leech emphasizes that such an artificial, formal language has two properties: It is unambiguous and it is arbitrary. I will now turn to a detailed explanation of the individual types of semantic feature, following the order in diagram (24).

1. *Denotative features* are the most important and central features of a lexeme. They are inherent, i.e. always obligatorily present or absent. They capture and formalize what Lyons calls *descriptive meaning*, which corresponds to Leech's *conceptual* or *cognitive meaning*, as well as his *sense*. Denotative features are normally based on cognitive features, properties, or attributes of the extralinguistic denotatum. They may also be derived by purely language-immanent procedures, on the basis of acceptable paraphrases. Different languages may draw on different properties for the linguistic categorization of the extralinguistic world (for example the presence or absence of a shell). Consequently, the use of a specific property of the denotatum, as a metalinguistic feature, is not identical with the description of the extralinguistic objects themselves. Only features or attributes which are relevant for linguistic distinctions may be used for semantic analysis and description.
2. *Connotative features* are needed to capture differences like those between *steed* and *horse*, or *to smite* and *to strike*. Thus, *steed* will have an additional feature [+ARCHAIC] which is missing in the unmarked lexeme *horse* (2.2.5.). The opposite value [-ARCHAIC] can be used as a notation for neologisms.[8] Connotative features are inherent components of a lexeme and do not concern properties of the denotatum. The latter is identical e.g. in the case of *steed* and *horse*. What is at stake here, are stylistic nuances and attitudes of the speaker. For this reason Leech in 1974, in the first edition of his book, speaks of *stylistic meaning* (relabelled in 1981 *social*) and of *affective meaning*.

   English dictionaries use labels like "archaic, literary, humorous" for such features. In fact, "humorous" really characterizes the function or effect of a stylistically marked lexeme in an incongrent context. We have already discussed connotations at great length in 2.2.5. I would therefore simply like to maintain again that connotative features are properties of a lexeme, not properties of the referent or denotatum. Such features are relatively secondary, additional, or marginal compared to the central, denotative features.

[8] Obviously, since both archaisms and neologisms are marked forms, the binary feature [ARCHAIC] does not symbolize a privative opposition and thus has a status different from that of [VOICE].

3. *Relational features* are essential and indispensable for the explanation of the opposition of *father* and *son* and the semantic analysis of similar lexemes. They are furthermore required for describing *converses* (see 4.2.3.3.) like *teacher* and *pupil*, or *own* and *belong to*. Such words are fundamentally relational and cannot be properly understood and explained with the help of properties. They always involve relations. Ascending and descending generation in kinship terminology, i.e. relations in a different sense, also cannot be represented as a binary contrast. Leech (^{2}1981: 103) introduces horizontal arrows, pointing in different directions, for symbolizing such "relative features", together with the common semantic component PARENT. Thus, e.g. the relational *father of* is symbolized by [→PARENT] and conversely *son of* (or *child of*) by the feature notation [←PARENT]. Relational words always relate to entities, which are called arguments in predicate logic (in the following A_1, A_2 etc.). Here, the direction of the relation marked by the linear order of the linguistic realization of the arguments is of vital importance. This can be represented in the following way:

A_1 A_2
(25a) James is the *father of* John [→PARENT]

A_2 A_1
(25b) John is the *son of* James [←PARENT]

Lexical pairs such as *father* and *son* are called *converses*. If these are substituted for each other and the syntactic position of the arguments is reversed, the denotative meaning of the whole sentence remains constant. Thus, *James is the father of John* is equivalent to *John is the son of James*. Syntagmatic lexical relations, i.e. the linguistic environment, influences the direction of the arrow in such relational features. Obviously, this type of feature is closely related to Leech's *thematic meaning*.

4. *Transfer features* are fundamentally syntagmatic in nature. As already mentioned, the concept and the term go back to 1966, when Weinreich first published his *Explorations in Semantic Theory*. We can make use of his own example *He was drinking carrots* and can represent it in the following way:

(26) He was *drinking* carrots
[+SOLID]
——→ <-SOLID>

The transfer feature <-SOLID>, which might also be formalized as <+LIQUID> or more adequately, as <2PENETRABLE>, is transferred from the verb *drink* to its grammatical object *carrots*, according to Weinreich's theory. There it replaces the contradictory inherent feature [+SOLID]. The combination of *drink* and *carrots* is not restricted or excluded. As a result of the transfer process, the object *carrots* is reinterpreted as 'carrot juice'.[9]

The symbolization of transfer features by angular brackets goes back to the introduction of the notation for selectional restrictions in Katz/Fodor (1963). Weinreich develops his own approach by starting out with a critical appraisal of Katz and Fodor's semantic theory. He adopts their notational device of angular brackets, at the same time reinterpreting them. In generative grammar, the notion of selection restrictions was the first attempt to capture semantic restrictions in the combination of lexemes on the basis of a syntactic theory. The mechanism was introduced to prevent the generation of deviant sentences. Weinreich's 'transfer features' are more active and less restrictive. They can explain the semantic interpretation of unusual combinations of lexemes and are therefore more adequate for describing phenomena which actually occur in natural languages.

Transfer features are also needed, in a language-immanent framework, for explaining metaphorical processes. Denotative features such as [+ANIMATE], [+HUMAN], and [+PERSON] may thus function as transfer features. In this way productive processes like animation and personification can be explained. From a referential and cognitive point of view metaphorical and metonymic processes are better explained as a secondary or dual categorization of the extralinguistic world (cf. Lipka 1988).

5. *Deictic features* are needed to explain certain locative and temporal relations, but also direction (with an additional dynamic component). They are not identical with the phenomenon of "directional opposition" discussed by Lyons, who clearly distinguishes this from deixis (cf. Lyons 1977:281 ff., 636 ff.). The feature [+PROXIMATE] contained for example in *now, here*, and *come*, symbolizes proximity. The reference point of orientation, the centre, in relation to which closeness or distance are expressed, generally lies in the speaker of an utterance at a specific time and place. Consequently, since the language user is involved, this type of feature is pragmatic in nature. But since, at the same time, it is an

[9] G. Pascoe finds this: "a highly eccentric way of referring to 'carrot juice', of borderline acceptability". Other examples for transfer features Weinreich gives are: <+WATER VEHICLE> in *to sail a craft*, <+MOVABLE ON LAND> in *to drive*, <–MALE> in *pretty children* (all with a neutral head), and <+ANIMATE> in *His fear ate him up* (with a feature conflict with [–ANIMATE] or [+ABSTRACT]). Tournier (1985 : 229; 1988 : 119) postulates a type of semantic feature labelled "sème de transfert", for the explanation of 'metaphor' (originally the Greek word for *transfer*). Cruse (1986 : 105) speaks of "traits" (his term for *semantic features*) which are "transferred to the head" in: *my pregnant neighbour/cousin/friend* and *Arthur drank the substance/it*. Leech (^{2}1981 : 141) speaks of an "apparent clash of features" which we resolve "through transfer meaning ... often metaphorical transfer", e.g. in *My gas meter eats up 10ps*. Cf. also Schneider (1988 : 67, 69 ff., 82).

inherent feature of a particular lexeme, it has to be treated and used in lexical semantics. This holds, for example, for the distinction between verbs such as *come* and *go, pull* and *push, bring* and *take*. Furthermore, the opposition between *here* and *there*, *this* and *that* as well as temporal relations in *now* and *then* can be explained and described by the use of deictic features.

Proximity and distance may also be of a psychological kind, and consequently *this* may refer to something with which the speaker identifies himself. On the other hand, *that* may point to something from which he distances himself. Fillmore has discussed such questions of deixis in great detail in a number of publications, in particular in his *Santa Cruz Lectures on Deixis*, which first appeared in 1971. The criterion for the postulation of deictic features is evidently a pragmatic one, since they depend on the temporal and locative orientation of the user of linguistic signs.

6. *Inferential features* (IFs) are unusual in several respects, as already mentioned. They do not occur in traditional Feature Semantics. From a synchronic point of view, only variable IFs can explain fuzziness of meaning, polysemy, and regional, stylistic, and other variation. In my opinion, the introduction of this type of semantic feature will neutralize the most important arguments levelled against the so-called "checklist theory of semantics". On the diachronic scale, it can capture semantic restriction, extension, shift and possibly other changes of meaning.

IFs are not discrete, obligatory, and inherent but rather optional, supplementary, and dependent on linguistic and extralinguistic context, from which they may be inferred. Thus, they can explain for example the lexicalization of *holiday*, and synchronic and diachronic variation of items like *starve, barn* and *mill* (cf. Lipka 1985).

IFs may be used for formalizing properties which are normally associated with a referent or denotatum. This corresponds to Leech's "connotative meaning", illustrated by slyness associated with *fox*, clumsiness with *ox* etc.[10] The contextual dependence captured by IFs also concerns the phenomena discussed by Leech under the heading "reflected" and "collocative meaning". Dictionaries often mark IFs by using labels such as "usually, especially, often". Thus, for example *beat* contains {WITH STICK} and the verb *nudge* the feature {TO GET ATTENTION}. Container terms may have IFs for the dimension MATERIAL

[10] This is not to be confused with my 'connotative features' (type 2), which are not optional but inherent in specific lexical units, although of secondary importance compared to the central 'denotative features'. Cf. also Ger *dreckig, Scheiße, abkratzen* 'die' vs. *schmutzig, Kot, sterben* and *crap, piss, fuck, snuff it* vs. *excrement, urinate, copulate, die*. Only IFs are a matter of fuzziness. Cf. also the distinction of criterial, expected, possible, unexpected, and canonical "semantic traits" in Cruse (1986:16f., 52f.), which may further be "promoted" or "demoted", "highlighted" or "backgrounded".

such as {GLASS} in *bottle* or {EARTHENWARE} in *pitcher*, but the features may also refer to content or other attributes, such as e.g. {DECORATED} and {FOR WINE} in *decanter*. In conclusion I would like to stress that IFs are also unusual in that the methods mentioned for the justification of features are not applicable. To be precise, this only holds for the first and third method of justification, because IFs may occur in paraphrases. So much for the discussion of the first six types of feature in schema (24). There is, however, a seventh class of feature which includes most of them.

7. *Distinctive features* include all the other classes discussed so far, with the exception of inferential features, since these are not inherent and obligatory. As already mentioned, this comprehensive super-class is based on the criterion of distinctive function, as originally introduced in phonology. All semantic features which serve to distinguish a pair of lexemes that are otherwise identical in meaning are distinctive features. They must be empirically justified. If we cannot find pairs of lexemes which only differ in a single feature, we cannot postulate a distinctive feature. Thus, for example *cat* and *kitten* are only distinguished by the denotative feature [ADULT]. *Steed*, if compared with *horse* bears an additional connotative feature [+ARCHAIC]. The transfer feature <+CAT> or <+FELINE> is contained in the verb *miaow*, and thereby distinguished e.g. from *bark* or *neigh*. The function of distinctive transfer features becomes especially clear, when the subject is not specified. This can be illustrated by comparing *The animal miaowed* with *The animal barked* and *The animal neighed* (cf. Leech ^{2}1981 : 139). The seventh type of features thus forms an inclusive, global category which can be further subdivided if additional criteria are used.

In concluding the presentation of my proposed typology of semantic features, I would like to give two examples for their justification, one for the paraphrasing method and the other for possible semantic tests. Paraphrasing is discussed in detail, in connection with lexical fields, in Lipka (1980). Let us consider the paraphrases for the following verbs:

(27)	*kick*	=	'hit (with foot)'
	punch	=	'hit (hard) (with fist)'
	nudge	=	'hit (not hard) (with elbow) esp. (in order to get attention)'

If these definitional paraphrases are accepted, we can extract a series of modifiers of *hit* and regard them as meaning-components. These modifiers of the object language can then be raised to the status of metalinguistic components (cf. Lipka 1972 : 42). We can therefore assign a denotative, obligatory feature [+HARD] to *punch*. In addition, we can postulate an inferential feature {IN ORDER TO GET ATTENTION} contained in *nudge*.

Various criteria and tests for establishing semantic features are discussed in great detail in Kastovsky (1982a:111 ff.). The possibility of semantic testing can be based on logical relationships such as contradiction and tautology, used in Leech ([2]1981), but also on various connectives like *but, and*, and *so*. In Lipka (1972: 60 f.) I have proposed a combination of the BUT- and SO-tests, which can be illustrated with the following example (see also p. 107):

(28a) *Sheila is a *spinster* BUT she is married
(28b) *Sheila is a *spinster* BUT she is not married
(28c) Sheila is a *spinster* SO she is not married
= [-MARRIED]

In (28a) and (28b) the two sentences are conjoined by *but*. The second sentence is negated in (28b) but not in (28a). Both coordinated sentences conjoined by *but* must be unacceptable (symbolised by *) if a specific component explicitly appears in the second sentence which is implicitly contained in a lexeme in the first sentence. Consequently in (28a) we have a contradiction and in (28b) a tautology. The consequence or implication in the pair of sentences (28c), which is marked by the connective *so*, reveals which value of the binary feature [±MARRIED] must be postulated as an inherent, denotative feature of *spinster*.

To sum up, I do not claim that all problems are solved in connection with the postulation and justification of semantic features in general, or of specific features of English in particular. The proposals made here are intended to show the direction which an applied practical word semantics of English might follow. At the same time they demonstrate which theoretical considerations must not be neglected. Clearly, the proposed classification of features crucially depends on the criteria used for the definition of the types. In principle, other criteria and a different weighting might be applied (cf. Schneider 1988: 64 ff.). I still believe, however, that the proposed typology comprises all the important and necessary aspects. Nevertheless, even for a language which has been as thoroughly described and analysed as English, a great deal of work remains to be done.

3.3.3. Feature Semantics vs. Prototype Semantics: An Alternative?

In 2.2.3. we already encountered the notions of *prototype* and Prototype Semantics, in connection with denotation and the question of categorizing extralinguistic reality in natural languages. The prototypical *bottle* and *cup* were mentioned and I have argued, in agreement with Cognitive Linguistics, that linguistic categorization is culture-dependent. Furthermore, I claimed that the distinction between Prototype Semantics and the "checklist theory of semantics" introduced by Fillmore sets up a false alternative, because they are complementary and there is a division of labour.

After discussing semantic features at such great length, I would now like to take up Prototype Semantics again and consider it in comparison with Feature Semantics, evaluating the advantages and weaknesses of both approaches (cf. Lipka 1986a, 1987a). In a recent paper, Cuyckens (1984: 175) also argued that Prototype Semantics alone is not an adequate model for word semantics, stating furthermore that it "at least implicitly assumes a componential/semantic feature approach to word meaning". He points out that certain lexemes cannot be described with the notion of prototype and distinguishes between "category features" and "identification features (IF)". The latter are very similar to my inferential features.

Aitchison (1987: 51 ff.) has a chapter on "bad birds and better birds" with the subtitle "Prototype Theories", thus hinting at the fact that there is not a single, unified Prototype Theory. She discusses "birdy" and "unbirdy birds", as well as "vegetably vegetables" and emphasizes that there may be "new or damaged examples" such as new inventions and a one-winged robin or a three-legged tiger which would still be categorized as a bird and a quadruped. Aitchison (1987: 59, 62) argues for a distinction "between identification criteria and stored knowledge" and notes further problems with prototypes which to her mind, however, "do not invalidate Prototype Theory".

In the following, I would like to summarize the most important general arguments against Feature Semantics, especially those advanced in recent publications. The attacks are often directed against the so-called "Aristotelian Semantics". Feature Semantics is usually characterized globally with a list like (29). It is said to involve the following points:

(29)
1. clear category boundaries,
2. features as discrete properties,
3. yes/no-decisions on the presence of features, and
4. equal status of all features (no weighting).

As opposed to this, a list of advantages of Prototype Semantics like (30) is often given. Thus, for example Geeraerts (1984) claims that only this approach can explain:

(30)
1. vague, continuous category boundaries (fuzziness),
2. gradual category membership, resemblance,
3. categories with prototypical kernels, and
4. the different importance of attributes (weighting).

As mentioned before, the weaknesses exposed in such criticism can be overcome in a modified and elaborated Feature Semantics which distinguishes various types of features, especially IFs, as presented in 3.3.2.

However, Feature Semantics can neither cope with the simultaneous presence of features from the same dimension, e.g. COLOUR, nor with the interdependence of criterial properties. In classical Feature Semantics all features have the same importance or weight. Furthermore, semantic features do not capture the psychological reality of prototypes for concrete denotational structure, for example with containers, animals etc. In spite of all this, semantic features, if objectively justified, can be and have been applied most fruitfully to (contrastive) linguistic analysis and description, language teaching, and historical semantics.

Prototype Theory, on the other hand, cannot adquately account for abstracts. Nor can it capture, unlike connotative features, differences between e.g. archaic *smite* vs. *strike*, or affective *town* (as in *London town, Chicago town*) vs. *city*. Furthermore, Prototype Theory is incapable of dealing with deictics (*come/go*), relational words (like *precede, love, hate, father*), and syntagmatic relations (selection restrictions or transfer features) in general. Yet, like Rosch, I believe that in dealing with the concrete world and our everyday experiences, prototypes free human beings from time-consuming, laborious cognitive processes (see 2.2.3.) providing matching models and mechanisms for our mental lexicon, which enable us to perceive quickly and store and process words in the mind. If necessary, however, prototypes as holistic units or gestalts (here used as a technical loanword, cf. LDCE, COLLINS) may be broken down into the "elements" or "attributes" of Prototype Theory. These are doubtless equivalent to semantic features.

Prototype Semantics is particularly suited for the description of concrete extralinguistic objects, especially those in which shape and proportion are relevant. There is considerable evidence for the belief that prototypical images, gestalts, and frames for situations (cf. Verschueren 1981) are stored in the brain and used for cognitive and linguistic processing. Metaphor and metonymy, as either individual or collective dual categorization, are also based on the psychological reality of prototypical models of shapes, objects, and situations (cf. Lipka 1988b). Neither Prototype Semantics nor Feature Semantics can claim that it alone is able to solve all problems and describe all phenomena adequately.

The integration of both approaches is the most urgent task of semantic theory and practice. This has become particularly clear at a conference on the lexicon and lexical semantics, documented in Hüllen/Schulze (1988) under the title *Understanding the Lexicon*. The second question hotly debated at this conference was the relationship between linguistic and encyclopedic knowledge, and consequently the alternative between a purely language-immanent or a referential approach to lexical semantics. Again, it was agreed that an all-or-none approach is misguided and that any claim to an exclusive methodology must be abandoned. Thus the limits and boundaries of traditional structuralist semantics have been transcended and the necessity of an interdisciplinary point of view in lexicology was recognized.

3.3.4. Relations between Components

A particularly knotty set of problems seems to be here to stay: the internal structure of lexemes or sememes, i.e. the relationship between semantic components within the meaning of a word. This question was raised as early as 1966 by Weinreich, who introduced a distinction between unordered and ordered sets of semantic features, which he labelled *clusters* and *configurations*. I will illustrate the distinction in the following, using Weinreichs examples (1972:46f., 54ff.).

(31a) cluster: (a, b) = (b, a) as in *daughter* (female, offspring)
(31b) configuration: (a → b) (b → a) as in *chair, dentist, spill, show*

If *daughter* is analysed into the components (a) 'female' and (b) 'offspring', the internal order of the two features is irrelevant – either (a, b) oder (b, a) – and they therefore form a *cluster*. A *configuration*, on the other hand, is an ordered set of features (a → b), symbolized by an arrow, which is said to represent transitivity or a causative relation. Thus, according to Weinreich, the two features (a) 'furniture' and (b) 'sitting' form a configuration (in *chair*), because the latter ought to be rendered by 'to be sat on'. In my terminology, *chair* contains a directed purposive relation. According to Weinreich (1972:56) transitive verbs contain a configuration. This is illustrated by the causative verbs *spill* and *show*, which he paraphrases as 'cause to flow' and 'cause to see'. Thus, for him, simple lexemes (e.g. *spill, dentist*) may have an underlying structure similar to a verb-object construction (e.g. *fix teeth*), which he labels a "nesting construction". I would like to represent the parallel analysis of *dentist* and *spill* in the following diagram (32) using Weinreich's symbolization. Nesting constructions yield *configurations*.

(32)				
	fix	→	*teeth*	
nesting construction:	(a, b	→	c, d)	= *dentist*
" " :	(a, b, K	→	, u, v)	= *spill*
	MANNER *cause*	→	*flow*	

Here, the "semantic feature of causation" is symbolized by K; and (u,v) are the features of *flow*. (K → u,v) represents '*cause* (something) *to flow*' and (a,b) specifies the manner in which this is accomplished (e.g. from a vessel). If the meaning of *fix* is represented by (a,b) and that of *teeth* by (c,d), the meaning of the "nesting construction" *fix* + *teeth* can be represented as the configuration (a, b → c, d). According to Weinreich (1972:54) the same configuration may be (part of) the meaning of the simple lexeme *dentist*.

Obviously, there is a close parallelism to the idea of lexical decomposition in the theory of Generative Semantics, discussed in 3.3.1., which is further enhanced by Weinreich's examples of causative verbs. This association is also strengthened by the following general statement in Weinreich (1972:84):

> Every relation that may hold between components of a sentence also occurs among the components of a meaning of a dictionary entry. This is as much as to say that the semantic part of a dictionary entry is a sentence – more specifically, a deep-structure sentence.

(cf. Lipka 1971:229, 1972:33). In fact, Kastovsky (1973:255) uses this very quotation as his starting point for a comprehensive and detailed discussion of causatives in the truly Generative Semantics spirit. Directly following this quotation, Kastovsky further states explicitly:

> In word-formation syntagmas, the components making up a word are directly observable, i.e. are explicit, and thus can easily be related to corresponding underlying structures, which will state the relations existing between the component parts of such a word-formation syntagma

and he illustrates this with the correspondence between *Someone has won a prize* and the compound *prizewinner*. Putting this into a larger theoretical context, one could claim that the theory of Generative Semantics is the continuation of the methods of word-formation below the unit of syntagma down to the level of simple lexemes.

Looking back at diagram (19) in 3.3.1., we see that Generative Semantics is the only theory which represents the internal semantic structure of simple lexemes as an explicit, hierarchic configuration (also in Weinreich's sense) of semantic elements. Unfortunately, these ideas have not been further pursued, and the Generative Semanticists themselves restricted the application of the theory to a limited number of exemplary verbs. With the shift of the scholarly paradigm in mainstream linguistics to cognitive theories, it is not suprising that e.g. George Lakoff himself did not further develop such a language-immanent methodology.

As far as I know, the only application of closely related ideas is to be found in Hansen et al. ([2]1985). Furthermore when the authors attempt to combine componential analysis and predication analysis ("Prädikationsanalyse") they start out from a modified Case Grammar model (cf. [2]1985: 165 ff.) and concentrate on complex lexemes and word-formation. It remains to be added, as already mentioned above, that atomic predicates and the deep cases of Case Grammar are to a large extent equivalent and that the two theories may also be regarded as complementary, as demonstrated in Lipka (1976).

3.4. Lexical Rules and Semantic Processes

In our discussion of the semantic structure of words, we have so far restricted ourselves mainly to an analytic perspective and to a discussion of existing lexemes, while in 3.2.4. morphological structure was also considered from the point of view of productivity. We will now adopt a more dynamic outlook, which at the same time breaks up or transcends to some extent the dichotomy of morphology and semantics. In order to do this, we must first discuss the comprehensive notion of *rule*, as advocated here, and will then look in some detail at a borderline case between derivation and purely semantic changes, namely metaphor and metonymy (cf. Lipka 1989a). In my view both semantic transfer and word-formation provide productive patterns for creating new lexical units. There are a number of similarities and these justify capturing both in a single very general *lexical rule*.

3.4.1. Rules and Tendencies

In the following, the concept of rule will not be used in the strict sense of generative grammar, where rules were formulated and formalized as processes to be either applied or not, if certain conditions hold. My use of the term here is nearer to the concept of "variable rule", as introduced into sociolinguistics by Labov. It is rather more like a tendency, which exists in a very wide sense, without precisely formulable conditions, and no absolute predictive power. A certain amount of individual variation is also possible for the application of a certain rule and there is furthermore a correlation with more or less permissive text types.

Let us take a concrete example: *Berlin is a splendid host to the Congress of Linguists*. Clearly, here *Berlin* does not refer to a place, but to the people who live in it and is thus an instance of a highly productive metonymic rule. From the noun *host*, a verb *to host* 'be, act as a host' can also be derived, just as the noun *patron* leads to a verb *patronize* 'be, act as a patron', with the addition of the derivative suffix *-ize*.[11]

(33)	*host* n.	-	*to hostØ*	v.	'be, act as a host'
	patron n.	-	*patron/ize*	v.	'be, act as a patron'

In fact, both denominal verbs are institutionalized in the 'norm' of present-day English (in Coseriu's sense).

I would now like to apply an approach developed by Leech (^{2}1981:216), who postulates a very general *lexical rule* for both semantic shift or transfer and word-formation (including 'conversion' or zero-derivation), which he represents as follows:

(34)

This formula is to be interpreted as follows: From the lexical entry A with the morphological, syntactic, and semantic specifications *p, q, r* we can derive an entry B with the specifications *p', q', r'*. In generative terminology such a very general formulation would be called a "rule schema". In fact, Leech derives several specific rules "of morphological derivation" and "of semantic transfer" from this, with further specific subclasses of rules. Leech (^{2}1981:220) states that all these lexical rules "are surprisingly powerful in their ability to generate new lexical entries" and that they are all "instances of the same general phenomenon" with a number of common characteristics. The first common property is "partial productivity", which will be illustrated presently in

[11] The metonymic noun *host* is an instance of semantic transfer, while the zero-derived verb *to hostØ* is the result of word-formation. Both are productive processes, but the former creates new lexical units and the latter new lexemes.

connection with metaphor. Lexical rules thus capture certain general, creative tendencies and represent productive morphological and semantic processes.

3.4.2. Metaphor, Metonymy and Categorization

With regard to semantic transfer, I shall now focus on metaphor, based on the notion of similarity, and metonymy, based on contiguity. For both, the boundaries of a language-immanent structuralist approach must be transcended and a semiotic model must include referents (in Ogden/Richards's sense) and the extralinguistic world. It is contiguity of the referents or denotata of linguistic signs in reality, or rather our cognitive models of it, as well as similarity in our view of the world, which are involved here, Leech (1969: 148) sets up the following general formula for all kinds of semantic transfer:

(35) "The figurative sense F may replace the literal sense L if F is related to L in such-and-such a way".

According to Leech (1969: 151) every metaphor has the following form, which I represent as diagram (36), in which the terms *tenor, vehicle* and *ground* go back to I. A. Richards.

(36)

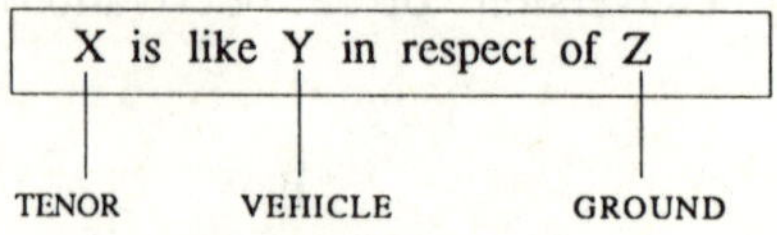

The terms *tenor* (X) and *vehicle* (Y) may be illustrated as in the following:

X Y
(37a) *Life* is a *walking shadow*

(37b) A *human elephant*
X Y

In (37b) the *ground* (Z) of comparison may be clumsiness or long memory, if *elephant* is figurative. As opposed to metaphors, in similes like (38) all three terms are explicitly mentioned:

(38) *His face* was as *white* as *a sheet*
X Z Y

In my opinion, there are three kinds of similarity between semantic transfer and word-formation. Both devices for extending the lexicon are characterized by: 1. productivity, 2. degrees of acceptability, and 3. the possibility of institutionalization (or lexicalization). The last one is particularly relevant if transfer of meaning is involved on the level of the lexicon, i.e. if we look at *word metaphors*, not at metaphors as stylistic devices or figures of speech (cf. Lipka 1989a). This term was introduced by Dirven (1985), who distinguishes it from three other types, namely *sound metaphors, phrase* and *sentence metaphors,* and *discourse metaphors*, on the levels of phonology, syntax, and discourse. Leech (^{2}1981:204ff.) only mentions the first two parallels between semantic transfer and word-formation under the terms "partial productivity" and "graded acceptability". Later, however, he stresses the "semantic open-endedness" of lexical rules in general. I agree, but furthermore claim that the rules are basically unrestricted, from a pragmatic point of view. In word-formation, this is particularly obvious in many languages where the compounding of two nouns and various types of zero-derivation are basically unrestricted processes (see 3.2.). They produce *contextuals*, interpretable with the help of Grice's maxims and our knowledge of the world.[12] These may become institutionalized or lexicalized, and then often combine various types of word-formation and semantic transfer, especially metaphor and metonymy.

Dynamic processes of semantic transfer impose a dual (or even multiple) categorization on extralinguistic reality. This observation can only be accounted for by a dynamic, interdisciplinary theory of semantics which transcends structuralism and includes referents and our perception and cognitive models of the world. For the naive speaker, there is a simple one-to-one correspondence between words and things, or classes of things. Words are simply names for preexisting categories of objects. Philosophers and linguists have long recognized that the relationship between language and extralinguistic reality is far more complex. In 1973, before the advent of Cognitive Linguistics, Ernst Leisi (^{2}1985:13), in the first edition of his *Praxis der englischen Semantik,* first emphasized that languages divide up the same world in different ways, by drawing boundaries between classes of objects differently (see diagram (6) in 2.2.1.). Of course there is a long tradition in the philosophical discussion of this problem, which could be labelled the "Sapir-Whorf-Humboldt-Weissgerber hypothesis" (cf. Lyons 1977:109 ff., 245 ff.; Leech ^{2}1981:26 ff.). Leisi (^{2}1985:13) stresses that: "Die Kategorien der Dinge, Vorgänge, Eigenschaften etc. ... [werden] erst durch die Sprache geschaffen", i.e. that categories only arise through language. Since then, this issue has become fashionable, and much work has been done on the concept of *categorization* by psychologists like Rosch and linguists like Fillmore, Lakoff, and Labov (cf. Rosch 1977, 1978, Lipka 1987a, 1988b, Craig 1986). While Labov, in his research on denotational structure (see 2.2.3.), concentrates on the question of the fuzzy boundaries of linguistic categories, Prototype Semantics focuses on their centre or kernel.

Simple categorization may refer either to the naive view of language, or to the correlation of a single lexeme with one category. In the first sense it

---

[12] See 3.2.5. p. 94. This term was introduced into linguistics in Clark/Clark (1979) and illustrated with examples like *The boy porched the newspaper* ('put it on the porch'), *He Houdinied his way out of the closet* ('escaped like Houdini'), *We were stoned and bottled by the spectators* (a complaint of demonstrators at whom stones and bottles were thrown).

is opposed to philosophical nominalism, in the second one to figurative language or semantic transfer. There is, furthermore, a twofold indeterminateness with lexical categorization (but cf. Schneider 1988:142f.). Referential boundaries may be vague as to where an object ends, e.g. a *mountain* and also about where to draw the line between the categories *mountain* and *hill, cup* and *bowl, green* and *blue, girl* and *woman* (see 2.2.1.). The first indeterminacy gives rise to metonymic semantic shift, for example with names of body parts, where no precise boundaries for the referents of a term exist. The second one is the main concern of Prototype Semantics and Cognitive Linguistics.

Categorization is certainly not simple in either sense of the term mentioned above. Semantic transfer, i.e. figurative use of language, is a widespread phenomenon in natural languages, both synchronically and diachronically. For this, I have proposed the term *dual categorization* in Lipka (1988b). As opposed to the literal meaning of a word (e.g. *rose, dog, house*), a figurative use can be said to impose a second way of categorizing extralinguistic reality.

Metaphor and metonymy, as the central types of semantic transfer, have been neglected to a very large extent in modern linguistics, in particular in works on lexicology and lexical semantics. This was certainly due to a structuralist bias, e.g. in the publications of Coseriu and Marchand, and the consequent ban on considering extralinguistic matters within linguistics. As so often in the history of thought, a neglected field is then rediscovered with great panache. Books and articles on metaphor and metonymy abound, so that I can only mention a few outstanding landmarks. The titel of Paprotté/Dirven's (1985) collection *The Ubiquity of Metaphor* is symptomatic and at least doubly ambiguous. Lakoff/Johnson (1980:41), perhaps the most influential book in the field, argue

> that metaphors and metonyms are not random but instead form coherent systems in terms of which we can conceptualize our experience.

Obviously, by doing so, we categorize the extralinguistic world around and in us. To my mind, Dirven (1985) and Tournier (1985), are the most relevant publications in our context, and perhaps the only ones in the field of English lexicology.

In Lipka (1988b) I have discussed a number of regularities in lexicalized cases of metaphor and metonymy, concentrating on SHAPE, as a semantic dimension responsible for similarity (metaphor), and PLACE, responsible for contiguity (metonymy). Culture-specific cognitive models of the world are shown to be relevant and the productive processes involved can only be accounted for by a dynamic, interdisciplinary theory of semantics. Examples are taken from English, German, and various Romance languages. Body parts and animal metaphors are considered in some detail. Following Leisi's approach in his *Praxis der englischen Semantik*, I have argued that metaphor does often not involve a single semantic feature or 'tertium comparationis', but rather a complete situation, i.e. a 'prototypical scene' (in recent terminology, cf. Verschueren 1981). I will come back to evidence for this position presently, but would like to modify this statement now, in view of the large amount of material analysed in Tournier (1985:199 ff.) to which I shall also return. I believe that this strengthens my argument against an alternative between Feature Semantics and Prototype Semantics (see 3.3.3.) and my plea for an integration of both approaches.

I believe that a further detailed discussion of metaphor and metonymy is justified in view of the long neglect of these matters in English lexicology. Let me therefore return to the problem of 'tertium comparationis', and to some theoretical models for *word metaphors*, which stress the systematic nature of the process and its relationship to the concept of field. Here, semantic transfer is not regarded as unique instances of stylistic tropes on the level of *parole*.

One of the first linguists to make this point quite explicit was Harald Weinrich, in a classic article on "Münze und Wort", originally published in 1958, since reprinted in slightly abridged and edited form in Weinrich (1976:276 ff.). I shall refer to this more accessible source in the following. Weinrich (1976:282 f.) introduces the term *Bildfeld* (i.e. 'image-field', in explicit analogy to *Wortfeld* and *Bedeutungsfeld*) and stresses the point that metaphors must not be seen as isolated phenomena. On the contrary, they relate a "bildspendendes" and a "bildempfangendes Feld", terms which are not equivalent to Richards's *vehicle* and *tenor*. Rather, they emphasize the insight that metaphor is based on certain conceptual and lexical fields, paradigms, or domains. The point is made quite clear (1976:283):

> Wie das Einzelwort ... gehört auch die Einzelmetapher in den Zusammenhang ihres Bildfeldes. Sie ist eine Stelle im Bildfeld.

Weinrich's examples of *Bildfelder* (1976:285) all combine semantic transfer and word-formation, e.g. Ger *Wortmünze, Liebeskrieg, Welttheater, Lebenssaft, Liebesjagd, Tierreich, Verstandeslicht, Textgewebe*. Furthermore, he stresses the point that certain field-correlations exist in Western languages, since there is a common literary tradition, and he thus concludes (1976:287): "Das Abendland ist eine Bildfeldgemeinschaft".

Basically the same point was made much later in Lehrer (1974:110 ff.), where field theory was applied to the "semantic extension" of English temperature words like *hot, warm, cool, cold*. Recently, Lehrer (1985) has again returned to the influence of semantic fields on semantic change, analysing in detail the development of sets of animal metaphors, gambling terms, and the transfer of dimension adjectives to the domain of taste for wine.

Leisi (^{2}1985:188 f.), who summarizes Weinrich's approach, stresses the point that Weinrich has transferred the study of metaphor into the more or less constant domain of the linguistic system. The situational interpretation of metaphor in Leisi (^{2}1985:183 f.) has already been briefly mentioned. He observes that we usually do not have a single 'tertium comparationis', but a complex plurality, because "eine Metapher enthält oft eine ganze Situation". He illustrates this with the comparison of a warrior with a boar in a Middle English poem, and with *crane*, in the sense of 'machine'. Not only is this metaphorical with regard to the shape of the bird's long neck and beak (and I would add, also with regard to their being joined at a particular point) but it furthermore involves typical actions, such as busily going to and fro and picking up things from the ground.

Rephrasing this in modern terminology, we could say that the 'ground' (in the technical sense, see (36)) for the metaphor is a whole prototypical 'scene' involving the bird *crane*. This explanation, in my opinion, would be further strengthened by a number of examples from English, German, and French (cf. Lipka 1988b).

A different kind of to-and-fro movement can be compared to weaving with a loom. This leads to the lexical item *shuttle* (a bus, railway, aeroplane, or spacecraft). In German, this movement is compared to that of a pendulum (*Pendel*), as in *Pendelbus, Pendelzug* 'commuter train', *Pendelverkehr* 'shuttle service', *Pendler* 'commuter', or a child's swing (*Schaukel*), as in *Schaukelbörse*, literally 'swing-stockmarket'. Movement[13] similar to that of a ship is certainly responsible, but not alone, for Ger *Wüstenschiff* (cf. E *ship of the desert*, for a camel, probably from Arabic). This lexicalized word metaphor evokes a complex situation, in which the desert is further compared to the sea through which the camel ploughs (another metaphor!), like a ship through the waves. In addition, camels were for centuries the only possible form of long-distance travel in the desert. In French the wide exit passages of a Roman theatre or amphitheatre are called *vomitoire* (E *vomitory* is not as common), which evokes the prototypical scene of spewing out people.

Perhaps the best example of a complete scene being visualized is the *bombardier beetle*. The COD explanation (not definition) "audibly releasing unpleasant vapour when alarmed" is not quite adequate. If you have once seen and heard in a documentary film how the little insect uses its body like a cannon when in danger, aiming with extraordinary precision, you will never forget the scene. With its use of a chemical weapon it is really like a bombardier. It can direct and aim and follow a shifting goal like a gun. It then mixes two liquids in its body, which explode with considerable noise and leave a noticeable mark very close to the goal. Obviously, we here have a very complex plurality and situation which cannot be adequately rendered by the metaphorical transfer of a single semantic feature.

Nevertheless, exactly this is possible in many other cases, as demonstrated in Tournier (1985 : 239 ff.) on the basis of a large list of English lexemes, including some contrastive observations on French. Thus, animal metaphors are highly culture-specific. While in English the *camel* may be a symbol of submission and endurance, in Franch malice is attributed to it. While one of the characteristics of a *pig* in English is egoism, this is not so in the French culture. Tournier also gives the example of *vache*, 'cow', the sacred animal in India, but the symbol for the policeman (stupid and vicious) in France. One

[13] As G. Pascoe points out, Ger *Weberknechte*, in England called *harvestmen* (because they mature in late summer), are not related to a specific movement, but probably to shape and habitat. Shape is also responsible for the names of the rather leggy flies called *crane-flies* or *daddy-long-legs*, equivalent to Ger *Schneider* (where weight also plays a role).

might add that the *dragon* has very different characteristics attributed to it in Western and Chinese culture.

Generally speaking, Tournier (1985:232) distinguishes four categories of metaphor according to four general classes of semantic features ("classèmes"), which can be further subdivided, yielding 16 types of metaphor altogether. He also points out (1985:293f.), in the tradition of Roman Jakobson, that the fundamental distinction between metaphor and metonymy is a psychological reality, because it can be related to two widespread types of aphasic disorders. These, in turn, are closely connected with the distinction between paradigmatic and syntagmatic relations in language. Thus, in the so-called "similarity disorder", where the ability for selection and substitution is impaired (corresponding to the paradigmatic access), the patient has recourse to metonymy, saying e.g. *fork* for *knife*. Conversely, in the case of "contiguity disorder" (affecting syntagmatic relations), the patient has recourse to metaphoric substitution, saying e.g. *spy glass* for *microscope*. This seems to prove that metaphor and metonymy, as fundamentally distinct lexical processes, are based on different mental or psychological processes.[14]

Tournier admits that in some rare cases the distinction between metaphor and metonymy may be difficult to draw or to verify. What is more important, however, is his observation that the two processes are very often combined, which he illustrates with the example *egghead*. This is said to imply one metaphor (*egg* – dome of bald head), and two metonymies (baldness – intellectual and *egghead* – egg-headed man). I would like to add that word-formation processes are obviously also involved and combined.

This brings us back to the general question of various types of semantic shift and change, also from a diachronic point of view. Tournier (1985:200) distinguishes two kinds which he calls: 1. "mutation par rayonnement", and 2. "mutation par enchaînement". The first type, which could be translated as *radial shift* or *radiation shift*, is illustrated by *head* with the first or central meaning or sememe (S_1) 'upper part of human body'. From this sense, or sememe, eight other senses (S_2 – S_9) can be directly derived as represented in diagram (39):

---

[14] Cf. the discussion of the different "types of link" in our mental lexicon in Aitchison (1987:74f., 194ff.). "Metaphorical extension" is also treated in detail in Lyons (1977:263f., 548ff.), who argues for accounting for it "in terms of strategies", since it is "a normal process in the everyday use of language" (1977:549), but prefers to use the term *metaphor* to include metonymy. For the position of Cognitive Linguistics cf. Lakoff (1987:271ff., 276ff.), who postulates "kinesthetic image schemas", especially the "CONTAINER schema", and deals with the "experiential bases of metaphors" and "cognitive models", including "metaphoric and metonymic models".

(39) S_2: 'seat of intellect'.
S_3: 'life (cf. 'it cost him his head')'.
S_4: 'image of head on one side of coin'.
S_5: 'knobbed end of nail'.
S_6: 'foam on top of liquor'.
S_7: 'top of page'.
S_8: 'fully developed part of boil'.
S_9: 'end of table occupied by host' ...

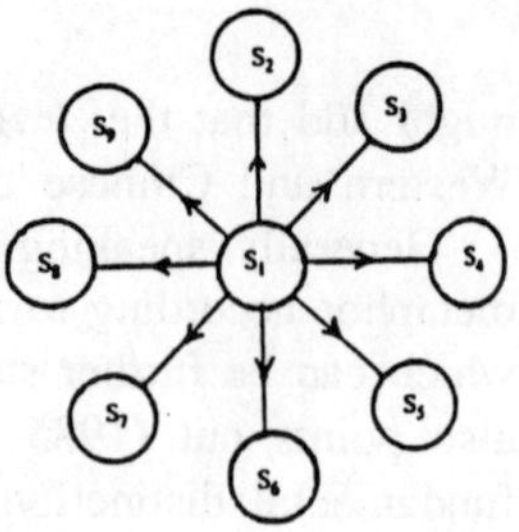

In the second type, perhaps best labelled *chaining shift*, one sense or sememe S_1 leads to the formation of sense, or sememe, S_2, and in turn to S_3, S_4 etc., thus each new sense deriving immediately from the preceding one. This can be represented as follows:[15]

(40)

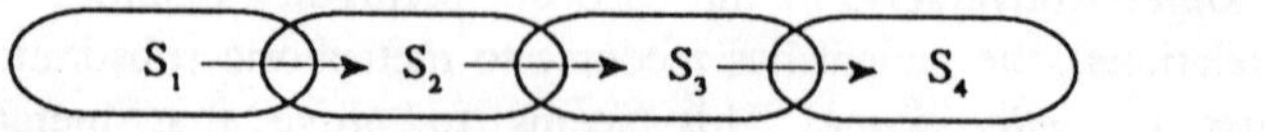

Tournier gives the example *volume*, with S_1 'roll of parchment', from which is derived S_2 'book tome', and in turn S_3 'size, bulk of a book', and S_4 'size, bulk of other things'. Tournier points out that S_1, obviously, has disappeared, and that with this type of chaining the motivation for the semantic shift often gets lost, and that of course the two kinds of semantic shift represented in (39) and (40) may obviously be combined in various ways.

As my final example from Tournier (1985: 207) and as an illustration of the combination of semantic shift and figurative language (metaphor and metonymy), I would like to introduce his analysis of the development of the various senses, or sememes, of *tea*. I have adopted his representation to English in (41), with the exception of the lexeme *le thé*, and have added further examples.

(41) TEA

A. Sense involving "le thé"	B. Sense not involving "le thé"
1. plant, shrub	
2. (dried, shredded) leaves of shrub	
3. beverage made by infusion of leaves ⟶	4. beverage made by infusion of leaves of other plants (e.g. *camomile tea*)
↓	↓
6. meal which consists of this beverage, cakes etc. (e.g. *afternoon tea, high tea*)	5. beverage not made of plants (e.g. *beef tea*)

---

15 From a synchronic point of view, diagram (40) could also be used as an excellent visual representation of Wittgenstein's concept of *family resemblances* (cf. Aitchison 1987: 47 ff.). The category denoted by the word *game* (ranging from cards, chess, tennis, to ring-a-roses) has no single common semantic element (e.g. skill or luck) but is related through chaining like the members of a family (e.g. by build, features, colour of eyes, gait, temperament). This also holds for other categories, like *furniture, vegetable* etc.

According to Tournier senses 1., 2., and 3. are instances of semantic shift (or shift in application), 4. and 5. instances of metaphorical polysemy, and 6. of metonymic polysemy. I would rather say that 1. is the original sense, and the shifts to 2. and 3. are classic cases of metonymy. This also holds for the shift to 6., while the change from 3. to 4. and from 4. to 5. are instances of the second figurative semantic process, namely of metaphor.

In my view, example (41) can furthermore serve as a good demonstration of language-dependent categorization. French *thé* is a narrower category then E *tea* or Ger *Tee*. The two senses, or sememes of E *tea* unter B can never be denoted by Fr *thé*. Other lexemes such as Fr *infusion, tisane, verveine*, come into play here.

This brings our discussion of lexical rules, semantic processes, in particular metaphor and metonymy, and categorization to a close. We have seen that all these phenomena are extremely important for a better understanding of the lexicon, both from a synchronic and a diachronic point of view. And we have seen again that both Prototype Semantics and Feature Semantics are necessary for a full understanding of the observable facts. The dynamic, interdisciplinary perspective can account for productivity, lexicalization, and language– and culture–dependent categorization. Prototypes, as well as the distinction between metaphor and metonymy, as the central processes of semantic transfer, have psychological reality. There is clear evidence that these two fundamental productive semantic processes depend on the equally fundamental distinction between paradigmatic and syntagmatic relations in language, to which we will now turn.

Chapter IV

The Structure of the Lexicon. Relations between Words

4.1. Units, Classes, and Relations

The lexicon, as the structured word-store of a language, consists of certain units which are related to each other in a twofold way. At the very beginning of this book, in diagram (4) (p. 12), I illustrated the fundamental distinction between syntagmatic and paradigmatic relationships in the lexicon. It was pointed out that the distinction between the two axes – the linear, horizontal one and the vertical one (which Saussure called associative) – can be found on all levels of language, from the smallest phonological units down to the level of extended texts.

In the following, we will first look at the nature of the units and introduce the new concept of *lexical unit*, as a technical term (4.1.1.). After reviewing various types of classes (4.1.2.), as possible generalizations, we will consider at length paradigmatic relations between words, lexemes, or lexical units (4.2.), and then discuss various approaches to the problem of syntagmatic relations (4.3.).

4.1.1. Lexical Entry and Lexical Unit

Before we can tackle the question of paradigmatic lexical relations, we must revise the simple, binary model of the linguistic sign introduced by Saussure and see what more technical, formalized characterizations of lexemes have been given in various linguistic theories. For the moment, we leave aside the question of the unity of the word, the distinction between homonymy and polysemy (see 4.2.1.), and the relationship between its different meanings or sememes. A formal specification of the various phonological, morphological, syntactic, and semantic properties of a word is commonly referred to by the term *lexical entry* (cf. Bauer 1983:190 ff., Kastovsky 1982a: 248 f., Lipka 1972: 37 ff.).

We have already encountered a very simple type of lexical entry in diagram (34) (p. 121) in connection with the general formulation of lexical rules given by Leech. Obviously, the three variables *p, q, r* used there do not specify the phonological properties of a lexeme, unless "morphological specification" is meant to include this. On the other hand, a schematic representation of a lexical entry like that given in Lyons (1977: 517) makes an explicit distinction between "inflectional class" and "syntactic properties", which apparently fall together in the variable *q* used by Leech. Lyons thus distinguishes within a lexical entry:

1. stem(s), 2. inflectional class, 3. syntactic properties, and 4. semantic specification(s).

If we conflated the two schemata and furthermore added the distinction between the spoken and the written medium, we would be forced to distinguish six variables: phonological, graphemic, morphological, inflectional, syntactic, and semantic properties. Many adjectives and especially verbs would need a seventh specification concerning the syntagmatic relations with other lexical items. In fact, Bauer (1983:196) gives a schema containing seven types of specification (with further subclassification) which does not, however, include syntagmatic restrictions, but explicitly mentions stylistic properties. What is more important, in our context, is his recognition of the relational nature of the term *lexical entry*. This becomes apparent in his distinct treatment (1983:190ff.) of lexical entries for "a simplex lexeme", "an affix", "a lexicalized complex form", and "institutionalized words". It will become clear presently that an even finer distinction is needed.

As discussed in Lipka (1972:37ff.), simple and more refined lexical entries were given, in the various strands of generative grammar, for items like *sincerity, boy, frighten, eat, chase, persuade,* and *kill.* In connction with Case Grammar, the question arose as to whether the adjective, the intransitive verb, and the transitive verb *open* were to be given a single lexical entry, a suggestion also made for *break* and *cook*, independently of their different environment or "case frame". The presence or absence of an Agent case clearly corresponds to the addition or subtraction of an atomic predicate CAUSE (cf. Lipka 1976:126f.), and the inchoative and causative *open* and *break* obviously differ in meaning like *die* and *kill.* This also holds for the ambiguity of derived verbs like *blacken, harden, redden, soften, thicken, solidify,* and *liquefy* (cf. Lipka 1982:10f.). Do we therefore assign them two lexical entries? What about the stock example *bachelor* and its "readings" or "paths" such as 'who has never married', 'fur seal when without a mate during the breeding time', etc. (cf. Kastovsky 1982a:248f., Fodor 1980:151f.)? Katz/Fodor (1963) explicitly labelled this hierarchic structure a "dictionary entry". Is *fox* with the meanings 'small, dog-like, wild animal' and 'person who deceives others' to be given one or two lexical entries?

In other words, the question really is whether we set up lexical entries for a lexeme or a unit smaller than the lexeme. This is closely related to the problems of the definition of *lexeme* (see 2.3.3.) and the tricky business of distinguishing between *polysemy* and *homonymy* (see 4.2.1.). At this point we must draw on a distinction first explicitly made in Cruse (1986:49), namely that between a *lexeme* and a *lexical unit.* Cruse (1986:76f.) defines the *lexical unit* as "the union of a lexical form and a single sense" and the *lexeme* as "a family of lexical units". For him, the *lexeme* is the appropriate unit for the lexicographer, since dictionaries contain an alphabetical list of the lexemes of a language. He defines *sense* as "the meaning aspect of a lexical unit" (1986:49). Cruse (1986:84) rightly claims that "semantic relations" (i.e. the *sense-relations* in the terminology of Lyons), which Cruse describes in detail in chapters 4–12 of his book, "hold between lexical units", not between lexemes. I will follow this terminological usage, namely the distinction between *lexeme* and *lexical unit*, in the remainder of my book.

It has to be noted here that the introduction of the concept *lexical unit* (although within the restricted technical language of linguistics) is itself an illustration of the concept-forming power of the word (see 4.4.1.). Many linguists (e.g. Hansen et al. ²1985, Gläser 1986, Schneider 1988) make a clear distinction between the *seme* (or semantic feature) and the *sememe*, defined as a complex or configuration of semes, which corresponds to a single sense of a lexeme. Sometimes the complete meaning of a lexeme is called a *semanteme*. However, up to Cruse (1986) a precise term was missing in lexicology and lexical semantics for the combination of a specific form with a single sense, i.e. a full linguistic sign in Saussure's sense. In the following we will distinguish two *lexical units* for example in the case of inchoative and causative verbs, or the literal and figurative meaning of a noun.[1] Thus, there are clearly two distinct *lexical units* $break_1$ 'BECOME NOT WHOLE' and $break_2$ 'CAUSE BECOME NOT WHOLE' and fox_1 'animal ...' and fox_2 'person ...'. Obviously, the introduction of the notion *lexical unit* has serious consequences for the distinction between homonymy and polysemy (see 4.2.1.). It must be recognized, however, that paradigmatic as well as syntagmatic relations between words are a matter of *lexical units*, not of *lexemes*.

4.1.2. Word Classes and Semantic Classes

In the preceding section of chapter IV we have looked at the units of the lexicon at various levels: the lexeme and the lexical unit. Before considering paradigmatic and syntagmatic relations between lexical units, we must briefly return to the overall structure of the lexicon and the possibilities of its organization (see 1.2.). The traditional approach of dictionaries, which give alphabetical lists of lexemes, is clearly insufficient and unstructured, and the alternative solution of presenting linguistic knowledge in the form of a thesaurus, e.g. *ROGET's Thesaurus* or the *Longman Lexicon of Contemporary*

---

[1] See 3.3.1. for the discussion of the lexical decomposition of verbs in Generative Semantics. In Lipka (1982: 9, 13) I have argued that there are basically two possibilities of interpreting causatives and inchoatives like *break, open, cook, dry, melt, burn* etc.: 1. as two distinct (possibly zero-derived, in/transitive) verbs, and 2. a single, contextually determined item, as in Case Grammar or in the sense of Clark/Clark's *contextuals*. Cruse (1986: 77 ff.) postulates two criteria for assigning 'lexical units' to the same 'lexeme': 1. the existence of a rule, which predicts recurrent semantic contrasts between 'senses', e.g. in *brilliant, sad* (person/book), *dog* (unmarked/male), *dry up, flatten out* (inchoative/transferred, as in *After Kendal, the countryside begins to flatten out*); and 2. "belonging to the same sense-spectrum", as with the various literal and metaphorical senses of *mouth*.

English, also has its drawbacks (cf. McArthur 1986: 120f., 148ff.).[2]

At the beginning of this book (p. 10f.), diagrams (2) and (3) were given, which represent the structure of the vocabulary of English and a general schema (Coseriu's) for the structure of the lexicon. Two alternative ways of structuring the lexicon of any language (if it is recognized that alphabetical listing is merely a convenient means of retrieval) would be its division into word classes (traditionally called "parts of speech") and into semantic classes. We shall look at both in turn.

In the various German versions of Coseriu's schematic representation of "lexematic structures" (cf. Coseriu/Geckeler 1981: 56), primary structures are subdivided into "Wortfelder" on the one hand and "klassematische Strukturen" or "Wortklassen" on the other. The latter, termed "lexical classes" in the English version (Coseriu/Geckeler 1981), are not to be confused with *word classes* (in the above sense). We will return to this presently. First, a brief discussion of "parts of speech". We will start with a simplified summary of the treatment in Quirk et al. (1985: 77ff.). The following categories of words can be distinguished in English:

(1) (a) CLOSED CLASSES: preposition, pronoun, determiner, conjunction, auxiliary verb
(b) OPEN CLASSES: noun, adjective, verb, adverb
(c) LESSER CATEGORIES: numeral, interjection

Category (a) is often referred to as *function words*, because of their grammatical function.[3] Traditional lexicology, however, is almost exclusively concerned with category (b); but dictionaries normally include (a) and (c). Category (b) is often called "major word classes", content words (contentives), or lexical items. Nouns, adjectives, verbs and adverbs may be further subclassified, according to various criteria. The non-hierarchic nature of the so-called "strict subcategorization" was an important problem for generative grammar, which was tackled with the help of the notion *cross-classification* and formalized with "syntactic features", taken over from phonology. It has long been recognized in linguistics (cf. Lipka 1971: esp. 234f.) that the major word classes have central and peripheral members, partly overlap, are characterized by certain formal elements (labelled "designators" by Crystal in 1967), and may be subclassified according to (weighted) phonological, graphemic, morphological,

---

[2] It is true that good dictionaries differentiate metaphorical, metonymic, and other related lexical units by means of numbers and/or letters (and the respective usage labels, e.g. *AmE apprec sl* for *fox* 4) and may even give cross-references to semantically related items (s.v. *fox, bachelor* – with reference to *spinster* –, *chair* in LDCE 2 and OALD 4). They also often include collocations, idioms, and sometimes explicit mention, under one lexeme, of items related through word-formation processes (OALD 4). However, alphabetical order may disrupt such structuring, e.g. when *charger*$_1$ 'a soldier's horse' is separated from *charge*$_1$ (verb) ... 3 'to rush (as if) in an attack', inter alia by *charge*$_2$ (noun), *charge account, chargé d'affaires,* and *charge nurse* in LDCE 2.

[3] See 2.3.1. and Jackson (1988: 15, 17) for the distinction between 'lexical words' and 'grammatical words'.

syntactic, semantic, and notional criteria (cf. Jackson 1988:17).

Recently, the parallelism between the fuzzy boundaries of grammatical classes (and thus of items of the metalanguage like *noun* and *verb*), and of words generally has been noted. Consequently, the notion of 'prototype' was applied also to word classes. Leech et al. (1982:26) compare the prototypes of *chair* and *bird* to the prototypical *noun* and *verb* and explicitly state that

> just as some chairs are less 'chairy' than others, and just as some birds are less 'birdy' than others, so some nouns are less 'nouny' than others, and some verbs less 'verby' than others.

The fuzziness of word classes is an obstacle for any attempt to structure the lexicon neatly, on the basis of such distinctions. Furthermore, the division of the entire vocabulary into the three categories (a), (b), (c) in diagram (1) – with special focus on the open classes and their finer subcategorization – would only result in a very global structuring. Finally, such a categorization would capture neither the morphological relations, nor the very essential semantic relations within the lexicon.

Semantic classes are a second alternative to dictionaries and thesauruses. Coseriu's "lexical classes" are "classematic structures" since they group together sets of words on the basis of their common classeme (i.e. very general features), e.g. 'living being', 'non-living being', 'person', 'transitive', 'intransitive' (cf. Coseriu/Geckeler 1981:59). Hansen et al. (^{2}1985:18 f., 221 ff.) also point out that words may be grouped together – on the basis of specific semantic components – into semantic classes like abstracts, persons, states, animals, but also according to other principles. They further distinguish two types of "paradigms" ("Wortbildungsparadigmen" and "semantische Paradigmen"), which are said to structure the lexicon in a systematic way since semantic classes alone are (indeed!) not easy to grasp ("unüberschaubar") and a grouping according to subject matter ("Sachgruppen") is boundless. We have dealt with word-formation in 3.2. and the second type of "paradigm" will be discussed here under the heading of *lexical fields* (see 4.2.4.).

4.2. Paradigmatic Relations

At the beginning of this book (see 1.1.) we reviewed the fundamental distinction between syntagmatic and paradigmatic relations on various levels of language. In diagrams (3) and (4) of chapter I, we distinguished – on the level of the lexicon – between paradigmatic and syntagmatic *lexical relations*. These were defined as relations between lexical items which are not necessarily *semantic relations*. Not all possible semantic relations between elements of the lexicon, however, are also *sense-relations* (in the sense introduced by Lyons in 1968) (see 4.2.3.). I will try to clarify these distinctions by drawing on the concept of the binary sign as defined by Saussure (see 2.1.). Basically, there are four possibilities of paradigmatic relations between pairs of linguistic signs:

1. Their *signifiant*, the phonological or graphemic form, is identical, the *signifié*, the meaning, is different and unrelated. In this case, the two signs, or lexical items, are traditionally called *homonyms* and the relation between them is labelled *homonymy*. If the meaning is partly identical, one also speaks of *polysemy*, or *multiple meaning*. The distinction between these two relations will be discussed in detail in 4.2.1.
2. The reverse is given when the *signifiant* is different, but the *signifiés* are almost identical. Such a relation has for a long time been called *synonymy*. Modern linguists believe that there is no perfect or total synonymy.

A further theoretical possibility for paradigmatic relations between signs is that both the *signifiant* and the *signifié* are different. Depending on the various relations between the contents of such signs, further distinctions are usually made. If the relation is one of oppositeness, one traditionally speaks of *antonymy*. An inclusion relation between the meanings, which corresponds to a hierarchic relation between the signs, is today normally labelled *hyponymy*. This term was coined in 1963 by Lyons and introduced into modern linguistics.

3. *Antonymy*, in the wider sense (for a more restricted use see 4.2.3.3.), is a paradigmatic relation between signs whose content is different but undoubtedly related. The meanings of such signs are opposed in various ways (cf. Mettinger 1988).
4. In the case of *hyponymy* the relationship between the contents is of a different kind, not one of oppositeness. In this case, the signs are related in a hierarchic order. The subordinate lexical item is called *hyponym*, the other one *hyperonym*, or (less confusingly) *superordinate (term)*, or *archilexeme*. Such hierarchic relations lead to the postulation of one type of *lexical field*.

Only the last three types of paradigmatic relations, synonymy, antonymy and hyponymy, are semantic relations between full signs (or more precisely between lexical units). Lyons (1968, 1977) has treated these under the label *sense-relations*. The first type of paradigmatic relation, homonymy, is not a meaning-relation or semantic relation between signs, lexical items, or lexical units. In the case of homonymy there is no relation whatsoever between the contents. On the other hand, polysemy too is not a paradigmatic sense-relation between lexical items, because we have a single lexeme and we can have no relations between one and the same lexeme. However, we may well discuss the relationship between different *lexical units* within a lexeme. The more serious question, on the other hand, which has troubled linguists for a long time, is how we can distinguish between homonymy and polysemy. We will now turn to this subject.

4.2.1. Homonymy versus Polysemy

The topic has already been touched on in 3.1. Criteria for the distinction which have been used by various linguists are thoroughly examined in Lipka (1986b).

Some linguists have also changed their mind over the years. Thus, Lyons (1968 : 406) claimed that

> the distinction between homonymy and multiple meaning is, in the last resort, indeterminate and arbitrary.

In Lyons (1977: 554) he argues that it is preferable

> to maximize polysemy. This will have the effect of producing a lexicon with far fewer entries than are to be found in our standard dictionaries.

One of his reasons for this change of position is the greater frequency of polysemy, compared to homonymy. More importantly, he argues (1977: 567) that polysemy is the result of metaphorical creativity of natural languages, and that this creativity is essential for the functioning of languages as efficient semiotic systems.

In order to distinguish one word with several meanings (i.e. polysemy or multiple meaning) from two different words with unrelated meanings (i.e. homonymy) basically three types of criteria have been used in research: 1. etymology, 2. formal identity or distinctness, and 3. close semantic relatedness. Also, various tests have been proposed, but it is not always clear what is actually being tested. In view of the importance of the problem and the consequences for distinguishing between words, lexemes, and lexical units, we will discuss the various criteria in some detail. This is also relevant for the understanding of zero-derivation, metaphor, and metonymy (see 4.2.2.) and our treatment of sense-relations (see 4.2.3.).

We will take up the criterion of etymology first. For ease of reference, it is useful to adopt a convention normally followed by dictionaries, which often distinguish words which are spelled identically, but belong to a different word class, by raised numbers. In order not to confuse these with the numbers of footnotes, it is better, however, to write them below the word as subscripts. *Ear*$_1$ 'organ of hearing' and *ear*$_2$ 'head of corn' are distinguished as homonyms, because they were formally distinct in Old English and thus have a different etymology. Consequently, they are treated as two separate words or lexemes in present-day English dictionaries. Following this argument, we would have to treat *flower* 'part of plant' and *flour* 'powder made by crushing grain' as a single, polysemous word with two meanings. The reason for this is that they are etymologically identical, since both go back to the same Middle English word *flour*. In spite of the different spelling, both are also identically pronounced. Lyons (1977: 550 f.) points out that also *port*$_1$ 'harbour' and *port*$_2$ 'fortified wine' – which are certainly considered as two words by most speakers – would have to be treated as polysemous, since ultimately they both derive from Latin *portus*. Wen can add a number of pairs of words with the same origin, which can demonstrate that etymology cannot be a decisive criterion. Thus, *glamour* and *grammar, person* and *parson, shirt* and *skirt* have a common source. Further well-known pairs in the history of English are: *catch* and *chase*, *mint* and *money*, and *inch* and *ounce*. It is furthermore true that the speaker of a language does not normally possess any etymological knowledge. In any case, this is irrelevant for a purely synchronic semantic analysis of English. From all this we conclude that etymology cannot be a useful criterion for distinguishing between homonymy and polysemy.

The second possible criterion is formal identity or distinctness of a linguistic sign. This must be further differentiated, although this is often not done. We must distinguish between the spoken and the written medium and also consider morphological and syntactic aspects. Hansen et al. (^{2}1985: 201) speak of complete homonymy ("vollständige Homonymie") only in the case of spoken, written, and grammatical identity of two signs. Traditionally, a further distinction is made between *homophony* and *homography*, as illustrated in the following diagram:

(2) homonymy vs. polysemy (= multiple meaning)

homophony		homography	
flower	: *flour*	*read*	: *read*
led	: *lead*	[i:]	[e]
[e]	[e]		

Flower and *flour* are homophonous signs, as well as *led* (past participle) and *lead* (noun), or *red* 'colour' and *read* (past participle). On the other hand, the infinitive *read* and the past tense and past participle of the same verb are only spelt the same way but pronounced differently. For this reason they are examples of homography. It must be mentioned, however, that the distinction illustrated in (2) is often not made and that the terms *homonym* and *homonymous* are frequently used in their wider sense, not only for complete homonymy.

The following is meant as an illustration of a clear case of complete homonymy. The identical form *bat* clearly has two different meanings and can therefore be assigned to two separate lexemes as in the following diagram:

(3) *bat*

1. 'a specially shaped stick for hitting the ball in cricket etc.' = BAT$_1$
2. 'a flying mouselike animal' = BAT$_2$

Obviously, there does not exist any semantic relationship between the two meanings or *signifiés*. The fact that in both cases we have countable nouns with a very general feature [+CONCRETE] or [-ABSTRACT] is irrelevant. Agreement in such an extremely common element of meaning is not an essential condition for assuming a single polysemous lexeme. We will return to the question of the necessary requirements for the close semantic relatedness of senses of a polysemous lexeme.

At this point, in connection with the sameness of the *signifiant*, an aspect of the formal identity must be mentioned which is neglected in all treatments of polysemy I know of. This is the formal distinctiveness of the *signifiant*, als already briefly touched on in 3.1., when *bachelor* and *cup* were compared. Monosyllabic words like *cup* and *cub* are not as formally distinct as complex lexemes like *topless* (cf. Cruse 1986: 49 f.), or *amphitheatre*, verb-particle combinations like *fall out, eat up* (which also have very specific syntactic properties), or hard words of Latin and Greek origin, like *vomitory, pedestrian,* or *hetero-paronymy* (coined by Cruse). Establishing the formal unity of word like *supercalifragilistic-expialidocious* (used in the musical *Mary Poppins*) is on a very different level from that of *bank* or *open*.

But even with monosyllabic words (as opposed to polysyllabic ones), different morphological and syntactic properties will lead to the postulation of separate lexemes. We can clearly distinguish between can_1, can_2, and can_3 because we have a modal auxiliary in one case, a noun in the second, and a transitive verb with the meaning 'put into a can' in the third case. Can_3 can be interpreted as a zero-derivation from the noun can_2 (see 4.2.2.). Thus, different word class and meaning must lead to the distinction of homonymous lexemes.[4]

To return to polysemy, let us look at the third criterion, close semantic relatedness. How much semantic overlap is required to decide on a single lexeme with different senses, i.e. on a family of *lexical units?* Hansen et al. ([2]1985: 202) speak of a "relativ engen Zusammenhang zwischen den Sememen" and opt for polysemy in two cases: 1. Semantic inclusion or hyponymy, and 2. semantic transfer, i.e. metaphor and metonymy. I will here adopt this delimitation of polysemy and will use the notation introduced above, distinguishing lexical units and lexemes by means of subscripts. Thus, the lexeme MAN_1 can be said to contain the lexical units, man_1 'human being' (Ger *Mensch*), man_2 'adult male human being' (Ger *Mann*), but not MAN_2 'to furnish with men' (Ger *bemannen*). Within the lexeme FOX we can distinguish fox_1 'wild animal', fox_2 'person as crafty as a fox', and fox_3 'fur of fox'. In the discussion of the distinction between polysemy and homonymy, psychological criteria have also been used, i.e. subjective association, for determining semantic relatedness. However, this is a different kind of relatedness. If a single speaker decides whether we have one word with two meanings or two different words,

---

[4] As in Lipka (1986b: 134), I here argue that the noun can_2 with the word-forms *can*, singular, and *cans*, plural) and the verb *to* can_3 (with the inflectional forms *he cans, canned*) constitute two homonymous lexemes in spite of the common meaning 'closed metal container'. Zero-derivation is an instance of 'lexeme-formation', and thus differs from the creation of new 'lexical units' by metaphor and metonymy. Basically, homonymy and polysemy are not absolute opposites, and total homonymy must be seen as the end-point of a continuum of degrees of formal and semantic relatedness and difference (cf. Lipka 1986b: 137, but also Lipka 1990 for parallels between word-formation and semantic transfer, namely metaphor and metonymy).

this is certainly not an objective procedure. Of course one could also use statistically relevant tests with a large number of informants to reduce the dangers of subjective intuition.

Tests of another kind for semantic relatedness are discussed in Kastovsky (1982a: 123). He claims that we must decide in favour of homonymy in three cases:

1. If two meanings of the same form belong to different lexical fields, they have to be treated as homonyms. An example is Fr *voler*$_1$ 'fly', which belongs to the field of movement verbs, and *voler*$_2$ 'steal', which does not.
2. Membership in different word-formation families ("Wortbildungsfamilien") is a second objective criterion. Thus, *man*$_1$ (Ger *Mensch)* is related to the compound *mankind.* On the other hand *man*$_2$ (Ger *Mann)* is related to *manly, manhood, to manØ,* and *to unmanØ.*
3. The third criterion is the coordination test. Thus, from the unacceptability of **He saw many fair girls and games* we must conclude that there are two homonymous adjectives *fair.*

We have seen in the discussion above that it is often not easy to distinguish clearly between homonymy and polysemy. I hope it has become clear that they are not absolute opposites, and that there are various degrees of formal and semantic unity. Thus they must be regarded as the two end-points of a scale with a continuum in between. There is certainly not a single criterion for drawing the line, but we must combine various criteria and tests in order to determine the degree of relatedness and difference in form and meaning.

To my knowledge, this was expressed explicitly for the first time in Cowie (1982:51), where we read:

> Polysemous words can differ considerably according to the degree of relatedness and difference which their meanings display ... homonymy (total distinctness of the meaning of identical forms) is properly seen as the end-point of the continuum.

From the point of view of the productivity of language and the psychological reality of human categorization (see 3.4.2.) we must support Lyons's decision to maximize polysemy. This solution is also most sensible from a historical point of view as Tournier (1985:199) clearly demonstrates. Furthermore, he rightly stresses the fact that polysemy is an eminently economical phenomenon, and that speech communities which did not use metaphor and metonymy would lack imagination, the ability to perceive analogies and to establish rational associations. He concludes that polysemy belongs to the properties which distinguish human language from animal communication.

4.2.2. Zero-Derivation and Word Metaphors

In 3.2.2. we have discussed zero-derivatives in connection with morphological structure and suffixal derivatives. Here we shall consider them briefly in comparison with word metaphors (see 3.4.2.). From our conclusions in 4.2.1. we can see that the latter must be interpreted as different lexical units belonging to the same lexeme. Zero-derivation, however, produces new lexemes with a different (though related) meaning and superficially identical, but grammatically distinct form, belonging to another word class. This can be illustrated with the following examples:

(4)	(a)	*tick*$_1$ 'parasitic insect'	→ *tick*$_2$ 'annoying person'[5]	= lexical units
	(b)	*tick*$_3$ 'sound of a clock or watch'	→ *tick*$_4$ / Ø, verb 'make ticking sounds'	= homonyms
	(c)	*tick*$_5$ 'a mark in a list'	→ *tick*$_6$ / Ø, verb 'mark with a tick'	= homonyms

The literal and figurative nouns *tick* in (4a) are two lexical units within the same polysemous lexeme. The verbs in (4b) and (4c) are derived by zero-derivation from the respective nouns and therefore homonyms. The three nouns in (4) are also homonymous lexemes, since they are semantically unrelated.

From the point of view of productivity, the two processes of derivation are very similar, and as we have seen in 3.4.2., word-formation and semantic transfer are often combined. We could therefore regard word metaphors and metonyms as the result of a special type of derivation, which might be labelled "semantic" or "inner derivation" (cf. Lipka 1986b: 134 f.). A further parallelism between word-formation and metaphorical and metonymic derivation is that the results of all three processes may be equally affected by lexicalization (cf. Lipka 1990). Having recognized that there is no sharp borderline between homonymy and polysemy, it is nevertheless advisable to include zero-derivation with homonymy, since there are clear grammatical differences (word class) and there is also the close parallelism with overt suffixal derivatives as illustrated in diagram (7) in 3.2.2.

4.2.3. Lexical Relations, Sense-Relations, and Lexical Semantics

We have already mentioned that lexical relations are not necessarily semantic relations and that lexical semantics is not exclusively relational. This caveat is not true for all approaches to semantics (see 2.2.2.), however. In particular, it must be stressed here that especially the semantic theory developed by Lyons since 1963, and also the type of lexical semantics propounded in Cruse (1986) – a book firmly based on Lyons's theory, but cast in rather idiosyncratic terminology – are fundamentally and also exclusively relational. To be fair, Cruse also draws on semantic features (which he calls "semantic traits"), and even mentions prototypes, but the bulk of his book (chapters 4–12) deals with

---

[5] *Tick*$_2$ is listed in LDCE 1 as *BrE infml* 'an annoying or worthless fellow' and in OALD 4 als *Brit sl* 'unpleasant or contemptible person'.

lexical relations such as hyponymy, hierarchies, part-whole relations (termed "meronomies"), opposites, and synonymy.

Incidentally Lyons has become increasingly sceptical, over the years, about componential analysis and critical of all metalinguistic meaning elements. In Cruse's book especially, the three types of opposites originally introduced into linguistics in Lyons (1968) – and then further subclassified and elaborated in Lyons (1977) – are re-classified and analysed in great detail.

In order to understand the situation, and also because lexical relations are so important within lexical semantics, we must have a closer look at the development of what Lyons termed *sense-relations*. It must be kept in mind, however, that these are only a special kind of both semantic relations and lexical relations, and that they do not at all cover the whole field of lexical semantics. Also, I would like to emphasize here that it is not true that sense-relations do hold only between the meanings of linguistic signs (as in Coseriu's theory; cf. Coseriu/Geckeler 1981:54, Kastovsky 1982a:25), or between lexemes as complete signs (as claimed by Lyons), but exclusively between *lexical units* (as the combination of a form with a single sense).

For Lyons neither homonymy nor polysemy are sense-relations. In his introduction to linguistics (1968:428) he defines the "sense of a lexical item" as

> the whole set of *sense-relations* ... which it contracts with other items

and explicitly recognizes that the items may be paradigmatically or syntagmatically related. In the following, he only deals with paradigmatic relations, which I will sketch presently. These are established – on the basis of logical relationships – between "lexical items" that are substituted for each other in the same syntactic slot of sentences. The main relations set up in 1968 are summarized in the following diagram:

(5) *sense-relations*:

1. synonymy : *rich* – *wealthy*
2. hyponymy : *flower* – *tulip*
3. oppositeness (= 'antonymy' in wider sense) :
   a) complementarity: *male/female*
   b) antonymy: *good/bad*
   c) converseness: *buy/sell*

At this point I would only like to make a few explanatory remarks. I will return to the five relations in detail presently. 'Synonymy', although defined on a logical basis, corresponds to the traditional usage of this term. The relation holds between two words with more or less the same meaning. The term *hyponymy* was coined by Lyons himself in 1963, on the analogy of *synonymy* and *antonymy*. It is closely related to *incompatibility*, and both are for Lyons the most fundamental paradigmatic relations of sense in terms of which the vocabulary is structured. Hyponymy relates a superordinate term to a subordinate *hyponym*. Lyons replaces the traditional term *antonymy* (in the wider sense) by *oppositeness* (of meaning) with a further subclassification into a) *complementarity*, b) *antonymy* (in the narrower, restricted sense) and c) *converseness*. Additionally, these three finer distinctions fall together under the term *antonymy* in the wider sense. As already mentioned, neither homonymy nor polysemy belong to the 'sense-relations', but in Lyons (1977: 559 f.) the possibility is discussed, whether "absolute, or complete, homonymy" should be defined as "a relation between lexemes".

I would now like to describe paradigmatic semantic relations in detail, with special focus on Lyons (1968) and (1977). Lexical fields, another important area of paradigmatic lexical semantics, closely related to hyponymy, will be treated in 4.2.4. Fields may be either hierarchic or non-hierarchic structures. Syntagmatic lexical relationships like those between *blond* and *hair, kiss* and *lips, bark* and *dog, kick* and *foot*, including purely lexical collocations which cannot be explained and described semantically, will be treated much later (see 4.3.).

As a last point, before beginning the detailed discussion of paradigmatic sense-relations, I would like to emphasize two methodological aspects of the theory underlying Lyons (1968) und (1977). Both publications are characterized by: 1. The lack of any meaning elements or semantic components, and 2. the logical basis of the relationships. As opposed to Leech and many other linguists, Lyons does not make use of a semantic metalanguage in his structural semantic theory. The sense-relations are established between lexical items, i.e. full linguistic signs, which are substituted for each other in the same syntactic position of sentences. This procedure is supposed to guarantee the objectivity of the methodology.[6]

4.2.3.1. Synonymy

I will start with the first sense-relation in diagram (5) and will not restrict myself to the opinions expressed by Lyons. In his *Introduction to Theoretical Linguistics* (1968: 428) he first defines synonymy provisionally in the following way:

> Two (or more) items are synonymous if the sentences which result from the substitution of one for the other have the same meaning.

He points out that neither "total synonymy" nor "complete synonymy" exist and then concentrates on "cognitive synonymy". This is defined precisely

---

[6] In Lyons (1981: 91–97) the logical notions 'entailment' and 'meaning postulates' are used to define the "substitutional" (paradigmatic) sense-relations: hyponymy, "descriptive synonymy", and incompatibility (with the sub-classes: complementarity, "polar antonymy", and converseness). Lyons (1981: 84) concedes that componential analysis is useful not for representing the meaning of lexemes, "but as a way of formalizing that part of their proto-typical, or focal, meaning which they share with other lexemes."

(1968: 450) in terms of "bilateral implication" or "equivalence" which may be illustrated with the following example:

(6) (S1) The Arabian sheikh was *wealthy*, and [x]
(S2) The Arabian sheikh was *rich* [y]

S1 $\supset$ S2 and S2 $\supset$ S1, therefore $\boxed{S1 \equiv S2}$ = equivalence

This can be explained as follows. Two sentences S1 and S2 must mutually imply each other ($\supset$ is the logical symbol for "imply, implication"). If this is the case, then S1 and S2 are equivalent ($\equiv$ stands for "is equivalent to"). In addition, the two sentences must have an identical syntactic structure. If, furthermore, one differs from the other only in that where one has a lexical item *x*, the other has *y* (in the same position), then *x* and *y* are synonymous.

On closer inspection we realize that synonymy does not hold between "lexical items" (as claimed by Lyons) but between lexical units. If, for example, we distinguish between $rich_1$ 'wealthy' and $rich_2$ 'fertile', then, obviously, the latter is not synonymous with *wealthy*. Let us look at some additional examples. We may distinguish e.g. the lexical units pig_1 'animal', pig_2 'greedy person', and pig_3 'policeman' (the German equivalent is *Bulle*, which can either denote an animal or a policeman). The lexical unit pig_3 is never synonymous with the lexeme *swine*, which may be split up into the lexical units $swine_1$ 'animal' (with an additional connotative label *archaic*, see 1.3., 2.2.5.) and $swine_2$ 'extremely unpleasant person' (with an additional label *old-fashioned slang*). Synonymy might only be claimed to exist between the lexical units pig_1 and $swine_{1,}$ as well as between pig_2 and perhaps $swine_2$. *Hog* (in the animal sense) is either connotatively marked as American English, or has a specific sense denoting a male, castrated animal. In the person sense, *hog* cannot replace *pig* in the collocation *male chauvinist pig*.

The examples demonstrate not only that synonymy is a matter of lexical units, but that cognitively more or less identical words usually differ in their connotations. It is perhaps worth pointing out that Lyons proposes to extend the notion of synonymy beyond equivalent lexical items to groups of lexemes. One could then call *drake* and its paraphrase *male duck* synonyms. This proposal results from the recognition of an important principle of the interrelation between paradigmatic lexical structuring and syntagmatic modification (cf. Lipka 1981a). Several other linguists even use the terms *synonym* and *synonymy* for relationships between sentences. I believe, however, that they should be reserved for purely lexical relations and that the term *paraphrase* should be used in other cases.

According to Lyons (1968: 452f.) synonymy is not "a structural relationship", especially if compared to hyponymy. In other words, it is fairly irrelevant for the structure of the lexicon of a language. If all instances of synonymy were eliminated from the vocabulary, this would not effect the structural relationship between the remaining lexical items. The so-called "impoverished" lexicon would no longer provide stylistic variety and choice, but everything could be said with the smaller "synonymy-free vocabulary".

4.2.3.2. Hyponymy and Incompatibility

Lyons characterizes hyponymy and incompatibility as the most fundamental paradigmatic relations of sense. Both are largely interdependent and extremely important for the structure of the lexicon. As opposed to synonymy, they cannot simply be eliminated without serious consequences.

Let us look at *hyponymy* first, which is the relation of lexical subordination or superordination. Lyons (1968: 455) gives a definition in terms of "unilateral implication", i.e. logical implication of lexemes in identical syntactic position. The subordinate term (or *hyponym*) necessarily implies the superordinate one, but not vice versa. The latter (which may sometimes be missing in a natural language, because there is a lexical gap in the system) is called *hyperonym* by some linguists. I shall avoid this term in the following, because of the danger of confusion with *hyponym*.

Following Coseriu's, Kastovsky's, and my own usage I shall prefer the unambiguous term *archilexeme*. This has been coined on the analogy of the phonological term *archiphoneme* ("Archiphonem") used by the Prague School of linguists. Thus the neutralization of the opposition between the phonemes /d/ and /t/ (in final position in High German e.g. in *Rad* and *Rat*) is symbolized by the archiphoneme /T/. Scholars of German often speak of *Auslautverhärtung* in this case.

This is another instance of the parallelism of phonology and semantics. In lexical semantics as well, the opposition between subordinate units is neutralized in the superordinate term. Hyponyms which are on the same level of the hierarchy are labelled *co-hyponyms*. The following simple diagram is meant to illustrate both the nature of the sense-relation and the terminology used by a number of linguists.

(7)

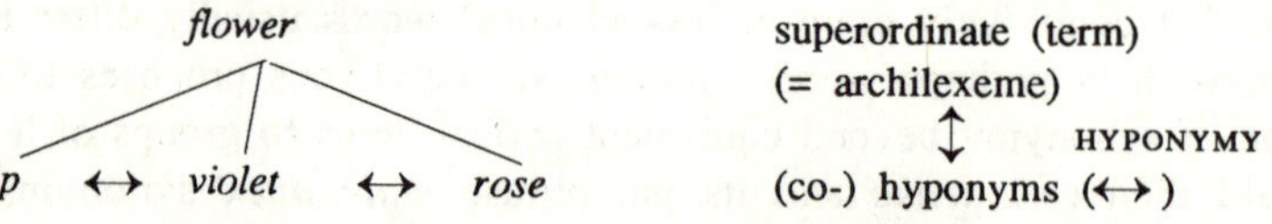

Lyons (1968: 455) defines the unilateral (or asymmetrical) implication between e.g. *tulip* and *flower* as "proper hyponymy". He also points out that the principle of hyponymy "enables us to be more general or more specific according to circumstances". On the same page, he points out that synonymy may be interpreted as a special case of hyponymy, namely as "symmetrical hyponymy". If *x* is a hyponym of *y* and if *y* is also a hyponym of *x*, then *x* and *y* are synonyms. Thus, logical implication can be made the underlying basis for both lexical sense-relations.

Again, it must be pointed out that hyponymy is a relation between lexical units, not lexemes. This becomes immediately clear if we look at the figurative senses of animal names, which are often used as terms of abuse in many languages. Thus, *tick*$_2$ (see 4.2.2.), *pig, ass, bitch* / Ger *Schwein, Esel, Gans* / Fr *vache, cochon, chien* do not at all logically or linguistically imply *animal*, as do their literal counterparts (cf. Tournier 1985:239 ff.).

Incompatibility is defined by Lyons (1968:458) on the basis of the logical *contradictoriness* between two sentences. If S_1 explicitly or implicitly denies another sentence S_2 and the two sentences only differ in that one has the lexical item *x* and the other has *y* (in the same syntactic position) then *x* and *y* are incompatible. This is illustrated by: *Mary was wearing a red hat* and *Mary was wearing a green (blue, white ...) hat.* Colour-terms are obviously incompatible lexical items. Within the same hierarchic lexical field, all those co-hyponyms are incompatible which belong to the same *dimension.* Such 'dimensions' (which group together a number of specific semantic features) are, for example, COLOUR, SEX, AGE, SHAPE, PURPOSE etc. (cf. Lipka 1980:100, 109 f., Kastovsky 1982a:81 ff., Schneider 1988:52 f., 147 ff.). Incompatible lexemes must therefore have important semantic features in common. Simple difference of meaning is not the same as incompatibility.

Again, we must stress that this sense-relation is a matter of lexical units. Senses which belong to different dimensions are not affected by incompatibility. Examples are *blue* and its senses 'depressed' or 'indecent' and *black* and its senses 'illegal' or 'sinister'.

To conclude this section on two closely connected sense-relations, it seems appropriate to draw attention to their functional aspects. Lyons (1968:455) points out that the principle of hyponymy "enables us to be more general or more specific according to circumstances". Cruse (1986:112 ff., 136 ff.), who distinguishes various "hierarchies" and "taxonomies" and relates these to the problem of categorization (143 ff.), discusses the pragmatic question of lexical over- and under-specification in particular situations, in connection with the notions "folk taxonomies" and "natural kinds". These will be discussed here under the heading of "lexical fields" (see 4.2.4.), which Cruse labels "lexical configurations".

4.2.3.3. Complementarity, Antonymy, and Converseness

As already pointed out (see diagram (5)), Lyons calls the traditional lexical relation of antonymy "oppositeness of meaning" and distinguishes three different types of oppositeness. He restricts the term *antonymy* to just one of those three types. We will review them in turn. In doing this, we should keep in mind that these sense-relations too are defined on the basis of logical relationships. The most recent (corpus-based) study of binary opposition in English is Mettinger (1988).

Complementarity can be illustrated by pairs of words like *male* and *female*, or *single* and *married* (cf. Kastovsky 1982a:96 f., 234 f.). It is characteristic of complementaries that the denial of the one implies the assertion of the other and vice versa. The definition of this sense-relation is therefore based on logical implication combined with negation.

Thus, e.g. *John is not married* implies *John is single*, and also *John is married* implies *John is not single*. There is no third possibility, which is also captured by the traditional Latin expression *tertium non datur*. This corresponds to the logical "contradictory statements", which are exclusive and exhaustive. This type of oppositeness is based on a yes/no-decision. Complementarity may be regarded as a special case of *incompatibility*, which only concerns pairs of lexical units.

Lyons (1968:461) emphasizes that the logical relation only holds for the "normal usage" of such pairs and that "dichotomization" is a very important principle in the semantic structure of language. Thus there may well be other possibilities besides the complementaries e.g. *male* and *female*, namely *hermaphrodite*. In our terminology we could say that the two complementaries do not cover the entire dimension of SEX. This is even more true today, 20 years after the publication of Lyons's book, of the pair *single* and *married*. He points out himself though, that under special circumstances an utterance like *more married* may well receive a sensible interpretation.

In this connection he also states that (besides logical criteria for the definition of complementarity) gradability is a linguistic characteristic. In normal usage such terms are neither qualifiable, nor gradable. In an article published in 1980, however, Cruse sets up a further subclass, namely "gradable complementaries" (cf. Kastovsky 1982a:98, 135; Cruse 1986:203). Examples are the following pairs: *clean* : *dirty, true* : *false, pure* : *impure*. In Cruse (1986) "opposites" are then discussed in very great detail in the three chapters 9–11.

Antonymy (in the narrow, restricted sense of Lyons) is the second subclass of oppositeness. It is distinguished from *complementarity* by being based on different logical relationships (cf. Kastovsky 1982a:131 ff., Cruse 1986:204 ff.). For pairs of antonyms like *good/bad, big/small, high/low* only the second one of the above-mentioned relations of implication (or entailment) holds. The assertion containing one member does imply the negation of the other, but not vice versa. Thus, *John is good* implies *John is not bad*. But *John is not good* does not necessarily imply *John is bad*. The negation of one term does not necessarily imply the assertion of the other. Using a further example, *The water is not hot* does not necessarily imply *The water is cold*. However, from *The water is cold* the negation *The water is not hot* does follow. Furthermore, *The water is hot* logically implies the negation *The water is not cold*.

Here, the principle *tertium datur* does hold, i.e. a third possibility exists. This corresponds to "polar opposition" in the terminology of Leech (^{2}1981:101 f.) and to the "contrary" in traditional logic (cf. Lyons 1977:272). Antonymous adjectives (in the narrower sense) behave like comparatives and are therefore often tied to specific norms as a point of reference (cf. Kastovsky 1982a:132). Cruse (1986:206 ff.) distinguishes a number of finer subclasses of antonyms.

An important linguistic difference from complementaries (like *single/married*) is that antonyms (in the narrow sense) are always fully gradable. This is true, of course, for *good/bad, hot/cold* and many adjectives. Additional criteria for the determination and subclassification of antonymy have been used in various publications by Cruse, Ljung, and Geckeler.

Converseness is the third subclass of oppositeness of meaning distinguished by Lyons (cf. Kastovsky 1981b; 1982a:136, Cruse 1986:231 ff.). This term introduced by Lyons derives from symbolic logic, where *converse* denotes an equivalent mirror-image relation, or function, in which the order of the arguments is reversed. We have already come across such cases when discussing 'relational features' (see 3.3.2.) and even earlier, when discussing the notion of *thematic meaning* introduced by Leech (see 2.2.4.). Examples are: *husband/wife, doctor/patient, teacher/pupil,* but also *precede/follow, above/below, in front of/behind, before/after*, i.e. not only nouns.

The criterion for the sense-relation of *converseness* is the possibility of permuting noun phrases, functioning as arguments, in sentences which remain otherwise equivalent. In other words, the sentences imply each other and thus have the same meaning. Thus, e.g. *John bought the car from Bill* implies *Bill sold the car to John* and vice versa. This example with the three-place predicates *buy* and *sell* is, of course, more complex than sentences with two-place predicates (cf. Lyons 1968:467; 1977:280). I would like to represent it schematically in the following way:

(8)	(NP_1)	*bought*	NP_3	from	(NP_2) $\supset\subset$
	(NP_2)	*sold*	NP_3	to	(NP_1)

Mirror-image sentences are in several ways similar to the relation between active and passive sentences. There is also a parallel to antonyms in the comparative form, and thus *X is bigger than Y* is equivalent to *Y is smaller than X.*

Converseness is thus characterized by the fact that pairs of sentences with lexemes like *buy* and *sell*, or *husband* and *wife* imply each other mutually. Thus, *John is Mary's husband* implies the sentence *Mary is John's wife* and vice versa. The substitution of lexical converses – with constant meaning – thus causes a permutation of the noun phrases functioning as arguments. This provides the possibility of assigning a different theme/rheme-structure with different 'thematic meaning', for purposes of information presentation in texts (cf. Kastovsky 1981b).

Cruse (1986:232 f.), who characterizes *converses* as "relational opposites", draws attention to the "dual semantic nature" of many nouns that belong to pairs of lexical converses. Adapting one of his examples to our purposes, I would like to demonstrate that converseness – as well as the other types of opposites – is a matter of lexical units too, not of lexemes. The lexeme CHILD contains two lexical units *child*$_1$ and *child*$_2$, of which only the latter is relational. It does not contain a feature [–ADULT] and only this lexical unit is an instance of converseness (together with *parent*). This is illustrated by (9a) vs. (9b):

(9a) She was a *child*$_1$ when her parents died

(9b) All their *child*$_2$ren are now grown up.

We have seen that the three kinds of sense-relations between lexical items (or more precisely, lexical units) that are traditionally summed up under the term *antonymy* differ clearly in many ways. Complementaries, antonyms and converses always occur in pairs, which are treated and interpreted as two-member lexical fields by some linguists. For all three types of oppositeness Lyons (1968), in his classical treatment, bases his definitions on the relation of logical implication, or entailment. In more recent research (Lyons 1977:281 ff.; Cruse 1986:223 ff.) this logical basis loses its importance, the subclassification becomes much more detailed and refined, and a fourth type of oppositeness is introduced, which is called *directional opposition.* We shall now look more closely into these developments.

4.2.3.4. Contrast and Opposition: Recent Work

As already mentioned, Lyons (1977) modifies, enlarges, and refines his earlier work on sense-relations. The most important change is the introduction of a fourth type of oppositeness, labelled *directional opposition.* This has also been adopted by Cruse and further subclassified and modified. The position in Lyons (1977) can be schematically represented as in the following diagram (10). This has been adopted (with minor modifications) from Geckeler (1980:46). As in many other cases, Lyons only gives a verbal explanation, and does not summarize his many distinctions in diagrammatic form.

(10)

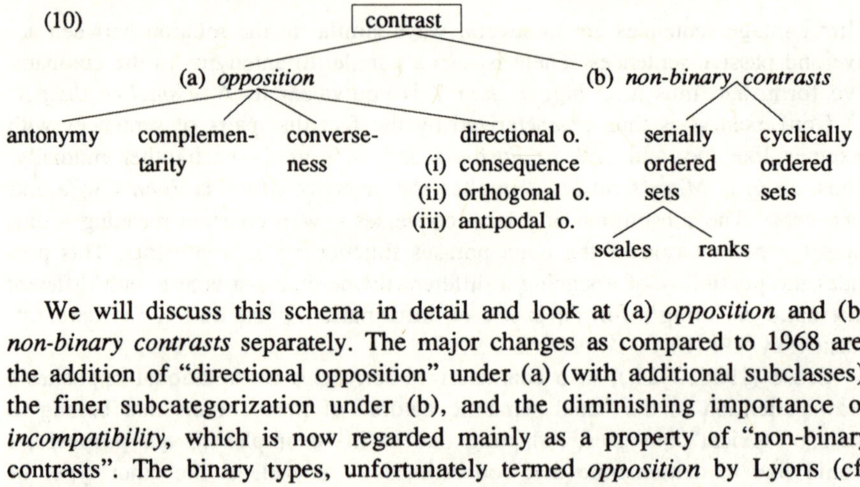

We will discuss this schema in detail and look at (a) *opposition* and (b) *non-binary contrasts* separately. The major changes as compared to 1968 are: the addition of "directional opposition" under (a) (with additional subclasses), the finer subcategorization under (b), and the diminishing importance of *incompatibility*, which is now regarded mainly as a property of "non-binary contrasts". The binary types, unfortunately termed *opposition* by Lyons (cf. Geckeler 1980:46) may be represented and illustrated as follows:

(10a)

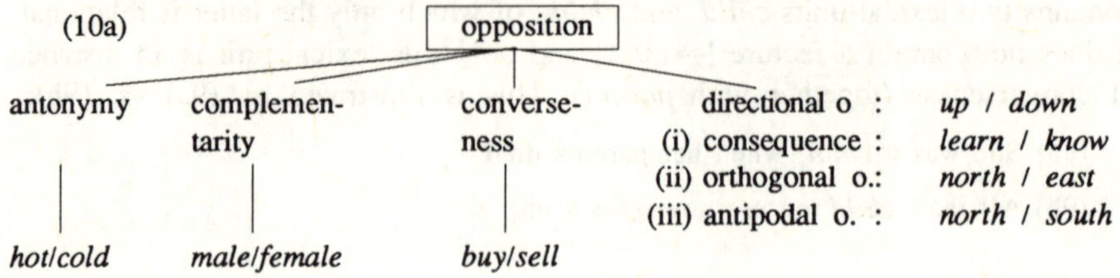

We have already discussed the first three types of opposition. *Directional opposition* (with its subclasses) is based on the notion of contrary motion (i.e. in opposite directions). This is seen most cleary in the pair *up/down.* According to Lyons (1977: 281) the pairs *come/go* and *arrive/depart* also involve motion in two opposed directions, with respect to a reference point *P*. In *up/down,* however, the opposition is drawn within motion away from *P*. *Come/go* is different again, in that it involves deixis, as does the opposition e.g. between *here/there.* Here, the reference point is normally the speaker. We have already discussed this phenomenon in connection with deictic features (see 3.3.2.).

Direction and motion can also be understood in a more abstract, figurative sense. This is often referred to as "the localist hypothesis" or "the thesis of localism". Motion from a place as well as abstract motion produces certain results. Lyons therefore distinguishes two possible types of "consequence": positive and negative consequence. The first one may be illustrated by *learn/know, get/have*; the second one by *forget/not know* and *die/not be alive.*

Antipodal (or diametrical) opposites are illustrated by *north/south* and *east/west.* Lyons distinguishes this type from orthogonal (or perpendicular) opposition, as in e.g. *north*, opposed both to *east* and *west*, or *east*, opposed both to *south* and *north.* Although the distinction between antipodal and orthogonal opposition may seem far too specific, since it applies only to a very restricted number of lexemes, it is helpful in explaining why certain lexical items do not have a single opposite (cf. Lyons 1977: 285). Thus, *girl* is opposed orthogonally to both *boy* and *woman.*

Cruse (1986), however, has given up this distinction and only recognizes *antipodals* as one of a number of subclasses of directional opposition. Among the others, converses and "reversives" (in most cases realized by complex lexemes) are perhaps the most important ones.

The category of "non-binary contrast" is newly introduced in Lyons (1977: 287 ff.), with further possible subcategorization as represented in diagram (10b). Lyons also speaks of "many-member lexical sets", which he discusses in connection with incompatibility.

(10b)

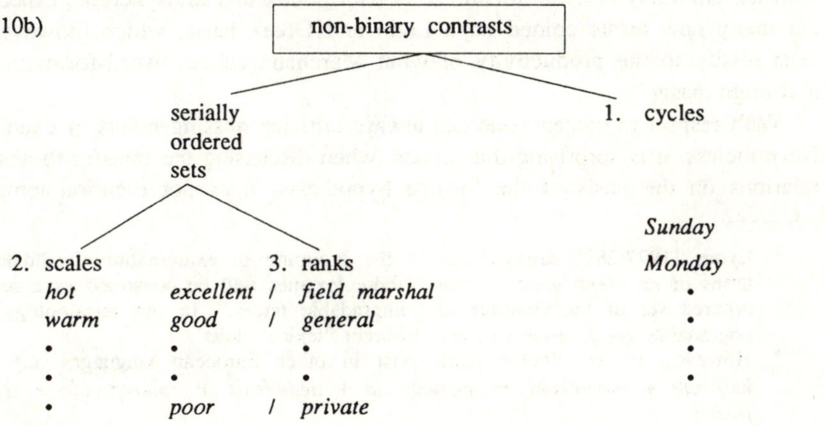

I will make some brief explanatory remarks concerning the three subcategories. 1. 'cycles' (or cyclical sets): like *spring, summer, autumn, winter* or *January* to *December, Sunday* to *Saturday*, are mainly to be found among words denoting units or periods of time. There are no "outermost members", or extremes, although there is a conventional beginning and end. Serially ordered sets or groups of words are subdivided by Lyons into: 2. 'scales' (which are gradable) e.g. *hot, warm, cool, cold* on the one hand and 3. 'ranks' (which are not) on the other. The latter are exemplified by examination marks like *excellent, good, average, fair, poor* and terms for military ranks.[7]

It might seem that this subclassification is too delicate, but as Lyons (1977:290) points out, it may contribute to a better understanding of the basic colour words in English, which combine a scale (*black, grey, white*) with a cycle (*red, yellow, green, blue, purple*). Lyons also argues that the scale of temperature words in English is unusual in that it contains an outer and an inner pair of antonyms (*hot/cold* and *warm/cool*).[8]

Finally, it has to be emphasized once more that "many-member lexical sets" do not really consist of lexemes, but of lexical units. As mentioned above, *black* and *blue* are polysemous words. This is also true for examples such as *hot, warm, fair, poor* etc.

Non-binary groups of words which belong to the same word class and cover a certain semantic area may clearly be understood also as non-hierarchic semantic or lexical fields. In fact, Lyons explicitly mentions both of these in 1968 and 1977 in connection with colour terms and examination marks. We will return to this subject presently.

Before doing this, a few critical remarks on Lyons (1977) and Cruse (1986) will not be entirely inappropriate. They concern both their terminology and the delicacy of the fine subcategorization. The terminological distinctions introduced by Lyons are not all of them entirely fortunate. In particular, his definition of *opposition* as 'binary contrast' may be and has been critized. A detailed critique can be found in Geckeler (1980), whose own terminological proposals, however, have not found favour with other linguists. The terminology used by Cruse, with its extremely fine ramifications, is unorthodox and idiosyncratic, especially the many new terms coined on a Latin and Greek basis, which, however, at least testify to the productivity of what Marchand called "word-formation on a foreign basis."

With respect to content, one can always criticize missing points or examples. Nevertheless, it is surprising that Lyons (when discussing the transfer to abstract relations on the basis of the localist hypothesis) does not mention temporal

---

[7] Lyons (1977:289) stresses that in the grouping of examination candidates in terms of *excellent, good, ... poor* "these lexemes will be construed as a serially ordered set of incompatible and ungradable terms.". In our terminology, the ungradable *good, poor* etc. are different 'lexical units'.

[8] However, similar double pairs exist in other European languages, e.g. Ger *heiß/kalt + warm/kühl*, Fr *chaud/froid + tiède/frais*, It *caldo/freddo + tepido/fresco*.

opposites like *now/then* and *first/last* (cf. also *before/after*). This also holds for Cruse and his account of directional opposition. In many languages such lexical units are derived from locative lexemes.

It is important, however, that both Lyons and Cruse clearly demonstrate the inadequacy of the traditional, global notion of antonymy. This comprehensive concept obviously covers and confuses many important differences which exist between the various types of binary and non-binary lexical "contrasts". The two linguists must certainly be credited with demonstrating the variety of distinctions which exist in the area of lexical opposites.

On the other hand, one can also go too far in refining an analysis and setting up an ever finer subclassification. It must be emphasized here that the more distinctions are introduced, the fewer general statements, rules, or so-called generalizations remain. This problem, which has also been discussed in linguistics under the term *delicacy*, does not have an absolute solution. In principle, one can make ever finer or more delicate discrimination and subclassification in many areas of language. It depends on the subject matter as well as on the purpose of a description, where the boundary line is drawn between a detailed analysis and an insightful generalization. For didactic purposes, a certain simplification is always more advisable than a too detailed description. There is always the danger of no longer seeing the wood for the trees.

Lyons (1968:152f., 164) himself has expressed this very clearly, by drawing on the concept of the "principle of diminishing returns". He illustrates this with the example of the ever finer subclassification of word classes. In his own words (1968:153):

> The linguist will be faced with a situation in which he is establishing more and more rules, each covering very few sentences; and he will be setting up so many overlapping word-classes (sic!) that all semblance of generality is lost. This is what is meant by the principle of 'diminishing returns'.

And he continues:

> There comes a point (and where this point is might be legitimate matter for dispute) at which the increase in the complexity of the rules is too 'costly' in proportion to its 'yield'.

One might well argue that both Lyons and Cruse have gone beyond this point and have overstepped the boundaries of a sensible balance.

4.2.4. Lexical Fields and Hierarchies

In the following, we shall first look at linear lexical fields and quasi-hyponymy and will then deal with the ambiguous concept of inclusion again, in connection with the notions of intension and extension. Finally, this will be related to a discussion of hierarchies.

Field-theory has a long tradition in European linguistics and all sorts of typologies have been proposed for it. Recent theoretical and practical work on the subject has been done mainly by Coseriu, Geckeler, Lehrer, and myself. The terminology is extremely confusing (cf. Lipka 1980: 94–97, Kastovsky 1982a : 125 f.). Cruse (1986 : 112 ff.) speaks of *lexical configurations*, while for Lehrer (1974) the terms *semantic field* and *lexical field* are synonyms. Coseriu, who uses *Wortfeld* (translated as *lexical field* in the English version) distinguishes these (cf. Coseriu/Geckeler 1981 : 58 f.) from: a) scientific taxonomies, b) categories of subject matter ("Sachbereiche"), c) associative fields, and d) conceptual fields. For him, all lexical fields are necessarily conceptual fields but not vice versa.

My own ideas on the subject are derived from Coseriu's, especially in considering fields as necessarily paradigmatic and opposed to syntagmatic structures. But I have introduced a finer distinction between the more comprehensive *lexical field* (consisting of simple or complex lexemes) and the *word-field* (exclusively containing morphologically simple items), in Lipka (1980). One of the reasons for doing this is the concept of 'lexical gap', which can only be proved to exist in structures of simple words. If complex lexemes are admitted in such a field, the productive word-formation processes may close such a gap at any time. In the article just mentioned, I have also adopted Coseriu's distinction between a "*micro-field*" and a "*macro-field*". Another, more important, subcategorization in our context is the differentiation between linear and hierarchic fields.

In Lipka (1980:98) the following conditions for membership in a field were set up (partly following Coseriu):

> 1. items must be in direct opposition in the same syntactic slot, i.e. belong to the same word class, 2. they must have at least one specific semantic component in common, 3. field-membership must be established by objective procedures.

With non-hierarchic, i.e. linear fields, criterion 2 for the definition of fields is equivalent to the statement that the field covers a whole 'dimension' such as SEX, AGE, COLOUR, TEMPERATURE etc. Hierarchic fields are based on the sense-relation of hyponymy (or inclusion) and can normally be replaced by an archilexeme. Note that this does not hold for the "hierarchic oppositions" in Leech (1981:106ff.) such as *inch/foot/yard* etc., *January/February* etc., *one/two/three* etc.

Hierarchies normally consist of several levels, usually not more than five (cf. Cruse 1986: 112ff., 145). If a hyponym is missing on any level we may speak of a "specification-gap". Conversely, the lack of an archilexeme may be termed "generalization-gap" (cf. Lipka 1980: 107). The latter case is called "quasi-hyponymy" by Lyons. In the case of a two-level hierarchy with a missing archilexeme, quasi-hyponymy results in linear fields, which we will now sketch briefly.

As we have seen in diagram (10b) Lyons (1977) distinguishes three kinds of "non-binary contrast": 1. cycles, 2. scales (gradable) and 3. ranks (non-gradable). Cruse (1986: 192 ff.) (within his treatment of "non-branching hierarchies" in chapter 8 of his book) uses two different criteria for distinguishing between "ranks, grades and degrees", namely 1. continuous or discontinuous variation on an underlying scale, and 2. gradability. Thus for him *ranks* "vary in discrete jumps", while *grades* (gradable) and *degrees* (non-gradable) vary on a continuous scale. The terminological confusion is complete and returns of the subclassification do not only diminish, but may seem to approach zero. I therefore prefer to treat all these subcategories as instances of linear lexical fields. Let us look at a concrete example:

(11) ← O →

hot	warm	tepid	cool	cold

- TEMPERATURE = scale

Here we have gradual oppositions, i.e. degrees on a scale (both in their literal sense!). An archilexeme is missing (or even, perhaps, inconceivable) which covers the whole lexical field, or more precisely word-field. But all members of the field have the semantic component [TEMPERATURE] in common, because they all belong to this dimension.

Both Lehrer and Lyons use the term *scale* for this type of opposition, because the members of the field are gradable (e.g. *warmer, cooler* etc.), except for the zero-point *tepid.* This (Lehrer's centerpoint) is in the middle of the field, which is exceptional, and the increase is directed to both ends of the scale.

This particular linear field is also exceptional in other respects (cf. Lehrer 1974:110–112; Lyons 1977:289), because it contains an outer and an inner pair of antonyms. A third, not so exceptional property, is the possibility of adding and inserting further lexemes, such as *scorching, burning, lukewarm, freezing, icy.* Since these are morphologically complex, they do not (in my terminology) belong within the *word-field.* However, together with the simple lexemes, they would constitute a complex *lexical field.* Collectively, all these adjectives of temperature constitute a linear field, a *scale.* Other scales (which we cannot deal with here) are treated in Lehrer (1974 : 28 f.).

My second example of a linear field is taken from the simple words for colours in English. Basic colour-terms have been investigated in many languages (cf. Leech [2]1981 : 24 ff.) from various points of view, including universality, psychological reality, and prototypicality. As already mentioned, colour is denoted in English both by a 'scale', namely *black, grey, white* and a cyclical opposition, which may be represented as a linear field in the following way:

(12)

red	yellow	green	blue	purple

– COLOUR = cycle

This linear field is a *cycle* in Lyons's classification. No single element in the chain of oppositions is above any other, nor does it show a greater degree of some quality. The items all have the same status. This type of opposition was called equipollent by Trubetzkoy in his theory of phonology (cf. Lyons 1977:279). An archilexeme is missing, although Kastovsky (1982a:90) proposes the complex lexeme *coloured* for this function. However, this usually has the meaning 'non-white'.

A third type of linear fields is formed by what Leech (²1981:100) calls "multiple taxonomy", e.g. *gold, copper, iron, mercury*, kinds of animal like *bird, fish, insect, mammal,* species of animal like *cat, dog, horse, cow, wolf*, and breeds like *alsatian, terrier, spaniel, collie* etc. These examples show that linear fields are not restricted to adjectives. Leech posits the common semantic components: METAL, KIND, SPECIES, BREED. The subclasses (*gold, copper* etc., *bird, fish,* etc., *cat, dog* etc., *alsatian, terrier* etc.) are distinguished in his notation by arbitrary, typographical symbols.

The reason for this procedure is explained better in Cruse (1986:140), who claims that e.g. *horse* cannot be paraphrased as 'equine animal' and be opposed to *cow* in the same way as *stallion* may be paraphrased as 'male horse' and be opposed to *mare*. He argues convincingly that in this case modification of *animal* is impossible, because *horse, cow* etc. are "natural kind terms", which resemble proper names in that both are "rigid designators". His argument is further strengthened by the observation that metalinguistic elements like EQUINE, BOVINE, CANINE, FELINE etc., and the paraphrases they are derived from, have doubtful status as evidence.

According to Cruse natural kind terms and their relations with their superordinates "can only be described encyclopaedically". Consequently, only those linear fields which do not denote natural kinds can be described with the help of dimensions such as TEMPERATURE, COLOUR, SHAPE, LENGTH, TASTE, SEX, AGE and (for verbs) MANNER, INSTRUMENT, PURPOSE (cf. Lipka 1980:109).

If we now turn from linear to hierarchic fields, both the concepts of inclusion and hyponymy must be reconsidered. In 2.2.1. we found (see esp. diagram (8) (p. 51), when looking at the relationship between language and reality, that the ambiguity of the term *inclusion* can be resolved, if we make a clear distinction between "sense inclusion" and "referential", or better "denotational inclusion". There is an inverse relationship between the two and they are complementary. The sense, or meaning component ANIMAL is necessarily included in the sense HORSE, but the class of *horses* is a subclass, and thus included in, the class of the denotata of *animal.* The sense FLOWER is included in the sense TULIP, but the class of *tulips* is included in that of *flowers*.

Because of the ambiguity of the term *inclusion*, Leech (²1981:93) thinks it is safer to avoid using the term altogether and to prefer *hyponymy* instead (see 4.2.3.2.). Unfortunately, *hierarchy* and *hierarchic* are also ambiguous. As already mentioned, Leech uses the terms for oppositions like *inch/foot/yard* etc., *January/February* etc. and opposes it to "multiple taxonomy" (e.g. *gold, copper*, etc.). Clearly, this is not what is meant when Lyons (1977:295ff.) deals with "hierarchical structure in the vocabulary". For Cruse (1986:112ff., 145) "hierarchies" must also have several (usually up to five) distinct levels, of which the "generic level" (exemplified by *rose*) is the most important one in natural (or folk) taxonomies. I here reproduce his example of *plant* in modified form, with additional branching and terminology indicated.

(13)

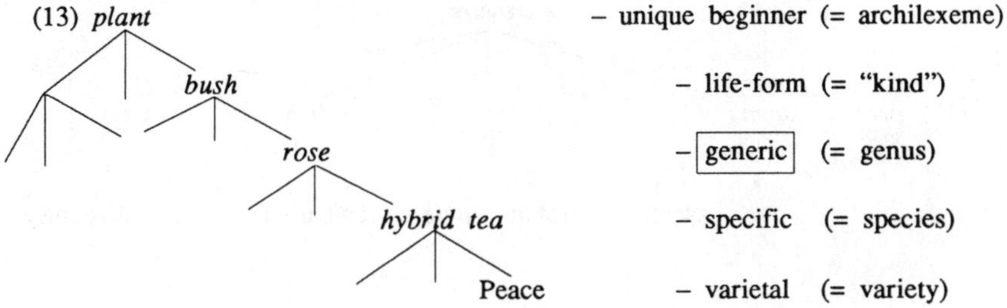

Just below the most important *generic level*, complex lexemes like *tea-rose, moss rose*, and *dog-rose* set in. This is the point where we change from a hierarchic *word-field* (with simple lexemes) to a *lexical field*. In my opinion, Cruse's *hybrid tea* is a technical term and denotes a subclass of *tea-rose*. Other problems with the diagram are where *flower* comes in, and whether *tree, flower*, and *vegetable* are to be treated as co-hyponyms of *plant*, because they can all be defined as 'a kind of plant'.

In principle, the differences between co-hyponyms are always neutralized in the archilexeme, and there are archilexemes on all levels, except for the lowest one. This is so because hyponymy is a relative concept. In order to illustrate this further, let us look at a possible, simplified, hierarchic field for *animal* (see diagram (8b) in 2.2.1. and the theme *A* "Life and Living Things" in the *Longman Lexicon of Contemporary English* (LLCE)).

(14)

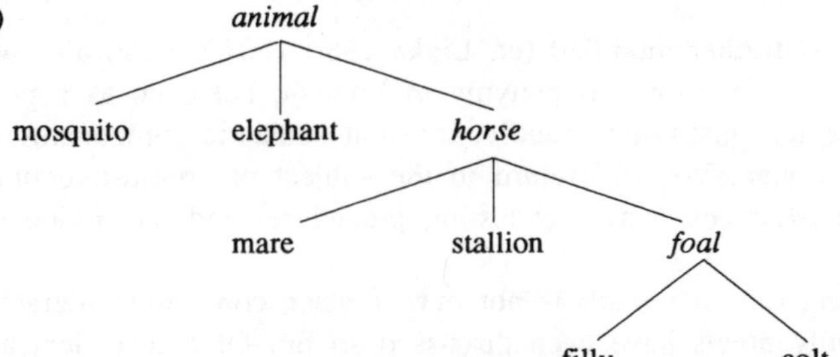

Here, as in diagram (13) and (15), only the items functioning as archilexemes are italicized. There are problems for this hierarchy too.[9] Lyons (1977:296, 298) points out that in ordinary everyday English *animal* is not superordinate to *fish, bird*, and *insect*. Rather, *creature* is the archilexeme to all four, including also *person* (cf. Cruse 1986:136, 146).[10] This can be represented as follows:

---

[9] It is certainly not homogeneous as is evident from a comparison of 'A *horse* is a kind of *animal*' but (??) 'A *mare* is a kind of *horse*'. Cf. also *pony* (kind/type of horse), *Arab, mustang, bay, chestnut, piebald, pacer, jumper, (fox)hunter*.

[10] It is important to make a distinction between 'folk (or natural) taxonomies' and 'scientific (or technical) taxonomies' as pointed out in Cruse (1986: 145).

(15)

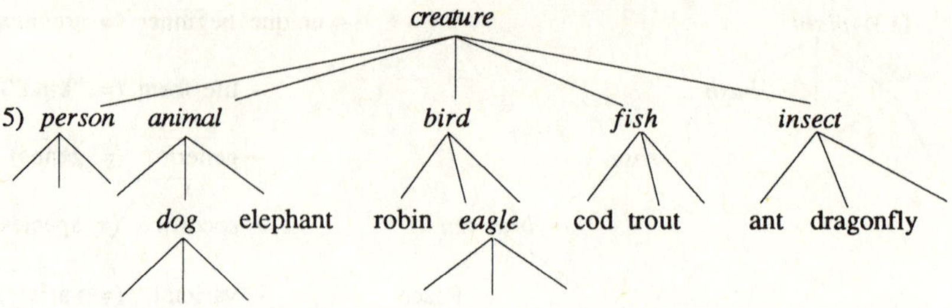

Since complex lexemes are normally hyponyms of their determinatum (cf. Kastovsky 1982a: 185), all the italicized lexemes can also function as archilexemes, but in a lexical field, not a word-field. Further hyponyms are indicated in diagram (15) by empty branches. Note that we here leave out of consideration polysemy and the figurative use of such words, and thus do not go beyond the level of lexeme to that of lexical unit.

For testing hyponymy (and thus the position in a hierarchic lexical field) Lyons (1977: 292) has proposed the formula: '*x* is a kind of *y*' (where *x* is the hyponym, cf. Cruse 1986: 137). With the slight modification suggested by Cruse, the following test-frame may be used:

(16)

A(n)	X	is a kind/type of	Y
A	*poodle*	is a kind of	*dog.*

If the formula is further modified (cf. Lipka 1980: 100f.) it can also be used, not only as a test for proper hyponymy in English, but even as a procedure for discovering and justifying specific, inherent semantic components in both English and German. We will return to the subject of contrastive linguistics and the relationship between strict testing procedures and the notion of field presently.

Before doing this, a remark is not out of place concerning hierarchies of verbs, since only nouns have been discussed so far. Of course, lexical fields consisting of verbs can also be hierarchically structured. A detailed analysis of an English word-field with the archilexeme *strike* is given in Lipka (1980). It contains dimensions like INSTRUMENT, MANNER, and PURPOSE. A treatment of further hierarchic word-fields can be found in Lehrer (1974). The notion

---

'Natural taxonomies' have been extensively studied by anthropologic linguists, especially Brent Berlin and his associates, as mentioned by Cruse and Lakoff (1987: 32f.), who both draw heavily on their work. The results are particularly relevant for the problem of the psychologically 'basic level' in categorization (what Berlin called the "folk-generic level"), illustrated by the genus (*oak, maple*) – as opposed to the "unique beginner" (*plant, animal*), the "life form" (*tree*), the "intermediate" (*leaf-bearing tree*) above, and the "species" (*sugar maple*) and "variety" (*cutleaf staghorn sumac*) below. See 5.2.1. and diagram (13) p. 155.

of lexical field can also be fruitfully applied to verb-particle constructions with *out* and *up*, as demonstrated in Lipka (1972: 216–221). The results show that constructions with *out* can be described with the help of archilexemes like *discover, distribute, obliterate, remove, utter*, while those with *up* are hyponymous to *begin, consume, fill, improve, increase, remove*, and *spoil*.

In my opinion, field theory is particularly helpful in the area of contrastive linguistics. The following example may serve as rather sketchy evidence for this claim.

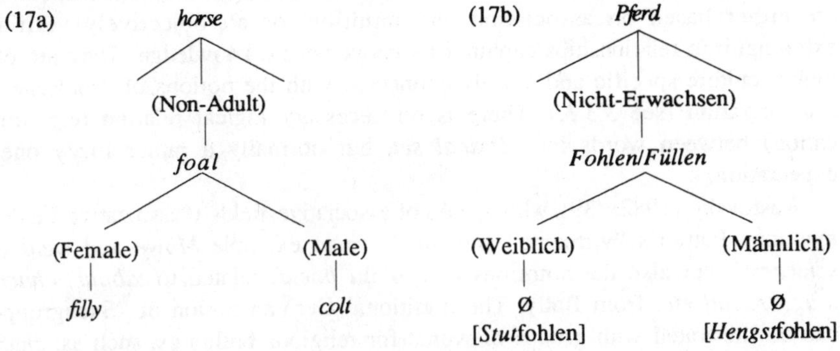

(17a) and (17b) only represent sections from the two word-fields *horse* and *Pferd*. In (17b) *Fohlen* and *Füllen* in present-day German are synonymous and there is no specification with regard to the dimension SEX. We thus have two specification-gaps (symbolized by ø) which in the technical language of horse-breeders are filled by complex lexemes. This demonstrates why lexical gaps can only be posited with assurance for word-fields, not lexical fields.

4.2.5. Association and Lexical Sets

Before we bring to a close our section on paradigmatic lexical relationships, we must have a look at some problematic cases. Obviously, we need a concept for lexical relations which are not sense-relations and which cannot be captured and described by strictly linguistic principles and procedures.

Thus, for example, tests for proper hyponymy or the criteria set up for synonymy cannot be applied to all the words grouped together in ROGET's *THESAURUS* or the *Longman Lexicon of Contemporary English*. Purely linguistic methods are not applicable either to the conceptual fields and the categories of subject matter ("Sachgruppen") which Coseriu excludes from his "lexical fields".

Words may also be related through their denotata, for example in a part-whole relationship (e.g. *finger - hand*), a type dubbed "meronomies" by Cruse (1986: 157ff.), and treated in a separate chapter of his book. Cruse (1986:194) also mentions "awkward and marginal" cases like *egg, caterpillar, chrysalis, butterfly*.

Finally, words are also psychologically related in our mental lexicon, a fact that can be tested with "word association responses", and then *butterfly* may be linked with: *moss, insect, wing(s), bird, fly, yellow, net, pretty, flower(s), bug* (cf. Aitchison 1987:74).

We will therefore introduce here, as a notational term, *lexical set*, which is intended as a cover term for all paradigmatically related groups of words which cannot be described by purely linguistic methods. On the syntagmatic level, this is paralleled by the term *collocation*, in the sense originally used in the British linguistic tradition (cf. also COBUILD 1987:xvii). *Lexical sets* are either based on association and intuition, or on objectively verifiable extralinguistic relationships captured by encyclopedic knowledge. They are often highly culture-specific and closely connected with the notions of prototype and categorization (see 3.3.3.). There is no necessary logical relation (e.g. implication) between words in a *lexical set*, but normally a rather fuzzy one of expectation.

Kastovsky (1982a:39), who speaks of associative fields ("assoziative Felder"), mentions Pottier's "virtuème" and the German example *Möwe* and *weiß* (not *schwarz*!), but also the notorious case of Fr *boeuf*, related to *labour, charrue, joug, travail* etc. from Bally. The traditional German notion of "Sachgruppen" can be illustrated with groups of words for religious buildings, such as: *church, cathedral, minster, chapel, vicarage, rectory, seminary, monastery, temple, mosque, synagogue* etc. and for human dwellings like: *farm, hamlet, village, borough, town, city, capital, port, settlement, colony, slum, ghetto* etc. Further examples of lexical sets can be easily collected from the *Longman Lexicon of Contemporary English*, e.g. *oyster, cockle, mussel, whelk, winkle*, which may be subsumed under the (more or less technical) archilexeme *mollusc*, but also "other sea creatures" like *jellyfish, starfish* (both not *fishes*!), *urchin, sponge, coral*, which may not be. To return to *butterfly* (not a *fly*!), the LLCE subsumes the relation between it and *egg, caterpillar, larva (grub), chrysalis (pupa)* as well as *housefly* under "stages in the lives of insects". The latter, together with *dragonfly* (also not a *fly*!), *mosquito, beetle, bee, wasp* etc. are categorized as "common insects", another illustration of a "Sachgruppe".

The author of the LLCE, Tom McArthur, does not tell us in the preface or elsewhere in the Lexicon how he arrived at his "list of sets" for organizing the words in the book. This information is to be found only in McArthur (1986:148 f.), where it is explained that the "word sets" given, and their micro- and macrostructure, are the result of a combination of two approaches. The first one is "the kind of thematization" which has a long tradition in European culture, from Pliny onwards, in the work of compilers of knowledge, ending in ROGET's *THESAURUS*. This is blended with "the kind of semantic structuring proposed by linguists like John Lyons".

One last remark on lexical sets and the possible relation between its members. They also may denote the same extralinguistic entity from different points of view. Thus, the surface of the world when compared to the sea is called *land*, when compared to the sky *earth* etc., and thus *land, earth, soil, ground, floor* form a lexical set (cf. LDCE 2 s.v. *land*).

4.3. Syntagmatic Relations

We now turn to syntagmatic structures in the lexicon and, in connection with this, to syntagmatic relations between lexemes and lexical units in the sentence. We have already dealt with one specific kind of syntagmatic relation between lexemes, or rather lexical morphemes, while analysing and describing complex lexemes (see 3.2.). We have seen that word-formation must be regarded as a syntagmatic process for the formation of new lexemes. In the following, those problems will be left aside.

Research on syntagmatic lexical relations has been carried out within different theoretical frameworks. Basically, we can distinguish between generative and non-generative (mostly structuralist) approaches. Within the latter, we can further separate those using a metalanguage from descriptions without semantic elements of any kind. Amongst research without metalinguistic elements, the notion of *collocation*, as developed within British linguistics, has to be particularly emphasized. The reason for this is that a number of linguists using this concept do not refer to semantic relations at all. They merely state that particular lexemes co-occur frequently. I therefore consider this asemantic approach to collocation as a parallel to the concept of lexical set as introduced in 4.2.5. For syntagmatic incompatibility of lexemes in the British tradition the terms *collocation restrictions* and *co-occurence restrictions* are often used (cf. Lipka 1972:47ff., 72ff.).

4.3.1. Various Approaches

I will now briefly sketch the various approaches, developments, and concepts. First the suggestions made within the framework of generative grammar in the wider sense. Here, the notion of *selection(al) restrictions* has played a crucial role. For determining and describing these, syntactic and semantic features have been used and generally descriptions were based on a highly formalized metalanguage. The features were intended to restrict and prevent the co-occurrence of certain lexemes. As late as 1965, the features used by Chomsky for this purpose were understood as exclusively syntactic.

The semantic nature of the phenomena was only recognized rather late. A survey of the whole development can be found in Lipka (1972:30ff.). In 1968 McCawley still argued that selection restrictions are semantic in nature and do not concern single nouns, but complete noun phrases. Five years earlier, Uriel Weinreich had proposed (as already mentioned) in his critique of Katz/Fodor (1963) to replace selection restrictions by the more active concept of "transfer features". In the later development McCawley (also in 1968), following Charles

Fillmore, had stated that selection restrictions are "presuppositions about the intended referents", not language-immanent phenomena.

In this connection it must be stressed that the term *presupposition* and the different notions related to it in linguistics and philosophy are used very differently by various authors. In any case, what is at issue here is "lexical presupposition", not "existential presupposition" (which is more relevant in philosophy). Obviously, when the concept is understood as presuppositions made by speakers or hearers about an intended extralinguistic referent, we have left the domain of linguistic semantics proper and entered the realm of pragmatics.

Within structuralist proposals for capturing syntagmatic semantic relations, there are also rather different positions. At first, before the impact of Katz/Fodor (1963), lexical semantics was almost exclusively paradigmatic. Under the overwhelming influence of Trier's field theory, attention and effort was concentrated on paradigmatic relations (cf. Lyons 1977:250 ff.). It is true, however, that as early as 1934 Walter Porzig focused on syntagmatically connected lexemes, labelling such relations "wesenhafte Bedeutungsbeziehungen" (cf. Leisi ²1985:200). But on the whole, there is a long tradition of neglecting these, from Leisi's, Coseriu's and Lyons's early work on semantics right through to Cruse (1986).

In Coseriu (1967) Porzig's proposals are explicitly taken as a starting point for developing a syntagmatic, structuralist approach using semantic features. Coseriu relabels the phenomenon *lexical solidarities* ("lexikalische Solidaritäten"). In Kastovsky (1980) lexical solidarities and selection restrictions are compared. He arrives at the conclusion that the two concepts are not mutually exclusive, but rather complementary from an analytic and synthetic point of view, respectively. Solidarities are positive semantic implications, while selection restrictions are constraints in a synthetic linguistic theory. In Kastovsky (1982a: 145, 262) the terms *contextual features* ("kontextuelle Merkmale") and *indirect semic information* ("indirekte semische Information") are also used for solidarities. In his opinion, these correspond to Weinreich's transfer features.

4.3.2. Selection Restrictions and Projection Rules

The term *selection restrictions* was first introduced in Katz/Fodor (1963) in connection with their suggestions for a semantic theory. As already mentioned, Chomsky still believed in 1965 that the combination of lexemes is a purely syntactic problem. In his proposals for the subcategorization of verbs, he distinguishes between "strict subcategorization rules" and "selectional rules". The former refer to the categorial context, and thus determine e.g. whether a verb can be followed by an NP or not. On the other hand, "selectional rules" refer to the possible syntactic features in the subject or object of a verb. Thus, according to Chomsky, the restrictions on the verbs *frighten* and *admire* can be formalized as follows (in simplified form):

(18) *frighten* [+ V, ... ______ [+ Animate]]
admire [+ V, [+ Human] ______ .....].

In (18) the long underline indicates the position of the verb with respect to the following and preceding elements in the sentence, i.e. the inherent features of a noun functioning as subject or object. The formalization thus means that *frighten* requires an animate noun as object, while *admire* has a selectional feature [+ HUMAN] in the subject noun. If these conditions are not met, the verb cannot be inserted in the nominal frame. Thus, the generation of **John frightens sincerity* and **Sincerity may admire the boy* is blocked by selectional rules.

The *selection restrictions* proposed in Katz/Fodor (1963) are semantic in nature (cf. Fodor 1977: 64–69). Their complex and highly formalized proposals for a semantic theory were extremely influential but not always convincing. They cannot be discussed here in detail. The following brief sketch, however, seems useful in our context. The model consists of two components: 1. the dictionary and 2. the so-called "projection rules". The "dictionary entry" contains various meanings of a single homonymous or polysemous lexeme, e.g. *bachelor* (see diagram (2) in 3.1.). The theory is supposed to select the appropriate meaning, in a specific context, and thereby to resolve the ambiguity of a lexeme. Thus, the disambiguation of e.g. *bill, ball, colorful* is achieved. A certain so-called "path" (i.e. a chain of general and specific semantic features) or "reading" is selected, as illustrated for *bachelor* in (19). Here, round brackets symbolize "markers", and square brackets so-called "distinguishers".

(19) *bachelor* → Noun → (Animal) → (Male) → (Young)
→ [fur seal when without mate during breeding time]

As opposed to nouns, adjectives and verbs have selection restrictions in their lexical entries, symbolized by angular brackets. These control the combination with nouns. The following abbreviated example may illustrate this:

(20) *hit*: V, V_{tr} (Action) ... <SUBJECT: (Human) v (Higher Animal),
OBJECT: (Physical Object) ...>

Katz/Fodor's standard example *The man hits the colorful ball* has been discussed in many linguistic publications. It contains two or more homonymous lexemes *ball* with readings such as: 1. 'globular object' and 2. 'social activity'. The second reading is excluded in the sentence by means of the selection restrictions, because it cannot be combined with *hit*. Thus the disambiguation is achieved.

The combination of the various possible readings of words in a sentence is performed by the projection rules, the second component of the theory. These are said to "amalgamate" readings, i.e. meanings, on the basis of the syntactic structure of the sentence. The amalgamation starts at the basis of a tree diagram, representing the syntactic structure of the sentence. The projection rules always combine the paths, i.e. the sets of features, of two immediate constituents of the sentence, unless this is prevented by selection restrictions. Thus, working upwards through the hierarchy of the sentence, they are intended to combine the meanings of more and more constituents, until we arrive at the meaning of the whole sentence.

4.3.3. Transfer Features and Metaphor

As already mentioned (see 3.3.2.), Katz/Fodor's theory was harshly criticized by Uriel Weinreich, a critique which resulted in the postulation of transfer features to replace selection restrictions. Besides my own use of this concept in various publications, it can also be found in recent work in Tournier (1985: 229) as "sème de transfert" (claimed to be the basis of metaphor), and in Cruse (1986: 105) who says that semantic "traits are ... transferred to the head", e.g. in *my pregnant neighbour/cousin/friend.* Weinreich's arguments for preferring transfer features to selection restrictions are all very convincing for any semantic theory and practice that makes use of semantic features, be it more or less formalized.

His main objection against the Katz/Fodor theory, however, is that projection rules do not really build on syntactic structure, but rather destroy the semantic structure. Their application reduces the words of a sentence to a heap of features, and in fact the meaning of any complex expression becomes "an unstructured heap of features – just like the meaning of a single word" (Weinreich 1972: 34). The amalgamation of the paths for the sentences *Cats chase mice* and *Mice chase cats* "would yield the same unordered set of features". As we have seen, transfer features are more active and less restrictive than selection restrictions, and they can explain the interpretation of vague, unusual, and even conflicting combinations of lexemes, or rather lexical units, including metaphors. Thus, e.g. *The animal miaowed, He sailed (flew) the craft, He was drinking carrots* and *His fear ate him up* can all be assigned a sensible interpretation (see diagram (26) p. 112).

Besides verbs like *sail, fly, eat, drink* (but also Ger *essen/fressen*, cf. Lipka 1972: 48–51), adjectives like *buxom* and *pregnant* (cf. Ger *schwanger/trächtig*) are often found in the debate on syntagmatic semantic relations. In English, we do not have (within *eat* and *drink*) the further distinction between Ger *trinken/saufen* and *essen/fressen*, which can also be explained on the basis of transfer features. If the subject of the verb *saufen* or *fressen* contains an inherent feature [+HUMAN], this is overridden and dominated by a feature <+ ANIMAL> transferred from the verb. This then leads to the interpretation 'drink like an animal' and 'eat like an animal'.

The same factual linguistic state of affairs might also be explained differently by drawing on the notion of presupposition. Thus, in the manner of McCawley and Fillmore, we could say that the items *fressen* and *saufen* presuppose that the subject of these verbs is non-human or an animal, or more precisely still 'like an animal'. In such a pragmatic explanation, however, we are no longer concerned with syntagmatic relations between lexemes as elements of the linguistic system. We would then, rather, make assumptions about extralinguistic referents or denotata. At the same time, this means giving up the possibility and the advantages of formalization.

Within the structuralist, language-immanent framework of Lyons's theory, the same facts are accounted for by the concept of *encapsulation*. Lyons (1977: 262) explicitly starts from Porzig's "essential meaning-relation" between *kick* and *foot, punch* and *fist*, and coins the term *encapsulation* for "the lexicalization of this syntagmatic modifying component". Kastovsky (1982a: 68) implicitly identifies this term with Coseriu's *lexical solidarities* (to which we will come presently) and draws attention to the parallel with word-formation syntagmas. In the latter, one word is semantically and formally contained or implied in the other, as e.g. *Telefon* in *telefon/ieren* and *knife* (noun) in the zero-derived verb *to knifeØ*. In the case of encapsulation and lexical solidarities, according to Kastovsky, one item is only semantically implied or contained in the other, namely *Zahn* in *beißen, lips* in *kiss, foot* in *kick*. Other relevant examples in English would be *teeth* and *gnash, lips* and *purse, lips* and *pout, shoulders* and *shrug*. For Lyons (1977: 262) this is not a matter of lexical relations, but of sense-relations, because

> the sense of *with the foot* is encapsulated in the sense of *kick*, as the sense of *with the teeth* is encapsulated in the sense of *bite*.

Encapsulation and lexical solidarities are both positive implications between the content of two given lexical items. Selection restrictions and transfer features attempt to capture such semantic relations with the help of features, either in a negative, restrictive way or a positive, dynamic one. All four concepts or theoretical approaches to the same problem and facts are within the bounds of a purely language-immanent view.

This perspective is transcended as soon as we move to a pragmatic level and include lexical presuppositions, as beliefs of speakers and hearers. If we further shift the focus along this line to a psychological, cognitive point of view – which in my opinion is complementary, not mutually exclusive – metaphor is understood as dual, or secondary, categorization, and metonymy (which is banned from most structuralist models) is easily explained (see 3.4.2.).

To the mind, the connection between two lexical units related through metaphor is simply similarity; in the case of metonymy it is simply contiguity. This semantic shift between the lexical units, both synchronically and diachronically, is extremely economical, since the form of the lexeme remains the same (as opposed to most word-formation processes). The mental effort is limited in both shifts, although it is not always easy, in the case of metaphor, to see the likeness in two things (*biting cold*, a *fox*). Poets are often specially gifted at doing precisely this. Nevertheless, the two cognitive processes, metaphor and metonymy, are basic and fundamental and both involve categorization (see 3.4.2.).

4.3.4. Lexical Solidarities

The following presentation of the notion of "lexical solidarities", as a very prominent approach to syntagmatic lexical structures from a language-immanent perspective, will be based mainly on the classic article Coseriu (1967), and also on Kastovsky (1980) and (1982a: 144–156). Coseriu explicitly starts out from Porzig's concept of "essential meaning relation" ("wesenhafte Bedeutungsbeziehung") and his examples: *bellen – Hund, wiehern – Pferd, beißen – Zähne, blond – Haar*. Coseriu proposes to reformulate Porzig's insights and make them more precise by drawing on certain concepts of structural semantics, such as lexeme, archilexeme, and classeme. The latter is a kind of very general semantic feature, such as [±ANIMATE], [±HUMAN], [±MALE].

Coseriu (1967: 296) defines "lexikalische Solidarität" as "inhaltliche Bestimmung eines Wortes durch eine Klasse, ein Archilexem oder ein Lexem", i.e. the determination of the content of one word by a class of other words (represented by a "classeme"), by an archilexeme, or by a specific other lexeme. Kastovsky (1980: 70; 1982a: 249) contrasts lexical solidarities with selection restrictions, characterizing the former as positive implications between lexemes. Solidarities are directed, oriented, unilateral implications. Thus, e.g. the determined lexeme *kiss* contains the meaning of the determining lexeme *lips*, but not vice versa. The classeme [+HUMAN] is contained in the following verbs and their grammatical subject: *marry, apologize, admire, criticize, murder, assassinate*.

Generally speaking, Kastovsky argues that the two concepts, lexical solidarities and selection restrictions, are not contradictory, but supplement each other and that lexical solidarities describe the same phenomenon from an analytic perspective, while selection restrictions do this from the point of view of synthesis. Coseriu distinguishes three types of lexical solidarities (which he calls "Affinität, Selektion, Implikation"), depending on whether a classeme, an archilexeme, or a specific lexeme function as a distinctive feature in a word, namely 1. 'affinity', 2. 'selection', and 3. 'implication'. These may be illustrated with the following example from Kastovsky (1980: 87):

(21) (a) The *boy* apologized: classeme [+HUMAN] = 1. affinity

(b) A *week* elapsed : archilexeme *TIME* = 2. selection

(c) Henry shrugged (his *shoulders*): lexeme *shoulders* = 3. implication

Kastovsky argues convincingly that (21a) and (21b) should be taken together and thus the distinction between 1. 'affinity' and 2. 'selection' should be given up.[11] His reasons are that classemes often function as archilexemes and that in both 'affinity' as well as 'selection' semantic features are involved as

[11] The point of his argument, basically, is that he rejects the distinction between *seme* and *classeme*; the rest follows from this automatically.

opposed to 3. 'implication', which only concerns specific lexemes. In connection with linear lexical fields, we have seen in diagrams (11) and (12) (p. 153) that semantic dimensions (sometimes called "archisememes") like TEMPERATURE and COLOUR are equivalent to the (missing) archilexemes. Modifying Coseriu's typology of lexical solidarities thus seems justified.

In fact, Coseriu's system is a cross-classification, because in addition to the three types he makes a further distinction between unilateral and multilateral ("einseitige/mehrseitige") solidarities. Examples of both types are the following:

(22) (a) *bite - teeth, lick - tongue, kiss - lips* etc. = unilateral
(b) *bark - dog, neigh - horse, bray - donkey* etc. = multilateral

The unilateral solidarities are idiosyncratic, while the multilateral ones form paradigmatic sets. With the former, the absence of the determining lexeme is the rule. Therefore, utterances like **He kissed her with his lips* and **The dog chewed the bone with its teeth* are hardly acceptable. Kastovsky (1982a:147) draws attention to the fact that the explicit realization is perfectly normal, as soon as the determining lexeme is further modified. Thus, we may have *Romeo kissed Juliet with chocolate-smeared lips* and the dog may well *chew with its sharp teeth.* With multilateral solidarities, the determining lexeme may either appear in the context or not. Thus we have both: *the donkey brayed* and *the animal brayed.*

At the end of his famous article on lexical solidarities, Coseriu points out that non-solidarity also exists. According to him, if we have a contradiction between inherent features and those deriving from syntagmatic relations, a metaphor may arise. Obviously, the conflict does not lead to excluding or discarding such a non-solidary utterance. There are thus no restrictions in Coseriu's approach. He gives the example of the verb *beißen*, which is said always to contain the syntagmatic feature "mit den Zähnen" and thus in the utterance *Die Kälte beißt*, according to Coseriu (1967: 302), "wird dadurch die Kälte als ein Wesen mit Zähnen dargestellt", i.e. coldness is represented as a toothed being. Incidentally, *beißende Kälte* and *biting cold* are habitual collocations in German and English (see 4.3.5.) but could also be interpreted as dead or "half-dead" metaphors.

Coseriu's method of dealing with non-solidarity clearly corresponds to Weinreich's use of transfer features. Kastovsky (1982a: 148) explicitly refers to these when dealing with metaphor, which for him is the result of 'contextual features' being superimposed on inherent features. In conclusion I would like to quote some of his examples of such reinterpretation:

(23) (a) His irony was biting
(b) Jim is married to his car
(c) The policeman barked at the suspect.

4.3.5. Collocation as a Neutral Syntagma

The concept of collocation, which plays an important role in British linguistics, where it originated (cf. Lipka 1971:214 f.; 1972:72–75), is neutral in several respects. The term designates the co-occurrence or syntagmatic combination of lexical items (or lexemes), independently of word class and syntactic structure.

According to J. R. Firth, we "know a word by the company it keeps" and this "keeping company" he called 'collocation' and considered it part of its "meaning" (in the widest sense; cf. Lipka 1971:214 f., 1972:72 ff., Palmer 1976:94 ff., Carter 1987:36 ff., 48 ff.). Thus, for example *open* and *window* form a collocation, irrespective of whether *open* is a verb or an adjective. As opposed to selection restrictions, the syntactic relation between subject and predicate, or verb and object, does not matter. The term collocation is also neutral with respect to which element is primary or dominant in the relation (cf. Lipka 1972:74). Finally, in the traditional British approach, a semantic analysis is also not carried out and thus lexical units (in our sense) do not play a role (cf. Carter 1987:48 f.).

Precisely because of this vagueness and neutrality, the concept of collocation has, in my opinion, certain advantages for capturing syntagmatic relations between lexical elements. This holds for syntagmas both on the syntactic level and on the level of word-formation, i.e. compounds and nominalizations. Collocations can therefore be called neutral syntagmas. This neutrality is particularly relevant for applied linguistics and the teaching and learning of vocabulary (cf. Carter 1987:155 ff.). Collocations are thus syntagmatic lexical relations, but not necessarily semantic relations. They are therefore parallel to the 'lexical sets' on the paradigmatic axis (see 4.2.5.) which are not necessarily sense-relations. A further parallel between the two is caused by the psychological notion of association. Just as lexical sets are paradigmatically linked by association (cf. Saussure's terminology mentioned in 1.2.) collocations are syntagmatically associated, learned and memorized.

The lexical items which form a collocation need not necessarily be contiguous, as demonstrated by the following example:

(24)	(a) They *collect stamps*	V + NP
	(b) They *collect* many things, but chiefly *stamps*.	

Word class and syntactic structure are also irrelevant for collocations, as illustrated by the following classic example (cf. Lipka 1971:214):

(25)	(a) His *argument* was *strong*	N + Adj
	(b) He *argued strongly*	V + Adv.

In both cases we have the same collocation between *argue* and *strong* that appears in *strong argument, the strength of his argument*, and *his argument was strengthened.* The same holds for the German items *rauchen* and *stark* in *Er raucht stark* and *Er ist ein starker Raucher.* All these examples demonstrate that collocation affects both the levels of syntax and word-formation.[12] Further proof of this point, as well as of the independence from word class and syntactic structure, is the sentence *A bullfighter fights bulls at a bullfight.* It contains three instances of the collocation of *fight* and *bull.*

For the learner, it is often difficult to establish and use the correct, significant, habitual, or fixed collocations in a foreign language, especially if the items concerned are semantically very close (e.g. *large, big, great / male, masculine / fat, plump, stout, obese* cf. Carter 1987:53) or formally similar (e.g. *electric, electrical / optic nerve, optical illusion*). But even in other cases, languages often differ in unpredictable ways. Although Ger *Wasser kochen* corresponds to E *boil water*, the similar collocations *Kaffee kochen, Tee kochen* have to be rendered by *make/brew coffee (tea)*, and **boil (coffee/tea)* is unacceptable.

Specialized dictionaries are not of great help, in particular with items from the general vocabulary (see 1.4.). This is true of Friederich/Canavan (1979), the DEWC, and Benson/Benson/Ilson (1986), the BBI dictionary of English, where one searches in vain for the collocations of *male* and *masculine* (but see s.v. *outstanding* in the sense 'not yet paid'). Ordinary modern dictionaries like the LDCE 2 (^{2}1987), the OALD 4 (^{4}1989), or the COBUILD *English Language Dictionary* (1987) are much better sources of information. In the latter, based on a computerized corpus of about 20 million words (cf. Carter 1987:140ff.), we find the following collocates (i.e. items collocating) of *male: nurse, hormones, attitudes, unemployment, roles, sex, plant, part of a device* and, as separate entries, the fixed collocations *male chauvinism, male chauvinist, male chauvinist pig.*

In an empirical study carried out by one of my students, with the help of a restricted number of native speaker informants (two English, two Scottish, two American), *male* was found to collocate most frequently with *choir, child, nurse, animal* and *masculine* with *style, woman, pronoun.* The judgement and elicitation tests also yielded the collocations: *electric light (shock, chair)*, but *electrical engineer (engineering, appliance, industry)*. Such collocations must be learnt as complete expressions, which are automatically triggered and reproduced. Syntactic or semantic rules cannot be formulated for them.[13]

G. Pascoe (personal communication) claims that there is a rule about *electric* ('powered/driven/caused by electricity') and *electrical* ('concerned/connected with electricity'). Similar rules for this pair in grammars and dictionaries are reviewed in Marsden (1985:27, 29) who believes that *electrical* is the older form and that *-ic* is preferred in recent collocations – witness also *electronic.*

---

12 Syntactic restrictions connected with a collocation may serve as an indicator for possible idiomatization.

13 Cf. Marsden (1985) for a very thorough and comprehensive empirical study of current usage concerning adjective pairs in *-ic* and *-ical.* From his evidence he concludes that there is "undivided usage", namely 100% consensus among speakers on the collocations, only with two pairs: *economic/-al* and *electric/-al.* At the bottom end of the scale, with almost exactly divided usage (50%), is *poetic/-al.*

The OALD 4 distinguishes five different lexical units *electric* (of which one is metaphorical – 'causing sudden excitement'): 'producing (electricity'), 'produced by', 'used in conveying', 'using electrical power'. It illustrates these with the collocations *electric atmosphere (generator, current, plug, cooker)* and further defines the familiar collocations *electric blanket (chair, field, razor, shock, storm).* No collocations are given for *electrical* with the single relational meaning 'concerned with electricity'.

There may be, however, a certain amount of individual variation. Thus, for example, McArthur (1986:111, 124ff.) and Carter (1987:28ff.) consistently use *alphabetic* in collocation with *order, ordering, mode, sequence, lexicography* (cf. also OED III, s.v. *alphabetization*). Carter also uses *problematic (category, set, feature)* and *unproblematic (equivalence)* while Lyons and Cruse prefer *problematical.*

The conclusion about the impossibility of general rules is further supported by research reported in Leitzke (1989a:18ff.), based on the work of many linguists and in addition on the LOB Corpus.[14] The author discusses pairs of what she calls "(de)nominal adjectives", such as *industrial/ous* and *economic/-al*, derived from an identical base with different suffixes.

She arrives at the conclusion that for the single pair *historic* vs. *historical* we can draw a systematic distinction and assign specific meanings to suffixes, as in *historic spot (event, speech)* 'famous in history' vs. *historical events (people, studies)* 'belonging to history'. In all other cases, collocations are unsystematic and the same meaning (e.g. a positive value judgement in *economical* and *historic*) may be expressed by different suffixes.

Examples with the same base, either from a formal, etymological, or semantic perspective, collected from the LDCE 2 (^{2}1987) may further illustrate the unsystematicity of collocations. We find *kingly manner/feast, regal manners/old lady/~ally entertained, royal familiy/assent vs. right royal welcome, royal blue/flush, prerogative,* and *Royal Highness.* Furthermore, there is *queenly dignity, queen consort/mother, Queen's bench/Council/English* and *queen's evidence.* Obviously, a number of these examples are more or less idiomatic. There is no hard-and-fast dividing line between fixed collocations and idiomatic turns of phrase, but basically only a difference of degree.[15]

For many idioms (cf. Lipka 1972:75ff.) like *red herring*, or *kick the bucket* (and Ger *ins Gras beißen*), synchronic explanations cannot be given. They can often only be explained from a diachronic point of view. Consequently, in learning a foreign language, such extreme cases of fixed collocations can only be taught and learnt as units.

---

[14] The Lancaster-Oslo-Bergen Corpus of British English; see Chapter I, footnote 1.

[15] For a comprehensive, descriptive study of English "colour collocations", including metaphorical and idiomatic ones, cf. Bennett (1988). This book contains a long alphabetical list (197–301) of collocations and expressions with colour terms (in nominal or adjectival form and as parts of compounds), together with definitions, collected from a great number of reference works and other sources.

Idioms as well as fixed collocations are the expression of irregularity which remains in the lexicon, besides the many possible generalizations and the internal and external structuring. There is no rule-governed explanation for the fact that we have *country house* besides *rural residence*, or that in French *chemin de fer* exists side by side with *voie ferrée*. As we have seen in 3.2.5., such irregularity can be described on the level of the 'norm' of a language (in Coseriu's sense), which exists between the *langue*, the language system, on the one hand and its concrete realization, the *parole*, on the other. Different varieties of the same language system may have different norms, such as British and American English, or Swiss, Austrian, and so-called High German (see 1.4.).

The following quotation from Quirk (1972: 26) is my last example of how erratic collocations (on the level of syntax and word-formation) can be in the norm of British and American English:

> *Mail* and *post* are interesting examples of the complexity that is possible. While Americans handle their mail (or post) – which may include *post*cards – through the *post* office and the *postal* services with *postage* stamps, the British deal with the post (or mail) with the help of *mail*bags in *mail* vans, *mail* trains, *Royal Mail* steamers, and there is the air *mail* service. Yet although Americans sometimes speak of the *postman* delivering their letters, there is no corresponding British use of *mailman.*

We may add that the British usually *post a letter / parcel* etc., i.e. 'send by post', while the Americans *mail* it.

Textlinguistic aspects are also relevant for collocation. *Outstanding* in the sense of 'not yet paid' (see p. 167) is rare in many texts and there are only 5 instances of it in the LOB Corpus. If, however, we focus on a particular text type, namely reminders for payments due, it occurs quite often in the company of words like *account, debts, invoice, payment* etc. Thus a specific text type favours certain otherwise rare collocations. In journalese, certain collocations frequently occur as clichés or euphemisms, as in the following examples taken from Gill (1987): *shy spinster, devoted mother, nutty professor, doctors battle to save lives, the pound plunges, firemen struggle, confirmed bachelor, constant companion, fun-loving, party-going.*

A more fundamental textlinguistic aspect of collocations is the way in which they contribute to what Halliday/Hasan (1976) have called "lexical cohesion". In general, the term *cohesion* was used in early textlinguistic studies for denoting the inherent means by which texts are linguistically connected. Clearly, lexical means are an extremely important subclass of such cohesive devices, which link parts of text across sentence boundaries and thus constitute texts. Halliday/Hasan (1976: 274) define *lexical cohesion* as "the cohesive effects achieved by the selection of vocabulary" (cf. Carter 1987: 72 ff.). The most important kind for them is what they call "reiteration". This form of lexical cohesion involves the repetition of a lexical item at one end of the scale and the use of a so-called "general word" at the other one. In between, there are a number of other lexical relations, which I shall summarize and illustrate in the following diagram:

(26)	1. *Reiteration*	
	(a) same word (repetition):	*mushroom - mushroom*
	(b) synonym (or near-synonym):	*boy - lad*
	(c) superordinate:	*car - Jaguar*
		flower - tulip
	(d) general word:	*man, people, creature, thing, stuff, business, matter, move, question, idea*

The second important form of lexical cohesion, besides the various types of reiteration, is "collocation". Although Halliday/Hasan (1976:284) define *collocation* as "the association of lexical items that regularly co-occur", the term is obviously not used in exactly the same way as I have used it so far. It includes various types of oppositeness of meaning and other kinds of sense-relation, as can be seen from the following diagram, in which I illustrate and summarize the views they express verbally in the book:

(27)	2. *Collocation*	
	(a) complementarity:	*boy - girl*
	(b) antonyms:	*like - hate, wet - dry*
	(c) converses:	*order - obey*
	(d) co-hyponyms:	*chair - table / furniture*
	...	
	(h) proximity:	*laugh - joke, ill - doctor.*

Besides lexical cohesion (in Halliday/Hasan's sense) other lexical phenomena contribute to cohesion and coherence in texts, especially the productive processes of word-formation. It must be pointed out here that in more recent research on textlinguistics the terms *cohesion* and *coherence* are used differently from the way they are in Halliday/Hasan's book. Today, *cohesion* normally denotes the means of grammatical linking in the surface structure of texts. On the other hand, *coherence* is used for deeper, underlying semantic and conceptual relationships. Since the productive processes of word-formation (see 3.2.4.) create both formal and semantic linking in the co-text, morphologically complex lexemes establish both cohesion and coherence at the same time. With these remarks we have already entered a wider, fundamentally different field, namely the contextual relations of words in general. We will discuss these under a separate heading here.

Chapter V

The Function of Words. Co-Text, Context, and the Mental Lexicon

So far we have disregarded the function of words in texts, the distinction introduced in 1.3. (p. 24) between *co-text* (linguistic context) and *context* (extra-linguistic context, including the context of situation), and the function of words in the mind (not only for categorization), namely especially their storage and processing (cf. also Kastovsky 1982b).

This will lead to the question of whether lexical units can be at all sensibly discussed without linguistic and extralinguistic context (5.1.). We will finally (5.2.) consider briefly problems of the mental lexicon, i.e. how words can be stored, found and processed in the mind, and how far the linguistic organization and structuring of words corresponds to their organization in the brain.

5.1. Words in Context

As is customary today, we will make a terminological distinction in the following between *co-text*, denoting the verbal or linguistic environment, and *context* (in the wider sense), including situational and cultural surroundings. Textual environment thus refers to co-text, and we will first have a closer look at complex lexemes and their various possible functions in texts. We then turn to the problem of monosemization in co-text, i.e. the problem of how specific meanings of homonymous or polysemous items (see 4.2.1.) are selected and determined by the co-text. Finally, the appropriateness of certain words in different varieties of English (see 1.3.) and different cultural contexts will be discussed. This topic clearly goes beyond merely co-textual considerations.

5.1.1. The Functions of Word-Formation in Texts

Besides the general function of complex lexemes just mentioned, of creating cohesion and coherence simultaneously, several specific functions of word-formation can be distinguished (cf. Lipka 1987b). Perhaps the most specific function, which immediately comes to mind, is the high degree of information condensation achieved by various kinds of nominalization. In the following example from Kastovsky (1982a: 217) there is no preceding co-text, but the extreme formal and semantic condensation becomes obvious:

(1) I know *an alleged discoverer of time-travel.*

The compound *penfriend*, another isolated example, defined in the LDCE as

> a person, esp. in a foreign country, whom one has come to know by the friendly exchange of letters, but whom one has usu. never met

is a further striking case in point.

The second function of complex lexemes in texts (related to information condensation) is quite well known and is repeatedly referred to in research by the term "pronominalization" (in the wider sense) (cf. Kastovsky 1982a:217, 1982b :182 f.). I would like to illustrate this with an instance of the very regular and productive process of agent-nominalization, taken from TIME magazine (8/8/83:31):

(2) Not since ... 1941 when Rudolf Hess flew off from Berlin to Scotland ... had a private trip abroad by a German leader so *puzzled* his country-men. This time the *puzzler* was none other than Franz Josef Strauss.

A much more complex type of nominalization is illustrated by the following example (3) collected from an introductory book on text linguistics (cf. Lipka 1987b: 60):

(3) Der letzte Bus ... [war] längst abgefahren, als der ... Zug ... gegen Mitte*rnacht* in Nienhagen ankam. Der einzige Fahrgast, der dem Zug entstieg, war *ein Herr*. ... schließlich *ging* er entschlossenen Schrittes in die angezeigte Richtung davon ... Aber noch ehe *der nächtliche Wanderer* diesen Gedanken verfolgen konnte ...

In this example, the complex nominal takes up and incorporates semantic material from the co-text of the antecedent, namely *nächtlich* from *Mitternacht* etc. and *Wanderer* from *ging entschlossenen Schrittes* etc. On the morphological level, *nächtlich* is only partially and indirectly related to *Mitternacht* and the agent noun *Wanderer* is not at all derived from an absent verb *wandern* in the text, but semantically related to *ging*. We thus have no direct word-formation processes in the text, but a morphologically complex nominal. I therefore proposed (in Lipka 1987b: 61) to use the terms "semantic nominalization" or "semantic pronominalization" for cases like this, in which preceding semantic and lexical material is taken up in the form of a complex nominal. Such a process is not recognized within Halliday/Hasan's concept of lexical cohesion. I propose to treat cases like *der nächtliche Wanderer* as a third type of word-formational function in texts, since it is clearly distinct from the preceding one.

A fourth kind of function has also been noticed by various linguists (who often speak of "Benennungsfunktion"), namely the naming function of complex lexemes. In my opinion, this is a mixture of more specific subfunctions, related to classifying (cf. Lipka 1983: 928) and categorization (see 3.4.2.) on the one hand and to the positive and negative aspects of the concept-forming power of words on the other hand. The negative aspect of the latter has been referred to (see 1.2.) by the term hypostatization.

In addition to the four types of function distinguished here, we can also mention another group of purely textual functions, such as creating coherence and cohesion, stylistic effects, etc. (cf. Lipka 1987b: 59–63). In this connection, metatextual discourse markers ("Textgliederungssignale") must be mentioned, in particular those performed by headlines containing non-lexicalized complex lexemes. These function as attention-getting devices in titles of journalistic texts, because the resulting cataphoric relations of such nonce-formations create suspense.

5.1.2. Monosemization as the Resolution of Polysemy

The age-old question of the ambiguity and polysemy of lexical items is normally only a problem if words are considered in isolation. As soon as the co-text and context are taken into account, ambiguity and polysemy are resolved, unless they are intended not to be, as e.g. in humorous (puns), literary, tactful, or political language. This is particularly true of longer and clearly situated texts. In such a case, a single meaning or "reading" of a lexical item is selected by the context, i.e. a lexical unit (in our terminology). I propose to introduce the term *monosemization* for this phenomenon, a translation of the term "Monosemierung", which is quite current in German linguistics. The text, or more precisely its interpreter (in pragmatical terms), selects a single, actual, or textual sense from the greater number of potential, or multiple meanings. Hansen et al. (^{2}1985: 198 ff.) stress the point that monosemization ("Monosemierung") may be produced either by the situational or linguistic (grammatical, lexical) context and claim that a polysemous word is monosemized by a contextual partner ("wird durch einen Kontextpartner monosemiert", ^{2}1985:200). Clearly, "contextual partner" is a near-synonym of *collocation* (see 4.3.5.). Hansen et al. also speak of the mutual monosemization, e.g. in the case of the verb *plant* and the noun phrase *a bulb*, as opposed to the ambiguous and vague noun-phrase *a small bulb*.

We will take up their example and represent the polysemous item in the following way:

(4) *bulb*
1. 'underground stem of plant'
2. 'glass container of electric lamp'

Clearly, there is a metaphorical relationship between the two lexical units based on the shape of the concrete objects. Syntagmatic relationships (like those between verb and object above) will normally disambiguate the item. This also holds for coordinated noun phrases like *the bulbs of the lilies and the tulips* and for complex lexemes like *tulip bulb*. Hansen et al. further illustrate this with *The bombers were trained/manufactured* and the following example, which I represent as diagram (5), where a metonymic relationship exists (see 3.4.2. and cf. Lipka 1988b):

(5) They — *rebuilt* the whole house [+ARTEFACT]
They — *informed* the whole house [+HUMAN]

Obviously, the question of monosemization (either seen from a language-immanent or a pragmatic point of view) is a variant of the problem of disambiguation, hotly discussed in TG (see 4.3.2.) in connection with examples like *He was wearing a light suit* and *The man hit the colourful ball.* Weinreich (1972: 17 f.) in connection with his critique of the theory proposed by Katz/Fodor, speaks of the "determination of the number of readings of a sentence" and "the idea of contextual resolution of ambiguities", which was "a commonplace with neogrammarian and descriptivist semanticists".

5.1.3. Words at Work

In concluding the topic of words in context, I would like to draw on some examples used in Quirk (1986: 104 f., 114 f.), which establish a connection with the appropriateness of lexical items in a larger, cultural context. This collection of papers bears the subtitle "Lectures on Textual Structure". The examples given there are closely related to the topic of varieties of English, discussed in 1.3.

Quirk (1986: 108 f.) points out that some lexical items and only a few performative verbs are used "for a few common occasions" and in very specific text types, as e.g. *I do hereby admit you as a member of the Royal College* and *I do confer upon you.* Thus, ceremonies and charters provide the only suitable contexts for some verbs and adverbs (*hereby, henceforth*), which are otherwise very rare. Subject matter (e.g. tennis or cooking), and the corresponding text types (sports reporting and recipes), are responsible for the selection of items like *straight sets, top-seed,* or *kwali, stir-fry, chillies.* Quirk (1986: 113 ff.) speaks of "content-dependence" as opposed to "style-dependence" and stresses the fact that:

> Important as are grammar and sentence-structure … there is no area of language comparable with vocabulary in the extent of its influence in conferring a sense of appropriacy.

The use of vocatives (*Mrs. Wong, Mary, Tony, Vice-Chancellor, Your Excellency*) clearly depends upon situational as well as cultural context (e.g. British vs. American speakers). A particularly striking example of the combination of both factors, situation and culture, is the "choric declaration" of new graduates, on admission to the profession of veterinary surgeons in the U.K. [my italics, LL].

(6) *Inasmuch* as the privilege of Membership of the *Royal College of Veterinary Surgeons* is about to be conferred on me, *I promise* and *solemnly declare* that I will *abide* in all due loyalty to the Royal College of Veterinary Surgeons

and will do all in my power to maintain and promote its interests. I further ... my constant endeavour will be to ensure the welfare of animals committed to my care

and the response of the President, quoted by Quirk (1986:107f.):

(7) In the name of the Council of the Royal College of Veterinary Surgeons ... I do *hereby* admit you as members of the Royal College and by the same power *do confer upon you* the right to be styled Veterinary Surgeons and to be known and *deemed* and recognised *henceforth* as duly qualified members of the veterinary profession.

Finally, he emphasizes the importance of sustaining a metaphor and avoiding mixed metaphors, as features of "all good discourse" and the need for "internal lexical harmony" in texts (1986:115). This is a fitting conclusion for our discussion of words in context.

5.2. Words in the Mind

The psychological aspects of the lexicon have long been neglected in linguistics, but were recently rediscovered in connection with Prototype Semantics and Cognitive Linguistics. Interdisciplinary approaches in text linguistics have also stimulated an interest in the relationship between linguistic and mental structuring and processing, as well as in the problems of understanding and of storing, retrieving, and processing information. The psychological notion of *semantic memory* is sometimes equated with the subjective or mental lexicon of the individual and, indeed, also with world or encyclopedic knowledge generally (cf. Hörmann 1986:145f.). The question how knowledge is stored and represented in the brain is closely related to models of linguistic and mental representation and organization, and to the process of categorization, also from a developmental point of view. Insights in this area are obviously of the utmost importance for language learning and teaching (cf. Carter 1987).

The following part of my book will be based mainly on Hörmann (1986), an excellent introduction to the psychology of language written by a psychologist, and on Aitchison (1987), a very competent and palatable introduction to the mental lexicon proper by a linguist. The sketch of a possible organization of the lexicon of English draws heavily on McArthur (1986) and his thematic, non-alphabetically organized "wordbook", the LLCE.

5.2.1. Categorization and Psychology

Hörmann (1986:135ff.), in a clear and revealing chapter on the psychology of word meaning, starts out from the observation that the lexicon, as the storehouse of our knowledge, cannot be ordered alphabetically, but must be structured otherwise. For Hörmann, who applies many of Karl Bühler's insights into language, meaning is the "activation" of a relationship between linguistic and non-linguistic factual situations. Understanding is related to building groups, or categories, of things and words and to processes of differentiating. The similarities and connections, but also the differences, may be captured by using semantic features and also in other ways.

Hörmann (1986:147 ff.) describes three types of psychological models which have been used for representing how we conceptualize the inner structure of the lexicon or "semantic memory": 1. network models, 2. feature models, and 3. prototypes and family resemblances (following the research of Labov and Rosch). The psychological experiments for lending plausibility or falsifying the various hypotheses are all based on one specific working assumption: what is closely connected in semantic memory and the brain can be reached quickly and therefore needs very little processing time.

Let me concentrate on Hörmann's (1986:148 f.) summary and critique of a theory developed around 1970 by Collins and Quillian (later revised by incorporating "spreading activation"). This model tries to describe and explain how information is stored economically in the brain in the form of a network. In the hierarchic representation short distance equals semantic relatedness and two types of relation are incorporated: 1. an 'IS a'-relation between concepts, expressed by dominance in the hierarchy and 2. a 'HAVE a'-relation, which localizes attributes of concepts around the nodes of the network. Diagram (8) is a partial and modified version of the schematic representation given by Hörmann.

(8)

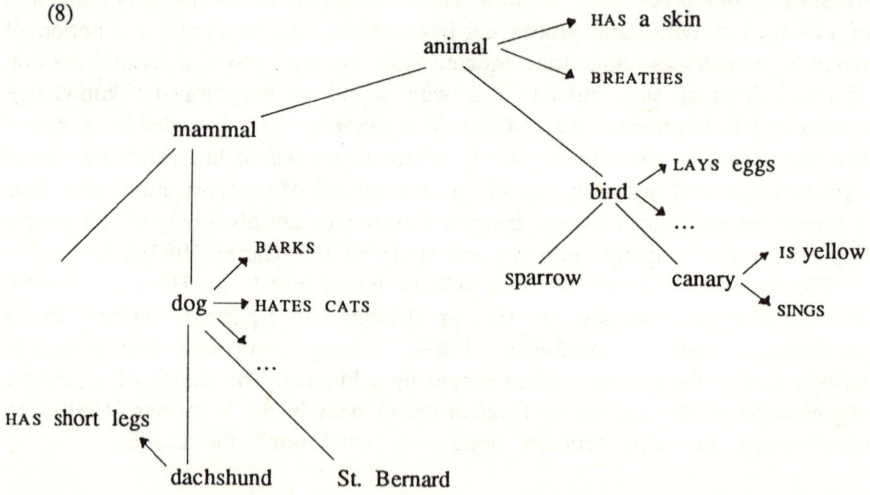

Hörmann rightly points out that many more relations are possible and necessary, besides 'IS a' and 'HAVE a', such as e.g. *contains, owns, hates, is offspring of* etc. He further notes that feature models, like networks, describe a certain categorization of extralinguistic reality and require yes/no decisions on the membership in a category (but see 3.3.3.). This naturally brings him to prototypes and the notion of *family resemblances*, originally developed by Wittgenstein for the problems of the category of *games* (cf. Hörmann 1986:155,

Aitchison 1987:47f.). As long ago as 1958, the philosopher Wittgenstein had noted that there is no characteristic attribute, or semantic feature, common to all sorts of games, such as *board-games, card-games, ball-games*, and *Olympic games*. However, there is a complicated network of overlapping similarities, for which he therefore coined the term *family resemblances*. Hörmann stresses the fact that Rosch sees the prototype as a gestalt, in the sense of gestalt psychology, but that all three models for semantic memory fundamentally consider the things stored (words, lexemes, semantic features, concepts) as having a verbal character.

If, however, concepts which we express with words are represented in memory by an "image", many problems of the three models of representation do not occur. In fact, Hörmann (1986:159f.) argues for such an "imaginal representation" of meaning, in which the word *car* is represented "as a *visual image* of a car". Strangely enough, he does not mention the concept (and word) *Gestalt* in this context, although it would be most appropriate, since its original meaning in German is 'shape'.[1] But shapes of concrete objects can only insufficiently be described in a verbal manner, and must be present before the inner eye in visual form (cf. Lipka 1987a for *cup, mug, bowl, tumbler, bottle*, and various types of *decanter*).

Hörmann's (1986:160) solution is the so-called "dual-coding hypothesis", originally introduced by Paivio. According to this proposal:

> Concrete words and sentences are stored as images and as words, whereas abstract words and sentences are stored only in verbal form.

This theory, which has two codes for concrete material, but only one for abstract words, can explain many research findings in psychology. Hörmann (1986:161) concludes:

> It seems to be rather well established that in many cases the meaning of a word is either completely or partially represented by an image.

This ties in neatly with Leisi's admission, referred to in 2.2.2., that a referential approach to semantics cannot be applied to abstract words. Thus, not only are Feature Semantics and Prototype Semantics complementary and not alternatives (cf. Lipka 1987a) – as analytic vs. holistic processes – but both have to be supplemented by language-immanent paraphrasing techniques.

Aitchison (1987:51–85) discusses the three models of word meaning in the chapters 5–7 of her book, and semantic memory, i.e. the organization of the mental lexicon, in her chapter 17. Her starting-point is the observation that the lexicon must be structured in some non-alphabetic way for two reasons: The

---

[1] To avoid misunderstanding: I do not claim that the German word *Gestalt* is to be identified with the technical term of psychology 'gestalt' (as a loan-word with a specific sense), nor with 'visual image' or 'shape'. Shape, with its inherently visual nature, is only one aspect of a holistic view of things as postulated by gestalt psychology. My point is to draw attention to the etymological and semantic connections.

enormous number of words and the extremely short time for retrieving them. In her presentation of semantic networks she argues convincingly (1987:74f., 85) that there are four important types of link between words in the human mind: 1. co-ordination, 2. collocation, 3. superordination, and 4. synonymy, of which especially co-ordinates and collocational links seem to be particularly strong.[2] For the problem of finding words in the mental lexicon, Aitchison (1987:165–176) discusses several models of the retrieval process, concluding that "spreading activation" is the most plausible one. The overall organization of the mental lexicon, with two major components – a semantic-syntactic and a phonological one – is then outlined in chapter 17. A very important insight into the workings of the mind is the conclusion (Aitchison 1986:199) that both in the search for a word and in processing links between them, many more words are activated than are eventually required and selected.

5.2.2. The Structuring of the Universe

In our minds, the organization of our cognitive views of the outside world can basically be described as derived from its categorization. Words serve as concept-forming tools, as crystallization points for semantic material, and as containers for the result of this process. Categories depend upon specific languages and it may be extremely difficult in some cases, if not altogether impossible (cf. Aitchison:1987:50, 195) to separate word meaning from encyclopedic knowledge.[3]

The distinction between the words and categories *camel* and *dromedary* (and the parallel German *Kamel* and *Dromedar*) may serve as an example. Many people remember that the property or attribute of having either one or two humps is relevant here, but are often at a loss to decide which is which. Obviously, we are not experts in this area, although most of us have actually seen the animals in question in the circus or the zoo. Turning to dictionaries for help, we find the following definition in the COD:

(9) *dromedary* = 'Light fast-moving (esp. Arabian or one-humped) camel bred for riding' ... [...f. Gk *dromas, -ados,* runner ...].

From this dictionary entry we can conclude either that the *dromedary* is a type or kind of the category *camel*, or that these are two closely connected

[2] The 'co-ordinates' of psychology correspond to the linguistic concept of 'co-hyponyms'. Thus psychological experiments appear to prove the dominance of horizontal, non-hierarchic relations (co-hyponyms, collocations) over the vertical, hierarchic, paradigmatic ones (hyponymy, homonymy, polysemy, sense-relations).

[3] Like Leech (^{2}1981:39) I believe that "language both determines and reflects the understanding of the world we live in" and that "the conceptual system of a language predisposes its users towards certain distinctions rather than others" and also that "the extent to which man is 'enslaved' by his language ... is mitigated by various forces of creativity in the system itself."

categories, like the *slug* and *snail*, or the *sheep* and *goat*, which fall together in a single class in Ger *Schnecke* or in Chinese *yang* (see 2.2.1.). Obviously, it is difficult in this case to distinguish relevant linguistic from encyclopedic knowledge. The COD (marking this by the label "esp.") treats both 'Arabian' and 'one-humped' as non-criterial meaning elements, i.e. as inferential features (in my terminology). In the COLLINS, *dromedary* is treated as polysemous, i.e. as the two lexical units: 1. 'a type of Arabian camel bred for racing and riding, having a single hump and long slender legs' and 2. 'another name for *Arabian camel*'. The LDCE 2 also considers one meaning of *dromedary* as synonymous with *camel*, but treats both as different animals in the following (abbreviated) entry:

(10) *camel* = "*n* either of two large long-necked animals used for riding ...
a also *dromedary* – the Arabian camel with one large HUMP ...
b the *Bactrian camel* from Asia with two large HUMPS ...".

It is clear that even well-known higher animaly may be classified or categorized in different ways and that the resulting structures of the animal kingdom will differ (see 4.2.4.). In this context, an experimental psychological study of the German field of *mammals* (Hejj/Strube 1988: esp. 77, 80 ff.) is revealing, also from a general theoretical point of view. The authors emphasize (cf. the subtitle of their article) that development and age are relevant factors here and that the structuring of this field crucially depends on instruction (e.g. *Wal-Fisch* is not a *Fisch* but a mammal), age, and the acquisition of specialized knowledge or expertise. It seems that these factors are more or less relevant in the cognitive and linguistic structuring of many aspects of our universe. This is the reason why many larger dictionaries draw on a staff of special consultants for a variety of subjects.

In concluding this topic, let us return to the most recent attempt at a non-alphabetical organization of the English lexicon: the LLCE (see 1.4.). It may be regarded as one possible proposal for structuring the universe (on a comprehensive but basic scale, containing "a core of some 15,000 words"), as represented and categorized through the English language (cf. McArthur 1981, 1986: 148 f.). We will only look at the first one of the 14 "semantic fields" (from A 'Life and living things' to N 'General and abstract terms') and its microstructure (A1 – A150), the "sets" in McArthur's terminology. The latter correspond to my own "lexical sets" (see 4.2.5.). The whole universe and the "theme", or "superset" A (on which I focus here, cf. McArthur 1986: 148 f.) are divided up in the following way:

(11)

A Life and living things
B The body: its functions and welfare
C People and the family
.....
.....
.....
N General and abstract terms

A1 Life and death
A30 Living creatures
A50 Animals/mammals
A70 Birds
A90 Reptiles and amphibians
A100 Fish and other water creatures
A110 Insects and similar creatures
A120 Parts of animals
A130 Kinds and parts of plants
A150 Plants in general

As already pointed out in 1.4., this framework is a combination of thematization and linguistic semantic structuring. In the preface to the LLCE, McArthur places himself in the tradition of the work of the Bohemian educator Comenius published in 1631 and of ROGET's Thesaurus (first published in 1852). But whereas Roget starts out with Class 1 'Abstract Relations' and deals with organic, inorganic, and matter in general, in Class 3 'Matter', McArthur finishes with abstract terms and mainly focusses on the concrete extralinguistic reality.[4]

The LLCE is not a thesaurus, however, but really a new kind of reference book (based on the LDCE) which contains information of various kinds and many illustrations. The use of the latter can be seen as conforming to the insights of gestalt psychology and Prototype Theory. This becomes particulary obvious if we look at the illustration given for *dromedary* (Africa, W Asia) and *Bactrian camel* (Asia) given in A 59. The illustrations provide the visual images for the categories and reveal the importance of the "slender legs" (in the COLLINS definition) and the runner qualities of the *dromedary* clearly.

In the "set" A 50 (animals/mammals) useful feature matrices (from linguistic theory) are given for many animals and also for some birds – in addition to visual images – like the following one:

(12)

Names for the horse according to age and sex		
sex / *age*	*male*	*female*
full-grown	stallion	mare
young	colt	filly
very young / *newborn*	foal	

[4] But s.v. Head 256 *Sharpness* for *nail, pin, needle, dagger, spire, steeple* and Head 258 *Smoothness* for *silk, satin, velvet, marble, glass, ice* in Kirkpatrick (1987). The LLCE makes extensive use of the relations: 'relating to', 'kind of', and 'part of' for structuring the lexicon and the universe. The last one provides empirical evidence for the importance of the 'part of' (not 'piece of'!) relation Cruse called *meronymy*, a term apparently coined by Ruqaiya Hasan in 1984 (cf. Carter 1987:21).

Matrices with meaning components, functioning as distinctive features, are also used in other areas of the lexicon, when appropriate, such as e.g. with ranks and titles, or in the following example from C 80:

(13)

general and smaller	town
larger	city
small	village
very small	hamlet

This schematic information, however, is supplemented in the lexicon by definitions (from the LDCE) for distinct lexical units, such as *town*$_1$ and *town*$_2$ (the latter with the label *affec*) and with illustrative quotations. All this information represents features (in the non-technical sense) not to be found in a thesaurus. That lexical sets, like A 100 and 110, group together similar creatures, while others, like A 120 and A 130, incorporate parts of animals or plants, is in my view a legitimate procedure for structuring the universe and forming lexical sets. These sets contain items which linguistically and psychologically belong together, although they cannot be justified by the strictly structuralist procedures discussed in 4.2., in particular in 4.2.4. Thus, the limits of for example the intricate testing procedures developed in Cruse (1986) are transcended in the structuring of the LLCE. Admittedly, the gain in descriptive adequacy and psychological reality is bought at the loss of rigorous linguistic methodology.

Chapter VI

Summary and Conclusions

6.1. Summary

The theme of this book was the nature of words and the development of our understanding of them. My aim has been to give a comprehensive and up-to-date survey of research on the vocabulary of English, of the most important dictionaries, of the foundations of general lexicology and lexical semantics, of the structure of words and of the lexicon, including some limited account of the function of words in context and in the mind. The book is intended both as an introduction to the field for the interested student and as a concise survey for the specialist. The open-ended nature of the lexicon and the basically unlimited productivity of various morphological and semantic processes have been stressed throughout. Although the focus was mainly on semiotic and structural phenomena from a synchronic point of view, pragmatic, sociolinguistic, textual, and cognitive aspects have not been neglected and the fundamental outlook is indeed interdisciplinary.

Chapter I discusses general problems, starting out from the words *lexicology* and *lexicon*, and others. A traditional, synchronic survey of the structure of the English vocabulary is then given and *lexical structure* is found to be ambiguous, meaning either 'the structure of lexical items' (Chapter III) or 'the structure of the lexicon' (Chapter IV). The former, the internal structure, may be further subdivided, according to whether the items are simple or mophologically complex, while the latter, the external structure, may be described from the point of view of paradigmatic or syntagmatic relations. Varieties of English are then considered in great detail, in particular on the basis of the schema of six variety classes proposed in the UGE and its possible application to lexicography in the form of "labels" attached to the entries in the LDCE. All variety classes can be correlated with specific labels. The chapter closes with an up-to-date sketch of the most important and relevant English dictionaries, where the OED, naturally, figures prominently together with various reference books derived from it. Special attention is given also to a characterization of medium-sized modern dictionaries and thematic "wordbooks". Diagram (10) summarizes the survey of British and American dictionaries most relevant for the present purposes and their interrelation. Lexicography is found to be "a never-ending story" and the future for dictionaries is surely electronic.

In Chapter II we turn to various aspects of the linguistic sign and the semiotic and semantic foundations of lexicology. Three models of the sign (Saussure's, Ogden and Richards's, Bühler's) are presented and its meaning and different kinds of 'meaning' are thoroughly investigated. Purely language-immanent approaches to semantics may be distinguished from those which take extralinguistic reality into account. If the abstract language system is separated from its concrete realization and application (Saussure's *langue* vs. *parole*) we must distinguish, following John Lyons, between *denotation* and *reference*. The latter is basically a *speech act*, in the sense of Searle and linguistic pragmatics generally. *Denotation* must also be distinguished from various types of *connotation*, for which a specific taxonomy is proposed. Finally, the basic structuralist notions *morpheme* and *lexeme*, necessary because of the ambiguity of the term *word*, are introduced. A schema for the classification of morphemes generally is suggested in this context, in which *lexical* vs. *grammatical morphemes*, related to word-formation and inflection (morphology in the narrow sense), are the most important subclasses.

The internal structure of words is then treated in Chapter III. Morphologically simple lexemes may clearly have multiple meaning, namely different 'senses' or *sememes*, i.e. they are polysemous. The *lexical entry* of such a lexeme consists of different *lexical units*. The preliminary discussion and illustration of polysemy, at the beginning of the chapter, provides a starting point for a survey of morphological structure, seen from a dynamic point of view, with the focus on the most productive processes of word-formation (compounding, derivation, nominalization). Word-formation produces new 'lexemes', while metaphor and metonymy (or 'semantic transfer') lead to new 'lexical units'. The results of both productive processes are then found to be equally affected by lexicalization and institutionalization. The semantic structure of words and its analysis and description by means of componential analysis and semantic features form another central part of this chapter. In this connection an original typology of features is proposed and Feature Semantics is found to be complementary to the newer, holistic approach of Prototype Theory. It is also pointed out that the problem of the internal relation of semantic components within lexemes and lexical units has still not been adequately solved, in spite of Weinreich's distinction between 'clusters' and 'configurations'. In the final part of the chapter Leech's proposal of a lexical rule common to word-formation and semantic transfer is taken up and dealt with in connection with metaphor, metonymy, and categorization.

Chapter IV covers the relations between words and thus the structure of the lexicon as a whole. It starts out with the introduction proper of the new concept of *lexical unit*, adopted from Cruse, which combines a single sense of a lexeme with the form of a lexical entry. The *lexeme* is defined as a family of 'lexical units'. Before continuing with the 'sense-relations' originally introduced by Lyons, which are now seen as holding between 'lexical units', not 'lexemes', other units of the lexicon are discussed which concern its organization and possible generalizations. These are the 'word classes' (parts of speech) and the 'semantic classes' postulated by Coseriu. Lexicology is mainly concerned with the 'open classes': noun, adjective, verb, adverb. These grammatical classes are found to have fuzzy boundaries, just like words, and the concept of *prototype* can therefore be applied to them as well. Paradigmatic and syntagmatic lexical relations generally, between lexemes and lexical units, are the main topic of this chapter. Besides the distinction between homonymy and polysemy, and the various kinds of paradigmatic sense-relations, linear and hierarchic *lexical fields* are considered. The notion of *lexical set* is then introduced to account for paradigmatic lexical relations which cannot be captured and described by strict linguistic procedures. Various prominent approaches to syntagmatic lexical relations (selection restrictions, transfer features, lexical solidarities) are then discussed and the concept of *collocation*, as a neutral syntagma, is seen to be parallel to the *lexical set* on the syntagmatic axis.

A book on lexicology would not be complete without at least a brief sketch of the function of words in context and in the mind. This is the topic of the last chapter (V). A distinction between *co-text* (linguistic context) and *context* (extralinguistic environment, situation) is made and the function of complex lexemes in texts is illustrated. Both co-text and context contribute to the resolution of polysemy, here called *monosemization*. Different text types also play a role especially for the function of particular words as speech acts. In the mind, words not only serve for the categorization of extralinguistic reality, but they are stored, processed, and retrieved. These problems have been tackled by psychology and a brief review of the relevant research is finally combined with remarks on the relationship between the linguistic organization of the lexicon and its function as a means of structuring the extralinguistic world.

6.2. Conclusions

6.2.1. Specific Results

A number of important insights emerge from this survey of the "state of the art" in English and general lexicology and from the discussion of individual examples. These are mostly compatible with previous work and are couched in generally accepted terminology, unless fundamentally new concepts require a new term. It must be recognized, however, that all technical terms are fundamentally *notational terms*, a concept introduced into linguistics by Nils Erik Enkvist, i.e. they have no "correct" sense, but may be defined differently by individual scholars in different theoretical frameworks.

This is particularly true of the crucial distinctions made here between: *denotation* and *reference*; *lexeme* and *lexical unit; polysemy* and *homonymy; lexical field* and *lexical set; selection restriction, lexical solidarity,* and *collocation; co-text* and *context;* and for the fundamental notions: *morpheme, sememe, lexicalization, categorization, sense-relations, syntagma, prototype, visual image, semantic networks,* and *monosemization.*

The terms of linguistics themselves, which belong to the metalanguage, exhibit the Janus-faced nature of words, which have often been compared to coins: their concept-forming power on the one hand and the dangers of hypostatization, as the reverse of the medal. This dual property may seem to support the binary model of the linguistic sign, but I hope it has become evident, throughout the book, that such a view is too narrow. Language-immanent approaches have to be transcended, in order to account not only for the prototypical kernel of linguistic categories, but for their fuzzy boundaries as well, and for our ability to structure and categorize the extralinguistic universe in specific natural languages and their words. Also, different functions of language, various kinds of meaning, and a variety of connotations must be distinguished for a full understanding of the social, pragmatic, textual, cognitive, and psychological aspects of words.

Various specific results are represented in diagrammatic form in Chapter II. The ambiguity of *inclusion* and the necessity to distinguish between *meaning/sense inclusion*, or intension, and *referential/denotational inclusion*, or extension, is illustrated in (8). The connotations of words (inherent properties of words), distinct from their denotation (the relation to classes of referents in the extralinguistic world), may be subcategorized, and possible schemas for doing this are given as (17), (17a), and (17b). The subclasses may be identified with different aspects of what Leech calls *associative meaning*. In contrast to neutral lexemes, or more precisely lexical units, which only have denotation (namely cognitive or conceptual meaning), those which contain additional connotations may be characterized as instances of 'marking' or 'markedness'. Diagram (20) presents a specific proposal for a cross-classification of morphemes. Besides *zero-morphemes*, better labelled *zero-allomorphs*, pseudo-morphemes called *formatives* are recognized. The lexeme may be defined syntagmatically as a combination of morphemes or formatives, and paradigmatically as a set of word-forms.

In Chapter III the concept of *sememe* is introduced for the specific sense of a lexeme, following Barbara and Klaus Hansen and their colleagues' work on English lexicology. In spite of the basically analytic approach to the internal structure of words in word-formation and componential analysis, the dynamic, productive aspect is stressed in connection with the notions *lexical rule* (34) and *semantic processes* (40), (41). The productivity and regularity of word-formation and semantic transfer is limited, or rather modified and superimposed upon, by the basically diachronic processes of lexicalization and institutionalization, which may result in idioms as the end-point of a scale of idiomatization. The combination of morphemes yields word-formation *syntagmas* (consisting of a determinant and a determinatum), while that of formatives results in idioms or *phrasal lexemes*, the domain of phraseology, not lexicology proper, as represented in (4). The distinction between *base* and *affix* leads to a general formula for affixation (6), originally postulated by Tournier. An improved version of Marchand's theory of *types of reference* (11) can explain differences between superficially parallel complex lexemes and nominalizations as well as the underlying identity of types in morphologically distinct words.

Semantic decomposition must be justified by objective procedures; evidence for specific analyses may be gained from morphological surface structure, from acceptable paraphrases, and from logical and semantic tests. An illustration of this procedure is given in (21) and (22) for verb-particle constructions with *out* and *up*. A typology of semantic features is presented in (24), in which denotative, connotative, relational, transfer, deictic, and inferential features are distinguished, all of which function as *distinctive features*, with the exception of inferential features. The postulation of this last class, which enables Feature Semantics to capture synchronic and diachronic variation and the phenomenon of semantic change, saves Feature Semantics from the charge of being unable to handle fuzziness of meaning and prototypicality. Nevertheless, Prototype Theory is needed to complement Feature Semantics, but the attributes of the former are found to be equivalent to semantic features. However, higher-level semantic *dimensions* (like SEX, AGE, SHAPE, FUNCTION) are also needed, which clearly function in both semantic theories. Metaphor and metonymy are considered as extremely productive semantic processes in the lexicon, and metaphor is explained as secondary or multiple categorization. Various illustrations are given of the fact that complete, prototypical scenes may be involved in this type of semantic transfer based on similarity, not only single features or attributes of the referent as 'tertium comparationis'.

Chapter IV reviews the most important research on possible generalizations within the lexicon, namely the structure of lexical relations and the overall organization of the vocabulary. Criteria for distinguishing between homonymy and polysemy are evaluated and the distinction is found to be based on a continuum on both the formal and the semantic side. Etymology is excluded as a proper basis for the distinction. Zero-derivation is found to produce new lexemes belonging to a different word class, and is therefore not to be identified with semantic transfer resulting in metaphors. Although both are extremely productive processes in English as illustrated in (4), metaphors are new lexical units. The ever finer subclassification of semantic opposites in the work of Lyons – as summarized and visually represented in (10), (10a), (10b) – and further developed by Cruse, is found to be an instance of the 'principle of diminishing returns'. Hierarchic lexical fields like (13), (14), (15) are not always based on the linguistic sense-relation of hyponymy, which can be tested by the general formula (16). *Word-fields*, consisting of morphologically simple words, must be separated from *lexical fields*, containing complex lexemes as well, if the problem of 'lexical gaps' (with a further subclassification into 'generalization gap' and 'specification gap') is to be adequately solved in connection with the productivity of word-formation. As originally claimed by Kastovsky, the *selection restrictions* of TG and the *lexical solidarities* introduced in Coseriu's structural semantic theory may be regarded as complementary theoretical constructs in a synthetic and an analytic framework. Weinreich's *transfer features* further contribute to a better understanding and formalization of syntagmatic semantic relations, although all three language-immanent semantic theories are limited, as especially shown by recent work in Cognitive Linguistics. Nevertheless, the notion of *collocation*, as a purely formal relation on the level of lexis, also has its merits particularly for pedagogical purposes. It is furthermore extremely relevant from a textlinguistic point of view, since it creates *cohesion* as shown in the theory developed by M.A.K. Halliday and Ruquaya Hasan, illustrated in (26) and (27).

The necessity of a contextual, functional, and interdisciplinary approach to lexicology is demonstrated in Chapter V. Complex lexemes are found to create both *cohesion* (in Halliday's and Beaugrande's sense) and cognitive *coherence*, understood as in the theory proposed by Beaugrande and Dressler. Apart from this fundamental property, four kinds of function in texts are distinguished: information condensation, pronominalization (in the wider sense), *semantic nominalization*, and the referential naming function which may be further subclassified. *Monosemization* is a function of both co-text and context, which normally leads to the resolution of the polysemy of lexemes. Quotations from specific text types discussed in original work by Randolph Quirk, as given in (6) and (7), show that certain words, used for performing particular speech acts, are only appropriate in very specific contexts and cultural settings.

Research by psychologists, particularly as surveyed by Aitchison and Hörmann, shows that the mental lexicon and its organization is only imperfectly understood so far. Nevertheless, *network models*, as illustrated by (8), have considerable plausibility. This also holds for the importance of *visual images*, related to the notion of *prototype*, in the so-called "dual-coding hypothesis" originally proposed by Paivio. Of the four types of link between words in the mind, namely co-ordination, collocation, superordination, and synonymy, psychologists have found that the first two are strongest. The 'coordination' of psychologists corresponds to the sense-relation of *co-hyponymy* set up by linguists, which means that horizontal, (non-hierarchic) relations between words are apparently dominant. Finally, linguistic categorization seen from the point of view of the psychologist, the linguist, and the lexicographer, is a matter of both linguistic and extralinguistic knowledge, and the categorization of the universe in specific languages must be seen as a socially, culturally, and linguistically determined structuring of reality.

6.2.2. General Conclusions and Consequences

The lexicon as a linguistic level, and lexicology as the discipline concerned with it, are today no longer the poor relations of linguistics, or the Cinderella of linguistic theory, as in the heyday of generative grammar, when the lexicon was regarded as "the full set of irregularities" of a language. Similarly, phenomena like metaphor and metonymy, which had been excluded from hard-core linguistics due to their connection with extralinguistic reality and their inaccessibility to formalization have been rediscovered with the advent of Cognitive Linguistics. Especially metaphor, with its close relationship to linguistic categorization, is now seen to have been an ugly duckling that has risen to prominence and respectability as an object of linguistic study. Research into the fuzziness of lexical meaning, triggered by experiments in denotational structure as carried out by William Labov and others, has come into contact with Prototype Theory, first hailed as an alternative to "checklist theories of meaning". This still-developing approach is itself the outcome of interdisciplinary contacts between linguists and psychologists, which have proved exceedingly fruitful in other areas as well.

Here are some of the consequences of recent lexical research for lexicography, language learning, and language teaching. Extralinguistic reality as well as social and cultural phenomena must no longer be strictly separated from linguistic science. Applied linguistics in all its forms must make use of insights from other fields, especially from psychology. This means that dictionaries, which have always made distinctions between the various senses of a word, should make more systematic use of the distinction between *lexemes* and *lexical units* and of the findings of research on polysemy and linguistic variation. Semantic transfer should be treated in a more systematic way. The importance of visual images is in fact already recognized by an increasing use of clear, prototypical illustrations. Pragmatic information is also already incorporated in some works in the form of "usage notes" and "language notes". The importance of collocations is fully acknowledged in many recent reference books. The productive patterns of word-formation also find special attention in the latest editions of some works. These are "steps in the right direction". What goes for lexicography also holds to a large extent for language learning and language teaching.

It is the duty of the lexicographer and the teacher alike to draw on the insights of linguistics into the internal and external lexical structure, without neglecting at the same time the limits of the discovered generalizations and the influence of extralinguistic factors. Above all, the function of words in context and the creative forces of lexical rules and semantic processes must be seen as the fundamental tools which help man to come to grips with the universe around him.

Abbreviations

A	argument
Adj	adjective
AHD	American Heritage Dictionary
AmE	American English
apprec	appreciative
BBI	Benson/Benson/Ilson Dictionary
BrE	British English
CED	Chronological English Dictionary
CN(s)	complex nominal(s)
COBUILD	COllins Birmingham University International Language Database
COD	Concise Oxford Dictionary
DAE	Dictionary of American English
DARE	Dictionary of American Regional English
derog	derogatory
DEWC	Dictionary of English Words in Context
DF(s)	distinctive feature(s)
dial	dialectal
dm	determinatum
DNE	Dictionary of New English
dt	determinant
E	English
EPD	English Pronouncing Dictionary
esp	especially
ET	English Today
fig	figurative
fml	formal
Fr	French
FSP	Functional Sentence Perspective
Ger	German
GSL	General Service List of English Words
humor	humorous
IA	Item and Arrangement
IC(s)	Immediate Constituent(s)
IF(s)	inferential feature(s)

infml	informal
IP	Item and Process
IPA	International Phonetic Association
It	Italian
LDCE	Longman Dictionary of Contemporary English
lit	literary
LLCE	Longman Lexicon of Contemporary English
LOB	Lancaster-Oslo-Bergen Corpus of British English
med	medical
N	noun
NEngE	North of England English
NP(s)	Noun Phrase(s)
O	Object
OALD	Oxford Advanced Learner's Dictionary
ODEE	Oxford Dictionary of English Etymology
OED	Oxford English Dictionary
OEDS	Oxford English Dictionary Supplements (1972–1986)
old-fash	old-fashioned
P	Predicate
poet	poetical
pomp	pompous
RDP(s)	Recoverably Deletable Predicate(s)
S	Subject
sl	slang
SOED	Shorter Oxford English Dictionary
tdmk	trademark
tech	technical term
TG	transformational-generative grammar
UGE	University Grammar of English
W 3	Webster's Third New International Dictionary
WP	Word and Paradigm

Dictionaries

The dictionaries are here ordered alphabetically under the names of their authors, editors, chief editors or editorial directors, in order to stress the fact that they are works of individual people, not of an abstract, supernatural authority (cf. Strang [2]1968:217). The latest edition is usually given, especially if it has clearly superseded earlier ones (see 1.4.).

Barnhart, C.L., S. Steinmetz & R.K. Barnhart (1973), *A Dictionary of New English (1963–1972 L)*, Bronxville, N.Y. etc.: Barnhart/Langenscheidt (= DNE).

– (1980), *The Second Barnhart Dictionary of New English*, Bronxville, NY.: Barnhart Books (= DNE 2).

Benson, M., E. Benson & R. Ilson (1986), *The BBI Combinatory Dictionary of English. A Guide to Word Combinations*, Amsterdam-Philadelphia: Benjamins (= BBI).

Burchfield, R.W. (1972–1986), *A Supplement to the Oxford English Dictionary Vol. I–IV*, Oxford: Oxford University Press (= OED Supplements).

– (1987), *The Compact Edition of the Oxford English Dictionary, Vol. III*, Oxford: Oxford University Press (= The Compact Supplements).

Cassidy, F.G. (1985ff.), *Dictionary of American Regional English*, Cambridge, Mass.: Harvard University Press (= DARE).

Cowie, A.P. (1948; 1989), *The Oxford Advanced Learner's Dictionary of Current English*, 4th ed., Oxford-Berlin: Oxford University Press/Cornelsen (= OALD).

Craigie, W.A. & J.R. Hulbert (1936; 1944), *A Dictionary of American English on Historical Principles*, 4 vols., London-Chicago: Oxford University Press/University of Chicago Press.

Craigie, W.A. & C.T. Onions (1933), *A New English Dictionary: Supplement*, Oxford: Clarendon.

Farrell, R.B. (1953; 1977), *Dictionary of German Synonyms*, 3rd ed., Cambridge etc.: Cambridge University Press.

Finkenstaedt, Th., E. Leisi & D. Wolff (1970), *A Chronological English Dictionary. Listing 80,000 Words in Order of their Earliest Known Occurrence*, Heidelberg: Winter (= CED).

Franklyn J. (1960; 1961), *A Dictionary of Rhyming Slang*, London-Boston: Routledge & Kegan Paul.

Friederich, W. & J. Canavan (1979), *Dictionary of English Words in Context*, Dortmund: Lambert Lensing.

Friedrichsen, G.W.S. & C.T. Onions et al. (1933; 1978), *The Shorter Oxford English Dictionary on Historical Principles*, 3rd rev. ed., 2 vols., Oxford: Clarendon (= SOED).

Gay, H., B. O'Kill, K. Seed & J. Whitcut, eds., (1984), *Longman Dictionary of the English Language*, Harlow: Longman.

Gove, P.B. (1942; 1973), *Webster's New Dictionary of Synonyms. A Dictionary of Discriminated Synonyms with Antonyms and Analogous and Contrasted Words*, 4th ed., Springfield, Mass.: Merriam.

Gove, P.B. et al. (1971), *Webster's Third New International Dictionary of the English Language. Unabridged*, Springfield, Mass.: Merriam (= W 3).

Heller, L., A. Humez & M. Dror (1984), *The Private Life of English Words*, London-Melbourne-Henley: Routledge & Kegan Paul.

Hofland, K. & St. Johansson (1982), *Word Frequencies in British and American English*, Bergen: Norwegian Computing Center for the Humanities.

Hoad, T.S. (1986), *The Concise Oxford Dictionary of English Etymology*, Oxford: Clarendon.

Howard, G. (1985), *A Guide to Good English in the 1980s*, London: Pelham Books.

Jones, D. & A.C. Gimson (1917; 1988), *Everyman's English Pronouncing Dictionary*, 14th ed., with revisions and Supplement by S. Ramsaran, London- Melbourne: Dent & Sons (= EPD).

Kenyon, J.S. & T.A. Knott (1944; 1953), *A Pronouncing Dictionary of American English*, Springfield, Mass.: Merriam.

Kirkpatrick, B. (1852; 1987), *Roget's Thesaurus of English Words and Phrases*, Harlow: Longman.

Klein, H.-W. & W. Friederich (1951; 1968), *Englische Synonymik für Studierende und Lehrer*, 3. Aufl., München: Hueber.

Lehnert, M. (1971), *Rückläufiges Wörterbuch der englischen Sprache/Reverse Dictionary of Present-Day English*, Leipzig: VEB-Verlag Enzyklopädie.

Manser, M.A. & N.D. Turton (1987), *The Penguin Wordmaster Dictionary*, Harmondsworth: Penguin.

McArthur, T. (1981), *Longman Lexicon of Contemporary English*, Harlow: Longman (= LLCE).

Mish, F.C. et al. (1986), *12 000 Words: A Supplement to Webster's Third New International Dictionary*, Springfield, Mass.; Merriam.

Morris, W. (1969; 1971), *The American Heritage Dictionary of the English Language*, New York: American Heritage (= AHD).

Moss, N. (1973), *What's the Difference? An American/British - British/American Dictionary*, London etc.: Hutchison.

Murray, J.A.H., H. Bradley, W. Craigie & C.T. Onions et al. (1884–1928), *A New English Dictionary on Historical Principles*, 10 vols., reissued as *The Oxford English Dictionary*, 12 vols., *Compact Edition*, vol. I, II (1971), vol. III (1987), Oxford: Clarendon (= OED).

Neufeldt, V.E. (1953; 1988), *Webster's New World Dictionary of the American Language. Third College Edition*, New York: Simon & Schuster.

Onions, C.T. (1966), *The Oxford Dictionary of English Etymology*, Oxford: Clarendon (= ODEE).

Partridge, E. (1937; 1974), *A Dictionary of Slang and Unconventional English*, 2 vols., London: Routledge & Kegan Paul.

Partridge, E. & P. Beale (1977; 1985), *A Dictionary of Catch Phrases. British and American, from the Sixteenth Century to the Present Day*, London: Routledge & Kegan Paul.

Pascoe, G. & H. Pascoe (1985), *Sprachfallen im Englischen. Wörterbuch der falschen Freunde. Deutsch und Englisch. Ein Lern- und Nachschlagewerk*, München: Hueber.

Pointen, G.E. (1971; 1983), *BBC Pronouncing Dictionary of British Names*, 2nd ed., London: Oxford University Press.

Procter, P. et al. (1978), *Longman Dictionary of Contemporary English*, Harlow-Berlin-München: Longman/Langenscheidt (= LDCE 1).

Simpson, J.A. & E.S.C. Weiner (1989), *The Oxford English Dictionary. Second Edition*, in 20 vols. Oxford: Oxford University Press (= OED 2).

Sinclair, J.M. et al. (1987), *Collins COBUILD English Language Dictionary*, London-Glasgow-Stuttgart: Collins/Klett (= COBUILD).

Stein, J. & L. Urdang (1966; 1987), *The Random House Dictionary of the English Language. Unabridged*, 2nd ed., New York: Random House (= RHD).

Summers, D. et al. (1978; 1987), *Longman Dictionary of Contemporary English*, 2nd ed., Harlow-Berlin-München: Longman/Langenscheidt (= LDCE 2).

Sykes, J.B. (1911; 1982), *The Concise Oxford Dictionary of Current English*, 7th ed., Oxford: Clarendon (= COD).

Urdang, L. et al. (1979; 1986), *Collins Dictionary of the English Language*, 2nd ed., London-Glasgow: Collins (= COLLINS).

Urdang, L. (1986), *Longman Synonym Dictionary*, Harlow: Longman.

Wentworth, H. & S. Flexner (1960; 1975), *Dictionary of American Slang*, 2nd ed., New York-Berlin: Crowell/Langenscheidt.

West, M. (1936; 1953), *A General Service List of English Words. With Semantic Frequencies and a Supplementary Word-List for the Writing of Popular Science and Technology*, 2nd ed., London: Longmans (= GSL).

Bibliography

Adams, Valerie (1973), *Introduction to Modern English Word-Formation* (English Language Series 7), London: Longman.

Aitchison, Jean (1987), *Words in the Mind. An Introduction to the Mental Lexicon,* Oxford-New York: Basil Blackwell.

Aronoff, Mark (1976), *Word Formation in Generative Grammar* (Linguistic Inquiry Monographs 1) Cambridge, Mass.-London: MIT Press.

Bach, Emmon & Robert T. Harms, eds., (1968), *Universals in Linguistic Theory,* London etc.: Holt, Rinehart & Winston.

Bald, Wolf-Dietrich (1972), *Studien zu den kopulativen Verben des Englischen* (Commentationes Societatis Linguisticae Europaeae 5), München: Hueber.

– (1988), "Anglistische Linguistik als Hilfswissenschaft", in P. Doyé, H. Heuermann & G. Zimmermann, eds., *Die Beziehung der Fremsprachendidaktik zu ihren Referenzwissenschaften,* Tübingen: Narr, 124–141.

Bally, Charles (1932; 1965), *Linguistique générale et linguistique française,* 4ᵉ ed., Bern: Francke.

Bauer, Laurie (1983), *English Word-Formation* (Cambridge Textbooks in Linguistics), Cambridge etc.: Cambridge University Press.

– (1988), *Introducing Linguistic Morphology,* Edinburgh: Edinburgh University Press.

Baugh, Albert C. & Thomas Cable (1951; 1978), *A History of the English Language,* 3rd ed., London-Boston-Henley: Routledge & Kegan Paul.

Bennett, T.J.A. (1988), *Aspects of English Colour Collocations and Idioms* (Anglistische Forschungen 197), Heidelberg: Winter.

Bloomfield, Leonard (1933; 1979), *Language,* 14th imp., London-Boston-Sydney: George Allen & Unwin.

Brekle, Herbert E. & Dieter Kastovsky, eds., (1977), *Perspektiven der Wortbildungsforschung. Beiträge zum Wuppertaler Wortbildungskolloquium vom 9. – 10. Juli 1976. Anläßlich des 70. Geburtstags von Hans Marchand am 1. Oktober 1977* (Schriftenreihe Linguistik 1), Bonn: Bouvier.

Bühler, Karl (1934; 1965), *Sprachtheorie. Die Darstellungsfunktion der Sprache,* 2. Aufl., Stuttgart: Gustav Fischer.

Bußmann, Hadumod (1983; 1990), *Lexikon der Sprachwissenschaft,* 2. Aufl., Stuttgart: Kröner.

Carter, Ronald (1987), *Vocabulary. Applied Linguistic Perspectives,* London etc.: Allen & Unwin.

Chafe, Wallace L. (1970), *Meaning and the Structure of Language,* Chicago-London: University of Chicago Press.

Chomsky, Noam (1965), *Aspects of the Theory of Syntax,* Cambridge, Mass.: MIT Press.

Clark, Eve V. & Herbert H. Clark (1979), "When Nouns Surface as Verbs", *Language* 55, 767–811.

Coleman, Linda & Paul Kay (1981), "Prototype Semantics: The English Word LIE", *Language* 57, 26–44.

Coseriu, Eugenio (1961; 1967), *Teoría del lenguaje y lingüística general. Cinco estudios*, 2ª ed., Madrid: Gredos.
– (1967), "Lexikalische Solidaritäten", *Poetica* 1, 293–303.
– (1970), "Die lexematischen Strukturen", in E. Coseriu, *Sprache, Strukturen und Funktionen* (Tübinger Beiträge zur Linguistik 2), Tübingen: Narr, 159–179.
– (1973), *Probleme der strukturellen Semantik. Vorlesung gehalten im Wintersemester 1965/66 an der Universität Tübingen* (Tübinger Beiträge zur Linguistik 40), ed. by D. Kastovsky, Tübingen: Narr.
Coseriu, Eugenio & Horst Geckeler (1981), *Trends in Structural Semantics* (Tübinger Beiträge zur Linguistik 158), Tübingen: Narr.
Cowie, Anthony (1982), "Polysemy and the Structure of Lexical Fields", *Nottingham Linguistic Circular* 11, 51–64.
– ed., (1987), *The Dictionary and the Language Learner. Papers from the EURALEX Seminar at the University of Leeds, 1–3 April 1985* (Lexicographica, Series Maior 17), Tübingen: Niemeyer.
Craig, Colette, ed., (1986), *Noun Classes and Categorization. Proceedings of a Symposium on Categorization and Noun Classification, Eugene, Oregon, October 1983*, Amsterdam-Philadelphia: Benjamins.
Cruse, D.A. (1977), "The Pragmatics of Lexical Specificity", *Journal of Linguistics* 13, 153–164.
– (1986), *Lexical Semantics* (Cambridge Textbooks in Linguistics), Cambridge etc.: Cambridge University Press.
Crystal, David (1971; 1985), *Linguistics*, 2nd ed., Harmondsworth: Penguin.
Cuyckens, Hubert (1984), "Prototypes in Lexical Semantics: An Evaluation", in H. Krenn, J. Niemeyer & U. Eberhardt, eds., *Sprache und Text. Akten des 18. Linguistischen Kolloquiums, Linz 1983* (Linguistische Arbeiten 145), Tübingen: Niemeyer, 174–182.
Dietrich, Wolf & Horst Geckeler, eds., (1981), *Logos Semantikos. Studia Linguistica in honorem Eugenio Coseriu*, vol. III, Berlin-Madrid: de Gruyter/Gredos.
Dirven, René (1985), "Metaphor as a Basic Means for Extending the Lexicon", in Paprotté/Dirven (1985), 85–119.
Dirven, René & Günter Radden (1977), *Semantische Syntax des Englischen* (Schwerpunkte Linguistik und Kommunikationswissenschaft 13), Wiesbaden: Athenaion.
Downing, Pamela (1977), "On the Creation and Use of English Compound Nouns", *Language* 53, 810–842.
Durrell, Martin (1988), "Some Problems of Contrastive Lexical Semantics", in Hüllen/Schulze (1988), 230–241.
Enkvist, Nils Erik (1973), *Linguistic Stylistics* (Janua Linguarum, Series Critica 5), The Hague-Paris: Mouton.
Farkas, Donka, Wesley M. Jacobsen & Karol W. Todrys, eds., (1978), *Papers from the Parasession on the Lexicon*, Chicago: Chicago Linguistic Society.
Fillmore, Charles J. (1968a), "Lexical Entries for Verbs", *Foundations of Language* 4, 373–393.
– (1968b), "The Case for Case", in Bach/Harms (1968), 1–88.
– (1969; 1971), "Types of Lexical Information", in D.D. Steinberg & L.A. Jakobovits, eds., *Semantics*, Cambridge: Cambridge University Press, 370–392.
– (1975), "An Alternative to Checklist Theories of Meaning", in C. Cogen, H. Thompson, G. Thurgood & K. Whistler, eds., *Proceedings of the First Annual Meeting of the Berkeley Linguistics Society*, Berkeley: Berkeley Linguistics Society, 123–131.

– (1978), "On the Organisation of Semantic Information in the Lexicon", in Farkas et al. (1978), 148–173.

– (1984), "Lexical Semantics and Text Semantics", in J.E. Copeland, ed., *New Directions in Linguistics and Semantics*, Amsterdam: Benjamins, 123–147.

Finkenstaedt, Thomas & Dieter Wolff (1973), *Ordered Profusion. Studies in Dictionaries and the English Lexicon.* With contributions by H. Joachim Neuhaus & Winfried Herget (Annales Universitatis Saraviensis 13), Heidelberg: Winter.

Fisiak, Jacek, ed., (1985), *Historical Semantics. Historical Word-Formation* (Trends in Linguistics. Studies and Monographs 29), Berlin-New York: Mouton.

Fodor, Janet D. (1977; 1980), *Semantics. Theories of Meaning in Generative Grammar*, (The Language and Thought Series), Cambridge, Mass.: Harvard University Press.

Funk, Wolf-Peter (1988), "On the Semantic and Morphological Status of Reversative Verbs in English and German", *Papers and Studies in Contrastive Linguistics* 23, 19–35.

Geckeler, Horst (1971), *Strukturelle Semantik und Wortfeldtheorie*, München: Fink.

– (1980), "Die Antonymie im Lexikon", in Kastovsky (1980), 42–69.

Geeraerts, Dirk (1984), "Prototype Theory and Diachronic Semantics: A Case Study", *Indogermanische Forschungen* 88, 1–32.

Gill, Liz (1987), "Journalese: The Inside Story", *English Today* 11, 24–27.

Gipper, Helmut (1959; 1973), "Sessel oder Stuhl? Ein Beitrag zur Bestimmung von Wortinhalten im Bereich der Sachkultur", in Schmidt (1973), 371–398.

Gläser, Rosemarie (1986), *Phraseologie der englischen Sprache*, Leipzig-Tübingen: VEB Verlag Enzyklopädie/Niemeyer.

Gleason, H.A. (1955; 1961), *An Introduction to Descriptive Linguistics*, 2nd ed., New York etc.: Holt Rinehart & Winston.

Görlach, Manfred (1987), "Abbreviating the Worlds' Englishes", *English Today* 11, 33.

Halliday, Michael A.K. (1978), *Language as Social Semiotic. The Social Interpretation of Language and Meaning*, London: Edward Arnold.

Halliday, Michael & Ruqaiya Hasan (1976), *Cohesion in English* (English Language Series 9), London: Longman.

Hansen, Klaus (1966), "Die Bedeutung der Worttypenlehre für das Wörterbuch", *Zeitschrift für Anglistik und Amerikanistik* 14, 160–178.

– (1977), "Gegenstand und Beschreibungsaspekte der Wortbildungslehre am Beispiel des Englischen", in A. Neubert, ed., *Beiträge zur englischen Lexikologie* (Linguistische Studien. Reihe A. Arbeitsberichte 36), Berlin: Akademie der Wissenschaften.

– (1978), "Problems in the Semantic Analysis of Compounds", *Zeitschrift für Anglistik und Amerikanistik* 26, 247–251.

Hansen, Barbara, Klaus Hansen, Albrecht Neubert & Manfred Schentke (1982; 1985), *Englische Lexikologie. Einführung in die Wortbildung und lexikalische Semantik*, 2. Aufl., Leipzig: VEB Verlag Enzyklopädie.

Hartmann, Reinhard (1987), "Yes, but WHICH Dictionary?", *English Today* 10, 10–17.

Hejj, Andreas & Gerhard Strube (1988), "Wortfeld im Wandel", in W. Marx, ed., *Verbales Gedächtnis und Informationsverarbeitung*, Göttingen: Hogrefe, 72–109.

Höhlein, Helga, Peter H. Marsden & Clausdirk Pollner (1987) *Auswahlbibliographie zum Studium der anglistischen Sprachwissenschaft. Mit Kommentaren* (Forschung & Studium Anglistik 2), Tübingen: Niemeyer.

Hörmann, Hans (1981; 1986), *Meaning and Context. An Introduction to the Psychology of Language*, ed. R.E. Innis (Cognition and Language), New York-London: Plenum.

Hoppenbrouwers, Geer A.J., Pieter A.M. Seuren & A.J.M.M. Weijters, eds., (1985), *Meaning and the Lexicon*, Dordrecht-Cinnaminson: Foris.

Hüllen, Werner & Rainer A.I. Schulze, eds., (1988), *Understanding the Lexicon. Meaning, Sense and World Knowledge in Lexical Semantics* (Linguistische Arbeiten 210), Tübingen: Niemeyer.

Ilson, Robert (1987), "Illustrations in Dictionaries", in Cowie (1987), 193–212.

Jackson, Howard (1988), *Words and Their Meaning* (Learning About Language), London-New York: Longman.

Jakobson, Roman (1969) "Closing Statement: Linguistics and Poetics", in T.A. Sebeok, ed., *Style in Language*, Cambridge, Mass.: MIT Press, 350–377.

Kastovsky, Dieter (1969; 1981), "Wortbildung und Nullmorphem", in Lipka/Günther (1981), 306–323.

– (1973), "Causatives", *Foundations of Language* 10, 255–315.

– (1977), "Word-Formation, or: at the Crossroads of Morphology, Syntax, Semantics, and the Lexicon", *Folia Linguistica* 10, 1–33.

– ed., (1980a), *Perspektiven der lexikalischen Semantik. Beiträge zum Wuppertaler Semantikkolloquium vom 2.–3.12.1977*, (Schriftenreihe Linguistik 2), Bonn: Bouvier.

– (1980b), *Selectional Restrictions and Lexical Solidarities*, in Kastovsky (1980a), 70–92.

– (1981a), "Lexical Fields and Word-Formation", in Dietrich/Geckeler (1981), 429–445.

– (1981b) "Interaction of Lexicon and Syntax: Lexical Converses" in J. Esser & A. Hübler, eds., *Forms and Functions. Papers in General, English and Applied Linguistics Presented to Vilém Fried on the Occasion of his 65th Brithday*, Tübingen: Narr, 123–136.

– (1982a), *Wortbildung und Semantik* (Studienreihe Englisch 14), Düsseldorf-Bern-München: Bagel/Francke.

– (1982b), "Word-Formation: A Functional View", *Folia Linguistica* 16, 181–198.

– (1986), "Diachronic Word-Formation in a Functional Perspective", in Kastovsky/Szwedek (1986), 409–421.

Kastovsky, Dieter & Aleksander Szwedek, eds., (1986), *Linguistics across Historical and Geographical Boundaries. In Honour of Jacek Fisiak on the Occasion of His 50th Birthday* (Trends in Linguistics, Studies and Monographs 32), Berlin-New York-Amsterdam: Mouton de Gruyter.

Katz, Jerrold & Jerry A. Fodor (1963), "The Structure of a Semantic Theory", *Language* 39, 170–210.

King, Robert Thomas (1988), "Spatial Metaphor in German Causative Constructions", in Rutzka-Ostyn (1988), 555–585.

Kittay, Eva & Adrienne Lehrer (1981), "Semantic Fields and the Structure of Metaphor", *Studies in Language* 5, 31–63.

Labov, William (1978), "Denotational Structure", in Farkas et al. (1978), 220–260.

Lakoff, George (1982), *Categories and Cognitive Models*, Berkeley: Cognitive Science Reports 2 and Trier: LAUT A 96.

– (1986), "Classifiers as a Reflection of Mind", in Craig (1986), 13–51.

– (1987), *Women, Fire, and Dangerous Things. What Categories Reveal About the Mind*, Chicago-London: University of Chicago Press.

– (1989), *The Invariance Hypothesis: Do Metaphors Preserve Cognitive Topology?*, Duisburg: LAUD, A 266.

Lakoff, George & Mark Johnson (1980), *Metaphors We Live By*, Chicago-London: University of Chicago Press.

Leech, Geoffrey N. (1969), *A Linguistic Guide to English Poetry* (English Language Series 4), London: Longman.

– (1974; 1981), *Semantics. The Study of Meaning*, 2nd ed., Harmondsworth: Penguin.

Leech, Geoffrey, Margaret Deuchar & Robert Hoogenraad (1982), *English Grammar for Today. A New Introduction*, London-Basingstoke: McMillan.
Leech, Geoffrey & Jan Svartvik (1975), *A Communicative Grammar of English*, London: Longman.
Lees, Robert B. (1960; 1968), *The Grammar of English Nominalizations*, 5th printing, Bloomington: Indiana University Press/The Hague: Mouton.
– (1970), "Problems in the Grammatical Analysis of English Nominal Compounds", in M. Bierwisch & K.E. Heidolph, eds., *Progress in Linguistics*, The Hague-Paris: Mouton, 174–186.
Lehrer, Adrienne (1974), *Semantic Fields and Lexical Structure* (North-Holland Linguistic Series 11), Amsterdam-London-New York: North Holland/American Elsevier.
– (1985), "The Influence of Semantic Fields on Semantic Change", in Fisiak (1985), 283–296.
– (1989), *Polysemy, Conventionality, and the Structure of the Lexicon*, Duisburg: LAUD, A 240.
Leisi, Ernst (1952; 1975), *Der Wortinhalt. Seine Struktur im Deutschen und Englischen*, 5. Aufl., Heidelberg: Winter.
– (1955; 1985), *Das heutige Englisch*, 7. Aufl., Heidelberg: Winter.
– (1973; 1985), *Praxis der englischen Semantik*, 2. Aufl., Heidelberg: Winter.
Leitzke, Eva (1989a), *(De)nominale Adjektive im heutigen Englisch. Untersuchungen zur Morphologie, Syntax, Semantik und Pragmatik von Adjektiv-Nomen-Kombinationen der Typen ATOMIC ENERGY und CRIMINAL LAWYER* (Linguistische Arbeiten 221), Tübingen: Niemeyer.
– (1989b), Review of Warren (1984), *Anglia* 107, 463–468.
Levi, Judith N. (1978), *The Syntax and Semantics of Complex Nominals*, New York-San Francisco-London: Academic Press.
Lipka, Leonhard (1969), "Assimilation and Dissimilation as Regulating Factors in English Morphology", *Zeitschrift für Anglistik und Amerikanistik* 17, 159–173.
– (1971), "Grammatical Categories, Lexical Items and Word-Formation", *Foundations of Language* 7, 211–238.
– (1972), *Semantic Structure and Word-Formation. Verb-Particle Constructions in Contemporary English* (International Library of General Linguistics 17), München: Fink.
– (1974), "Probleme der Analyse englischer Idioms aus struktureller und generativer Sicht", *Linguistik und Didaktik* 20, 274–285.
– (1975a), "Re-Discovery Procedures and the Lexicon", *Lingua* 37, 197–224.
– (1975b), Review of Adams (1973), *Lingua* 37, 382–389.
– (1976), "Topicalization, Case Grammar, and Lexical Decomposition in English", *Archivum Linguisticum* 7, 118–141.
– (1980), "Methodology and Representation in the Study of Lexical Fields", in Kastovsky (1980), 93–114.
– (1981a), "On the Interrelation of Syntagmatic Modification and Paradigmatic Lexical Structuring in English", in Dietrich/Geckeler (1981), 373–383.
– (1981b), "Zur Lexikalisierung im Deutschen und Englischen", in Lipka/Günther (1981), 119–132.
– (1982), "Causatives and Inchoatives in English and their Treatment in Recent Lexicographic Practice", *Studia Anglica Posnaniensia* 14, 3–16.
– (1983), "A Multi-Level Approach to Word-Formation: Complex Lexemes and Word Semantics", in S. Hattori & K. Inoue, eds., *Proceedings of the XIIIth International Congress of Linguists, Tokyo 1982*, Tokyo, 926–928.

– (1985), "Inferential Features in Historical Semantics", in Fisiak (1985), 339–354.
– (1986a), "Semantic Features and Prototype Theory in English Lexicology", in Kastovsky/Szwedek (1986), 85–94.
– (1986b), "Homonymie, Polysemie oder Ableitung im heutigen Englisch", *Zeitschrift für Anglistik und Amerikanistik* 34, 128–138.
– (1987a), "Prototype Semantics or Feature Semantics: An Alternative?", in W. Lörscher & R. Schulze, eds., *Perspectives on Language in Performance. Studies in Linguistics, Literary Criticism, and Language Teaching and Learning. To Honour Werner Hüllen on the Occasion of His Sixtieth Birthday*, Tübingen: Narr, 282–298.
– (1987b). "Word-Formation and Text in English and German", in B. Asbach-Schnitker & J. Roggenhofer, eds., *Neuere Forschungen zur Wortbildung und Historiographie der Linguistik. Festgabe für Herbert E. Brekle zum 50. Geburtstag*, Tübingen: Narr, 59–67.
– (1988a), "Variety is the Spice of Life: Language Variation and Sociolinguistics", in J. Albrecht, J. Lüdtke & H. Thun, eds., *Energeia und Ergon. Sprachliche Variation - Sprachgeschichte - Sprachtypologie. Studia in honorem Eugenio Coseriu*, vol. II, (Tübinger Beiträge zur Linguistik 300), Tübingen: Narr, 317–325.
– (1988b), "A Rose is a Rose is a Rose: On Simple and Dual Categorization in Natural Languages", in Hüllen/Schulze (1988), 355–366.
– (1989a), "Der Risalit und seine Folgen: Ernst Leisi und die Prototypensemantik", in U. Fries & M. Heuser, eds., *Meaning and Beyond. Ernst Leisi zum 70. Geburtstag*, Tübingen: Narr, 225–235.
– (1989b), "The State of the Art in Lexicology", in H.J. Müllenbrock & R. Noll-Wiemann, eds., *Anglistentag 1988 Göttingen*, Tübingen: Niemeyer, 250–263.
– (1990), "Metaphor and Metonymy as Productive Processes on the Level of the Lexicon", in W. Bahner, J. Schildt & D. Viehweger, eds., *Proceedings of the XIVth International Congress of Linguists, Berlin 1987*, Berlin: Akademie-Verlag (in print).
Lipka, Leonhard & Hartmut Günther, eds., (1981), *Wortbildung* (Wege der Forschung 564), Darmstadt: Wissenschaftliche Buchgesellschaft.
Lyons, John (1968), *Introduction to Theoretical Linguistics*, Cambridge: Cambridge University Press.
– (1977), *Semantics*, 2 vols., Cambridge etc.: Cambridge University Press.
– (1981), *Language, Meaning and Context* (Fontana Linguistics), Bungay, Suffolk: Fontana.
Lutzeier, Peter Rolf (1985), *Linguistische Semantik* (Sammlung Metzler 219), Stuttgart: Metzler.
Marchand, Hans (1960; 1969), *The Categories and Types of Present-Day English Word-Formation*, 2nd ed., München: Beck.
– (1964), "A Set of Criteria for the Establishing of Derivational Relationship Between Words Unmarked by Derivational Morphemes", *Indogermanische Forschungen* 69, 10–19.
– (1966), "On Attributive and Predicative Derived Adjectives and Some Problems Related to the Distinction", *Anglia* 84, 131–149.
– (1967), "On the Description of Compounds", *Word* 23, 379–387.
– (1974), *Studies in Syntax and Word-Formation. Selected Articles* (International Library of General Linguistics 18), ed. by D. Kastovsky, München: Fink.
Marsden, Peter H. (1985), "Adjective Pairs in -ic and -ical. Towards a Systematic Description of Current Usage", *Lebende Sprachen* 30, 26–33.
Matthews, P.H. (1970), "Recent Developments in Morphology", in J. Lyons, ed., *New Horizons in Linguistics*, Harmondsworth: Penguin, 96–114.

– (1974), *Morphology. An Introduction to the Theory of Word-Structure* (Cambridge Textbooks in Linguistics), Cambridge: Cambridge University Press.
McArthur, Tom (1986), *Worlds of Reference. Lexicography, Learning and Language. From the Clay Tablet to the Computer*, Cambridge: Cambridge University Press.
McCawley, James D. (1968a), "Lexical Insertion in a Transformational Grammar without Deep Structure", *Papers from the Fourth Regional Meeting CLS*, 71–80.
– (1968b), "The Role of Semantics in a Grammar", in Bach/Harms (1968), 124–169.
Mettinger, Arthur (1988; 1990), *Aspects of Semantic Opposition in English. A Corpus-Based Study of Binary Meaning-Relations* (Oxford Studies in Lexicography and Lexicology 1), Oxford: Oxford University Press.
Nida, Eugene A. (1975), *Componential Analysis of Meaning. An Introduction to Semantic Structures*, The Hague-Paris: Mouton.
Nöth, Winfried (1985), "Semiotic Aspects of Metaphor", in Paprotté/Dirven (1985), 1–16.
Ogden, C.K. & I.A. Richards (1923; 1949), *The Meaning of Meaning. A Study of the Influence of Language upon Thought and of the Science of Symbolism*, 10th ed., London: Routledge & Kegan Paul.
Palmer, F.R. (1976; 1981), *Semantics. A New Outline*, 2nd ed., Cambridge etc.: Cambridge University Press.
Paprotté, Wolf & René Dirven, eds., (1985), *The Ubiquity of Metaphor* (Current Issues in Linguistic Theory 29), Amsterdam-Philadelphia: Benjamins.
Porzig, Walter (1934; 1973), "Wesenhafte Bedeutungsbeziehungen", in Schmidt (1973), 78–103.
Postal, Paul M. (1970), "On the Surface Verb REMIND", *Linguistic Inquiry* 1, 37–120.
Quine, Willard V.O. (1960), *Word and Object*, Cambridge, Mass.: MIT Press.
Quirk, Randolph (1972), *The English Language and Images of Matter* (Language and Language Learning 34), London: Oxford University Press.
– (1986), *Words at Work. Lectures on Textual Structure*, Harlow: Longman.
Quirk, Randolph & Sidney Greenbaum (1973), *A University Grammar of English, London:* Longman.
Quirk, Randolph, Sidney Greenbaum, Geoffrey Leech & Jan Svartvik (1985), *A Comprehensive Grammar of the English Language*, London-New York: Longman.
Rohdenburg, Günther (1985), "Dogs Bitches and Other Creatures", *Journal of Semantics* 4, 117–135.
Rosch, Eleanor (1977), "Human Categorization", in N. Warren, ed., *Studies in Cross-Cultural Psychology*, Vol. 1, London-New York: Academic Press, 1–49.
– (1978), "Principles of Categorization", in E. Rosch & B.B. Lloyd, eds., *Cognition and Categorization*, Hillsdale, N.J.-New York: Erlbaum, 27–48.
Rosch, Eleanor & Carolyne B. Mervis (1975), "Family Resemblances: Studies in the Internal Structure of Categories", *Cognitive Psychology* 7, 573–605.
Rudzka-Ostyn, Brygida (1985), "Metaphoric Processes in Word Formation. The Case of Prefixed Verbs", in Paprotté/Dirven (1985), 209–241.
– ed., (1988), *Topics in Cognitive Linguistics* (Current Issues in Linguistic Theory 50), Amsterdam-Philadelphia: Benjamins.
Saussure, Ferdinand de (1916; 1965), *Cours de linguistique générale*, 3ième ed., publié par Ch. Bally, A. Sechehaye & A. Riedlinger, Paris: Payot.
Schäfer, Jürgen (1980), *Documentation in the O.E.D.: Shakespeare and Nashe as Test Cases*, Oxford: Clarendon Press.
Scheler, Manfred (1977), *Der englische Wortschatz* (Grundlagen der Anglistik & Amerikanistik 9), Berlin: Schmidt.

Schmidt, Lothar, ed., (1973), *Wortfeldforschung. Zur Geschichte und Theorie des sprachlichen Feldes* (Wege der Forschung 250), Darmstadt: Wissenschaftliche Buchgesellschaft.

Schmidt, Wilhelm (1963; 1967), *Lexikalische und aktuelle Bedeutung. Ein Beitrag zur Theorie der Wortbedeutung*, 4. Aufl. (Schriften zur Phonetik, Sprachwissenschaft und Kommunikationsforschung 7), Berlin: Akademie-Verlag.

Schneider, Edgar W. (1988), *Variabilität, Polysemie und Unschärfe der Wortbedeutung*, 2 vols. (Linguistische Arbeiten 196/197), Tübingen: Niemeyer.

Schwarze, Christoph & Dieter Wunderlich, eds., (1985), *Handbuch der Lexikologie*, Königstein/Ts.: Athenäum.

Searle, John R. (1969), *Speech Acts. An Essay in the Philosophy of Language*, Cambridge: Cambridge University Press.

Sprengel, Konrad (1980), Über semantische Merkmale", in Kastovsky (1980), 145–177.

Standop, Ewald (1985), *Englische Wörterbücher unter der Lupe* (Lexicographica, Series Maior 2), Tübingen: Niemeyer.

Stein, Gabriele (1971), *Primäre und sekundäre Adjektive im Französischen und Englischen* (Tübinger Beiträge zur Linguistik 22), Tübingen: Narr.

– (1973), *English Word-Formation over two Centuries. In Honour of Hans Marchand on the Occasion of His Sixty-Fifth Birthday* (Tübinger Beiträge zur Linguistik 34), Tübingen: Narr.

Strang, Barbara M.H. (1962; 1968), *Modern English Structure*, 2nd ed., London: Edward Arnold.

Summers, Della (1988), "ELT Dictionaries: Past, Present, and Future", *English Today* 14, 10–16.

Testen, David, Veena Mishra & Joseph Drogo, eds., (1984), *Papers from the Parasession on Lexical Semantics*, Chicago: Chicago Linguistic Society.

Tournier, Jean (1985), *Introduction descriptive à la lexicogénétique de l'anglais contemporain*, Paris-Genève: Champion-Slatkine.

– (1988), *Précis de lexicologie anglaise*, Paris: Nathan.

Trubetzkoy, N.S. (1939; 1971), *Grundzüge der Phonologie*, 5. Aufl., Göttingen: Vandenhoeck & Ruprecht.

Ulherr, H. (1986), Review of Hansen et al. (1982), *Journal of English Linguistics* 19, 137–141.

Ullmann, Stephen (1951; 1957), *The Principles of Semantics*, 2nd ed., Oxford-Glasgow: Basil Blackwell.

– (1962), *Semantics. An Introduction to the Science of Meaning*, Oxford: Basil Blackwell.

Verschueren, Jef (1981), "Problems of Lexical Semantics", *Lingua* 53, 317–351.

Viehweger, Dieter et al. (1977), *Probleme der semantischen Analyse* (Studia Grammatica 15), Berlin: Akademie-Verlag.

Wächtler, Kurt (1977), *Geographie und Stratifikation der englischen Sprache* (Studienreihe Englisch 16), Düsseldorf-Bern-München: Bagel/Francke.

Warren, Beatrice (1978), *Semantic Patterns of Noun-Noun Compounds* (Gothenburg Studies in English 41), Göteborg: Acta Universitatis Gothoburgensis.

– (1984), *Classifying Adjectives* (Gothenburg Studies in English 56), Göteborg: Acta Universitatis Gothoburgensis.

Weiner, Edmund (1987), "The New OED and World English", *English Today* 11, 31–34.

Weinreich, Uriel (1966; 1972), *Explorations in Semantic Theory* (Janua Linguarum, Series Minor 89), ed. by W. Labov, The Hague-Paris: Mouton.

Weinrich, Harald (1976), *Sprache in Texten*, Stuttgart: Klett.

Wotjak, Gerd (1971), *Untersuchungen zur Struktur der Bedeutung*, Berlin-München: Akademie-Verlag/Hueber.
– (1987), "Ansichten und Einsichten der lexikalischen Semantik im Lichte der Textlinguistik", in W. Neumann & B. Techtmeier, eds., *Bedeutungen und Ideen in Sprachen und Texten. Werner Bahner gewidmet* (Sprache und Gesellschaft 20), Berlin: Akademie-Verlag.

Index of Subjects

(Major or defining page references are printed in **bold** type)

Index of Persons